Why Schoolchildren Can't Read

iea

Bonnie Macmillan

Published by the IEA Education and Training Unit, 1997

First published in February 1997 by
The Institute of Economic Affairs
2 Lord North Street
Westminster
London SW1P 3LB

IEA Studies in Education No. 2
All rights reserved
ISSN 0073-909X
ISBN 0-255 36403-2

Printed in Great Britain by
Redwood Books, Trowbridge, Wiltshire
Set in Century Schoolbook and Bookman Old Style

Contents

LIST OF FIGURES

LIST OF TABLES

Foreword: Educating the Educators

Experimental psychology has always had an ambivalent relationship with common sense, never doing much more than tiptoeing ahead of it. Only seldom does any kind of gulf appear between widely accepted beliefs and its clear conclusions. Perhaps intelligence is one such topic. Another is reading.

There is now a significant gap between trustworthy experimental evidence and practice in the teaching of reading, the training of teachers in this valuable art (previously done with great success by mothers) and public policy in the area. Bonnie Macmillan has written the first account of this gap to cover all these different concerns in a single, generous sweep. Nor is she content to furnish a reprise of the findings of science. In the academic world there is little capacity or willingness to address pedagogy – the business that matters most to schools, children, teachers, parents, governments. Dr Macmillan firmly faces such real life concerns without shirking her scholarly commitment to expose the 'issues' to the light of knowledge.

Why do public discussions in the reading 'debate' (as the reading wars are politely known in this country) have such a crude character? Especially, why are they so *political*? Dr Macmillan enables us to rise briefly above the pedestrian dispute in which quite basic facts are never assimilated. Her scholarly approach to the richer, more recent literature is welcome. But the question remains: given that the research picture she describes was essentially complete in 1967, the year of publication of Jeanne Challs's *Learning to Read: The Great Debate*, why, thirty years later, are we still having a 'debate' about the best way to teach reading, a question that has been decided in favour of traditional phonics and which has long ceased to be controversial within the research community?

One factor is the avoidance of *history*. Schooling and the doctrines that drive it, seldom very prominent on the domestic agenda, are habitually regarded as mundane. Indeed educational history scarcely seems to get written. This must be one reason why we continually go round in circles, an experience congenial only to believers in reincarnation.

Then there are major differences in values. What for some is a degradation of education for others is a laudable objective: the enfranchisement of all pupils by the making easy of everything. To this end it has been necessary to take the grammar out of French and German, the number out of mathematics, the literature out of English, the phonics out of reading and the necessity for correct spelling out of writing. No doubt a history without facts and a geography without places do not linger far behind.

The pattern is clear: bring the work within the reach of all and we have a curriculum for all, an education for all. Who would be cavalier enough to intrude a note of discord into such social harmony?

> 'One Sunday after noon, four years ago, I was sitting out in a cafe in the Frederiksberg Gardens smoking my cigar and looking at the servant-girls and suddenly the idea struck me: you go on wasting your time without profit; on every side one genius after another appears and makes life and existence, and the historical means of conveyance and communication with eternal happiness, easier and easier – what do you do? Could you not discover some way in which you too could help the age? Then I thought, what if I sat down and made everything difficult?... From that moment I found my entertainment in that work.' (Kierkegaard, *Journals*, May 14th 1845.)

In her task Dr Macmillan has employed her preferred method of *patience*, in this, perhaps, somewhat unlike Kierkegaard. Especially valuable has been her gathering of specimens of perverse 'guidance' from many sources (teacher training, the BBC, the Department of Education, the Basic Skills Unit, the School Curriculum and Assessment Authority), an activity ordinarily as interesting as night-soil collection.

But perhaps a third, still more important consideration is needed to account for the time-warp in which discussions about reading seem to take place. Many of the intellectual leaders in state primary education and initial teacher education espouse a humanistic and literary approach to the whole business of education. While this seems appropriate to encouraging children who can read to do so, it side-steps the initial task of learning to decode, on which researchers bear from a very different tradition. Writers and lecturers genuinely seem never to have considered scientific evidence and, given a choice, always to prefer sentimental excitement. They have fallen for ideas about the teaching of reading whose wild romance is equalled only by their destructive and apparently irreversible effect upon children's lives. As Dr Macmillan writes:

> 'All of these approaches have in common an aversion to teaching a child how to read' (p.85).

No F.R. Leavis could today hope to justify a state of affairs in which those concerned to shape national education remain themselves ill equipped to read and evaluate serious research. C.P. Snow's *two cultures* rift valley runs right down the middle of the education community.

Many of the most persistent problems turn, in the end, upon a paradox. Human language capacity, for instance, and its biological programming, does not represent some fatal restriction of scope, except perhaps to would-be dictators. As Steven Pinker writes in his *Language Instinct* (1995, p. 287):

> 'Mental flexibility confines children; innate constraints set them free.'

Similarly in learning to read, there is no drastic divide between alphabetic, phonic teaching and the encouragement of meaning; *the meaning of a word or letter is its sound.*

These matters all become very much clearer thanks to the care and thoroughness of Dr Macmillan's work. The grounds for legitimate dispute continue to shrink and excuses for ignorance of the contours of basic research to dwindle. This book should be on the reading list of every course of initial teacher training concerned with the teaching of reading.

Martin Turner,
Windlesham, Surrey,
7 January, 1997

Martin Turner is Head of Psychology at the Dyslexia Institute

The Author

Bonnie Macmillan was educated in Victoria and Vancouver, receiving her doctorate from the University of British Columbia. She has taught in Canada and Australia at both the primary school and university level. She has two daughters, now at university, whom she taught to read before they went to school. Since 1991, she has been living in London, England where she has remarried and is working on a number of reading-related research projects.

Acknowledgements

There are many people who have helped me in the preparation of this book. They have given their time generously and I am indebted to them. I would especially like to thank James Tooley, who is largely responsible for bringing the project to completion. I am grateful to him for his kind support and his determination to see the book in print. I would also like to thank my reviewers. The time and thought they have so generously given have contributed enormously. I am grateful as well to the many people in schools, colleges, research institutes and other organisations who have supplied me with materials, information and help with my research. Finally, I am very grateful to the many friends and members of my family who have provided unfailing support and encouragement right from the beginning of the venture, and over a period of time much longer than I could have ever foreseen. If this book contributes to achieving higher standards of reading education, I know that everyone who has helped will share my satisfaction.

Bonnie Macmillan,
February 1997

Introduction

Probably the most important task of every primary school is to ensure that every child learns to read. Difficulty with reading will limit a child's experience in every school activity and area of study, while his or her future as a contributing member of society will also be blighted. Try to imagine for one second what it must feel like to be 12 years old and be unable to read the school notice-board, the cafeteria menu, or a railway timetable. What would one do? How would one behave? This is a prospect facing at least half the school population (DfEE, 1996a; Ofsted, 1996). And this is not just a passing phase, something that will become less noticeable with age, like a playground scar. This disability will be with the child for life. According to the researchers Sammons, Nuttall, Cuttance, and Thomas (1993), the single most important factor influencing GCSE results at age 16 is reading ability at age 7. If a child does not learn to read at an early stage, he or she is destined never to reach his or her true intellectual potential.

Although the government spends more than £32 billion on education (Hayman & Simpson, 1996), analysis of a number of sources suggests that at least a quarter of 7-year-old children are failing to learn how to read after two years of primary school (Cato and Whetton, 1991; DES, 1991a; DFE, 1992, 1995; DfEE, 1996b; HMI, 1990; Turner, 1990). This is a conservative estimate; there is evidence that the real incidence of failure may be as high as a third of children at this early stage (Davies, Brember, & Pumfrey, 1995). Indeed, in some areas, the figure is even higher, as shown by a recent Ofsted survey using standardised reading tests in forty-five inner London schools, representative of the schools in Islington, Southwark, and Tower Hamlets (Ofsted, 1996). Although one would expect scores in urban areas to be depressed relative to other areas, the results were disturbing. It was found that the percentage of 7-year-olds reading either at a level below their chronological age, or not actually reading was *nearly 80%*.

Moreover, there is evidence that reading standards are *declining*. The standardised reading test data for 7-year-olds from local educational authorities (LEAs) throughout England and Wales were examined throughout the period 1981-90 by the National Foundation for Educational Research (Cato & Whetton, 1991). Out of the LEAs that conducted tests and were willing to submit test data, 19 out of 26 LEAs showed evidence of a substantial decline in reading standards. Although NFER found, based on this sample, that the average decline over this period was about 4 months of reading age, it is likely that the true rate of decline was even more serious. For there was a selection bias in the data available to NFER; the 22% of all LEAs involved were those that had conducted appropriate tests and, at the same time, were willing to submit data. Turner, for example, through independent analysis of reading test data from 37 LEAs (or 32% of all LEAs), found evidence of a more serious decline of approximately 6·5 months of reading age over this period (Turner, 1990; 1991a; 1995). Another NFER survey indicated that the decline in reading standards was continuing. In one sample of 24 schools, reading scores of 7- and 8-year-olds were compared from the years 1987 and 1991 (Gorman & Fernandes, 1992). A drop of just over 5 months in reading age was discovered between these two groups. Another sample of 37 schools corroborated this rate of decline. Thus, the annual rate of decline represented over this four-year period was three times greater than that found in the earlier NFER investigation. In addition, since there was some degree of sampling bias (data was obtained solely from schools willing to participate), it is quite likely that the rate of decline may have been more serious (Pumfrey, 1991, p. 55; Davies, Brember, & Pumfrey, 1995).

The personal tragedy of this failure to assist young people to read must be enormous. A recent study undertaken by the Institute of Education, University of London, followed the progress of almost 800 pupils over nine years. It found that the most significant factor affecting achievement at GCSE level is reading and mathematics attainment at age 7. The degree to which this factor influences GCSE results at age 16 is almost three times greater than the extent to which a group of background factors such as sex, socioeconomic status, or ethnic group affect GCSE attainment (Sammons et al., 1993a).

A later analysis showed that reading attainment at age 11 exerts by far the most important influence on subsequent GCSE performance; this factor is *at least four times more important* than the influence of a number of background factors including age, sex, father's occupation, low family income, ethnic group, and fluency in English (Sammons, 1995).

Early success in learning to read also brings emotional and behavioural advantages. It has been found that reading achievement at age 7 is predictive of later 'self-concept' and attitude to school (Mortimore, Sammons, Stoll, Lewis & Ecob, 1988a). Apart from the loss of self-esteem, pupils who fail to learn how to read may suffer many other negative effects, including the inability to cope with other subjects (Stuart, 1995) and the avoidance of school altogether. According to data collected by Keele University from more than 7,000 pupils in 1993-4, 17 to 20% of 15- and 16-year-olds admitted to playing truant 'often' or 'sometimes', and about 25% admitted to behaving badly 'sometimes' or 'often'. This research also shows that boys aged 11 to 16 are twice as likely as girls to be unhappy at school, fail to do their homework, misbehave in lessons or play truant; as is pointed out, 'one of the most significant shifts in the education scene over the last decade is the growing disparity in achievement and attitude to school between girls and boys' (Barber, 1996, p. 6). This disparity may well have a significant cause in terms of the teaching of reading, as we shall see below.

The increased frustration experienced as a result of not being able to read exacts a serious toll. In a study of two different groups of delinquent adolescent boys, the one factor found to correlate significantly with aggression was reading failure (Hogenson, 1974). In a longitudinal study, it was found that reading disability at age 9 in boys was predictive of juvenile delinquency at age 15 (Williams & McGee, 1994). In a large government survey in the United States, a direct link between illiteracy and crime was demonstrated; it was found that more than 85% of minors entering the juvenile justice system could not read (Brunner, 1993). In England, a survey involving 16 prisons, chosen as representative of all those in England and Wales, found that 52% of inmates could only read at the level of a 9-year-old or below (BSA, 1994).

Personal tragedy aside, the cost of reading failure to the taxpayer is enormous. Moreover, extra training costs to industry as a result of poor literacy skills are estimated by employers to be £4·8 billion a year (ALBSU, 1992); more than 90 per cent of companies are dissatisfied with the literacy skills of their recruits (Lamb, 1994). Multinational companies rate British teenagers as the least literate in Europe (Layard, 1996).

Teaching children to read early in their school careers is thus of paramount importance; so important, in fact, that one would imagine that only the most effective methods would be used to teach them. And indeed, literally hundreds of experimental research studies over the past seventy years have been devoted to determining how best to teach children to read. In recent years, many studies have been conducted both in this country and abroad, using large sample sizes, rigorous statistical analysis, and controlled, repeatable conditions. These have contributed to and confirmed earlier research demonstrating the effectiveness of certain methods and the ineffectiveness of others. The scientific evidence is surprisingly consistent to the extent that it can be regarded as conclusive. It puts us in a position where it is now possible to define quite precisely what is the optimum programme for teaching children how to read.

It is, unfortunately, very far removed from that which is occurring in this country's primary schools. Exploring this mismatch between the research evidence and what goes on in schools is the main aim of this book, and will take up the majority of the next six chapters. Clearly, this mismatch provides a strong argument to support the claim that it is the inadequacies in the teaching of reading that are to blame for reading failure. However, before becoming immersed in the detailed arguments required to show this, we can see that there is also considerable circumstantial evidence to support the connection between teaching methods used in schools and failing readers.

The Connection between Teaching Methods and Failing Readers

There are three reasons for suspecting that poor reading standards are related to teaching methods. These relate to:

1. No corresponding decline in mathematics scores;
2. Gender differences in reading scores; and
3. Countries which use 'more traditional' methods of teaching reading do not show reading in decline - evidence from Scotland.

First, one period of notable decline in the reading standards of 7-year-olds was during the 1980s, particularly during the late 1980s (Turner, 1990; 1991b). During this period, as Turner pointed out, there was no corresponding decline in numeracy standards of the same children. One would expect environmental factors, often blamed for the decline in reading scores, also to affect number attainment. The fact that this did not occur throws suspicion on a factor occurring within schools, and a factor peculiar to reading instruction.

Second, in 1994, it came to national attention in England that girls had overtaken boys for the first time in their attainment at A Level examinations. While historical changes in attitudes to men and women were offered as one explanation of this phenomenon (BBC 1, 1994), another highly plausible alternative is suggested by recent evidence which highlights the importance of reading ability at age 7 as the most significant factor affecting later attainment, (Sammons et al., 1994). Given what we know - as we discuss later - about the detrimental effects on boys in particular of certain methods of teaching reading, one could easily have predicted the recent superior A Level performance of girls compared to boys. How? Simply by looking at the way both have performed on reading tests at age 7 over the last thirty years. As we shall see, gender differences have been increasing precisely during the period in which the teaching of reading has been dramatically transformed.

Trends in reading attainment of girls and boys over a period of years from 1957 to 1985 can be examined for 11-year-olds (DES, 1978; Douglas, 1969; Inner London Educational Authority, 1985; Morris, 1966; Start & Wells, 1972). Although different measures were used in these surveys, it is possible to detect changes in the way boys and girls performed. In 1957, a survey of over 2,000 children in Kent (age 10-11 years) found no significant sex differences in reading performance (Morris, 1966). In the years 1969, 1972, and 1977, other large surveys in England of 11-year-olds' reading ability confirmed this finding (Douglas, 1969; Start & Wells, 1972; DES, 1978). In general, even where girls have performed better than boys in reading at age 7, by the age of 11, boys catch up with girls. However, by 1985, with the increasing infiltration of child-centred, whole-word methods in the teaching of reading (methods explored in subsequent chapters), boys' performance was considerably worse than girls': among 11-year-olds with severe reading difficulties, 20% were girls and 28% were boys (ILEA, 1985).

From 1985 until 1996, there have been no large surveys of reading results by gender available for 11-year-olds which have employed standardised reading tests. However, the subjective tests that were given to 11-year-olds in 1988 by the Assessment of Performance Unit showed that girls performed better than boys in writing and reading comprehension and these differences were found to persist at the age of 15 (Gorman, White, Brooks & English, 1989; Ofsted, 1993a).

These gender differences did not exist in the past. Data from many years ago would suggest that there were certainly no sex differences in reading at the age of 14 since surveys of reading attainment at age 11 show that differences in reading ability disappear by this age (Chazan, 1971; DFE, 1978; Douglas, 1969; Start & Wells, 1972). Throughout the book we suggest that it is the transformation of the teaching of reading which is likely to be responsible for this gender difference.

Third, the evidence from Scotland is particularly interesting. In comparison to the 'progressive', discovery approaches used to teach children to read in English and Welsh primary schools, as we discuss in the remainder of the book, the methods used in Scottish schools have remained relatively traditional and phonics-based (Johnston, 1995; Maxwell, 1977; Scottish Education Department, 1985; Vernon, 1967). If environmental influences were to blame for the declining reading standards in England, one would expect that schools in Scotland would be equally exposed to these influences, and their reading standards would also be affected. However, in contrast to England, no corresponding decline in reading scores has occurred in Scotland (results for Year 4 and Year 7 pupils, age 8 and 11, in 1984 and 1989) (Foxman, Gorman, & Brooks, 1992-93). These differences between countries in reading trends strongly implicate the child-centred, whole-word methods of reading instruction used in

England as a decisive factor in the decline of England's reading standards.

Even more compelling is the absence of sex differences seen in the reading performance of Scottish children in contrast to that observed in English children. In 1977, Scottish 8-year-olds of either sex performed similarly on the Edinburgh Reading Test (Maxwell, 1977). In contrast, English 9-year-olds in this same year revealed a sex difference, with girls significantly outperforming boys on the Burt Standardised Reading Test (DES, 1978); this result was obtained in spite of the fact that by the age of 9, the expected trend is for the sex differences in reading performance to diminish or disappear. As a later example, in 1989, and 1992, in the Scottish Assessment of Achievement Programme (AAP) surveys, standardised reading tests of Scottish 8-year-olds revealed no significant sex differences (Scottish Education Department, 1989, 1992). By contrast, English children who were tested at the age of 8 in 1988, and the age of 7 in 1991, 1992, 1994, and 1995 on National Curriculum tests once again revealed significant sex differences favouring girls in their reading performance (Mortimore et al, 1988; DES, 1991a; DFE, 1992; DFE, 1995; DfEE, 1996c).

The Structure of the Book

In its six main chapters, this book examines the extent to which current teaching practice is informed by the findings from reading research. Research shows that virtually all children can be taught how to read, that the incidence of reading failure among the less gifted can be almost entirely eliminated, and that the rate of reading progress can be such that it allows all children of whatever ability or social background to reach their full potential, as long as teaching practice is aligned with findings from empirical research. Thus the very low standards of reading attained are a direct reflection of the disparity which now exists between reading research and practice.

This book seeks to expose this gap; it investigates to what degree teaching practice is at variance with important findings from empirical research. These chapters compare what research says about how best to teach a child to read with how a child is actually being taught to read in today's primary schools. All children can easily be taught to read: why is the system failing them? Can the reason for girls outperforming boys, and Scottish children outperforming English children, on standardised reading tests really be due to differences in teaching practices?

But while answering these questions, a number of others arise: Why are we told that reading standards are improving (DFE, 1994a; Shephard, 1995), when reliable evidence shows they are growing worse (Davies et al., 1995)? Why do half of trainee teachers feel inadequately prepared to teach reading (Brooks, Gorman, Kendal, and Tate, 1992)? Is there evidence that bias may have crept into teacher training? And how true is it that no evidence exists implicating reading methods as a likely cause for the decline in reading standards? In general terms, one may find oneself wondering if it is possible that educational bureaucrats, teacher trainers, teachers' unions and organisations, in collaboration with book publishers, and assisted by the rapid turnover of Secretaries of State for Education, may have conspired over a number of years to weave a complex veil of orthodoxy that has functioned most effectively to obscure the facts.

Uncovering the facts is the main aim of this book. Throughout, an attempt is made to review the most up-to-date scientific research pertaining to beginning reading instruction. Every effort has been made to ensure objectivity in reviewing the relevant research; relevant studies, providing that they have been well-conducted, statistical studies, have been included in this review, whether or not the results have supported a particular point of view.

It is important to note that the information about both research and practice presented here has been strictly confined to that which pertains to beginning reading instruction. A distinction is made between beginning reading and later reading; once a child has learned to read, the processes involved are not the same as those characterising the beginning stages.

The first five chapters of the book are each split into two sections: research and practice. Each chapter begins with a section presenting research findings pertaining to a particular aspect of beginning reading instruction, and is followed by a second section which examines the degree to which these findings are reflected in present-day teaching practice. This simultaneous juxta-position of research and practice is designed to throw any contrasts between the two into sharper relief.

Indeed, throughout these chapters, a consistent pattern is revealed: a disturbing gap between research and practice becomes increasingly apparent.

Chapter 1 answers two questions: what, according to experimental research, are *the key elements that must be taught* to children if all children are to learn how to read? Does current teaching practice reflect these findings?

Chapter 2 examines the *rôle of reading materials* in early reading instruction. What does research indicate are the most effective materials for promoting early reading development, and how does this compare with the nature of the reading materials currently used in English classrooms?

Chapter 3, while investigating *the efficacy of phonics methods*, explores the popular assumption that children should be taught to read through *the use of a mixture of methods*. Does empirical research support this idea? To what extent does the current teaching practice of employing a mixture of methods contradict research findings?

Should it be accepted as fact, however, that what most teachers use to teach reading is indeed a mixture of methods? The efficacy of *whole-word methods of instruction* are examined in Chapter 4: what support does scientific research find for the use of these teaching methods during beginning-reading instruction? This chapter, then, explores both the extent to which whole-word methods hide within 'the mixture' and the degree to which this teaching practice is at variance with research evidence.

Chapter 5 analyses the research and practice related to *children's individual differences*. It is thought that because all children are different, children learn to read in a variety of ways. (This belief is the main justification for the mixture-of-methods concept found, upon investigation in Chapter 3, to be so popular.) Chapter 5 seeks to reveal the degree to which this idea is justified when examining the related research, and the extent to which this idea – catering to individual differences – is implemented in practice.

The careful *monitoring and assessment of reading instruction* can help to fine-tune its quality and help to ensure that the highest standards of reading possible are achieved. The politics of reading assessment is investigated in Chapter 6, the purpose being to answer two questions: does experimental research demonstrate how one might most effectively monitor progress and subsequently modify teaching practice? And, if the assessment procedures adopted in practice do not reflect these findings, what political pressures are at work?

In conclusion, the high incidence of reading failure among today's young schoolchildren is a tragic state of affairs – the more so, *because it need not be*. Indeed, there *is* a solution. Many schools have discovered this solution already, and it need not remain a secret: the more closely a teacher's instructional practice follows the findings from empirical research, the better will be the resulting reading achievement among pupils.

1 | The Essentials of Reading

Part 1 Research: What a Child Needs to Know in Order to Learn to Read

All babies learn how to speak; it is a universal, natural phenomenon. However, all children do not learn how to read. It is easy to underestimate the unique challenge that the task of learning to read presents to children. As adult, fluent readers, we may find it difficult to appreciate the enormous scale of the conceptual leap that is involved in understanding the equivalence of little black marks on paper to speech. Reading is a cultural invention, not a biologically-programmed facility. Children do not suddenly start reading. They need to be taught.

The Alphabetic Principle

How children learn to read, and how best to teach them, are problems that have been addressed over the years by a huge amount of empirical research. As far as the fundamental basics involved in learning how to read are concerned, the results are unequivocal. The most important finding, consistently verified and no longer in question, is that in order for children to learn how to read in an alphabetic language, such as English, they must understand that print is a code or a cipher representing speech sounds. It is the writing system which is unique about reading. Children must learn the writing system that is used to represent the sounds of the language. Research confirms what common sense would lead one intuitively to believe.

An understanding of this basic relationship is crucial in learning how to read. At some point, and regardless of the method of instruction, children must grasp and make use of this principle that units of print correspond to units of speech. This principle is known as the *alphabetic principle* (Adams, 1990; Bradley, 1987: Byrne, 1992; Gough, Ehri, & Treiman,

1992; Rieben & Perfetti, 1991; Stanovich, 1992; Tunmer & Rohl, 1991; Williams, 1985).

The principle may be induced, it may be learned along with, or after, the accumulation of a *sight word* vocabulary (words recognised automatically on sight), or it may be learned through direct instruction. Whatever the method of instruction used, in order for children to read independently and be capable of decoding the many unknown words that will be encountered in the early stages of learning to read, this principle – the alphabetic principle – must be understood (Alegria & Morais, 1991; Byrne, 1991; Ehri, 1991; Perfetti, 1991; Stanovich, 1992). Recent advances in the science of reading, particularly in the field of eye movement studies (which confirm the importance of identifying individual letter sounds), mean that there is no longer any dispute about the processes involved in reading (Garrod, 1995; Perfetti, 1995a; Rayner, 1995). Because both historically speaking, and historically for each individual, speech came first, it does not seem so surprising that one of the first processes that takes place during reading is the translation of the printed symbols into speech sounds. Thus, as a preliminary process in reading, the printed symbols are translated into a form of language that is familiar and already understood.

Two Types of Knowledge Necessary

What does a child need to know in order to be able to read? When children come to school they know how to speak a language, but what they frequently do not know is the writing system. Thus, what needs to be taught is the writing system, and how to translate the written symbols into speech sounds. There are *two* kinds of knowledge required in order for a child to learn this translation process, the process which has been called the alphabetic principle. A child must:

1. be aware that spoken words are made up of separate sounds and be able to identify them (this is known as *phonological awareness*); and

2. learn the specific correspondences of letters or groups of letters to specific speech sounds.

Phonological Awareness

Simply being aware that speech is made up of separate sounds aids understanding of the alphabetic principle. There is consistent and wide-ranging research evidence that a child's awareness of this concept, or the child's level of *phonological awareness* (sensitivity to the sounds in speech), or even more particularly, *phoneme awareness* (sensitivity to the individual speech sounds in words), is the best single predictor of success in learning to read, not only in English (Blachman, 1984; Bradley & Bryant, 1983; Fox & Routh, 1980; Gough & Juel, 1991; Goldstein, 1976; Mann & Liberman, 1984; Stanovich, 1986), but also in Swedish, Spanish, French, Italian, and Russian (for reviews, see Adams & Bruck, 1993). Phonological measures are even better than standardised tests of intelligence in predicting reading ability (Stanovich, 1992).

It is quite logical that this should be so when one considers to what a large extent dealing with language sounds features in the process of reading. In fact, research evidence suggests that *all* readers make use of speech sound information while reading. Chinese readers, for example, are instructed in the alphabet first, for the purposes of pronunciation, before being introduced to Chinese characters. At first the alphabetic script is written with the characters until they are learned, and thereafter alphabetic writing is used only when introducing new characters (Hu & Catts, 1993; Perfetti, 1995a). And, remarkable as it may seem, it has even been discovered that the more successful among deaf readers also make some use of abstract phonological knowledge while reading (Liberman & Shankweiler, 1991). In contrast to these examples, adult illiterates do not possess any awareness of the phonological structure of words (Byrne & Ledez, 1994; Morais & Kolinsky, 1994; Pratt & Brady, 1988).

Letter-Sound Correspondences

In addition to knowledge about the sounds of language, a child must also learn the writing system. In English, there are twenty-six letters that either singly or in combination represent the forty-four sounds of spoken language (Morris, 1994). An abundance of research evidence has demonstrated that the ability to recognise letter shapes and to translate these to their corresponding speech sounds is also necessary in learning how to read (Anderson et al., 1985; Backman et al., 1984; Chall, 1983; Cunningham, 1990; Manis & Morrison, 1985; Share & Jorm, 1987; Williams, 1985).

A Reciprocal Process

Both phonological awareness and knowledge of letter-sound correspondences act in concert to generate an understanding of the alphabetic principle (Alegria & Morais, 1991; Ehri, 1991; Perfetti, 1991). Knowing that words are made up of separate speech sounds (or *phonemes*) and being able to hear these and identify them is not sufficient to understand the alphabetic principle. Supplementing this knowledge with information about how letters correspond to various sounds, however, will produce the necessary alphabetic insight. Learning the sounds that the letters represent is not sufficient on its own either. That needs to be supplemented by the ability to identify and segment sounds in spoken words.

Although most children by the age of 3 or 4 will have developed a minimal level of phonological awareness, being able to recognise rhyme, for example (Maclean, Bryant, & Bradley, 1987), there is evidence that the more advanced type of phonological awareness, being aware of individual or separate sounds in words, does not evolve from this rudimentary ability without intervention (Cary & Verhaeghe, 1992; Seymour & Evans, 1994). It appears that it is the introduction of an alphabetic code which is particularly instrumental in initiating the development of this specialised phonological knowledge. Although some of the more advanced phonological awareness skills examined in research investigations (such as being able to substitute different sounds in spoken words, for example) are not a prerequisite for learning to read (Perfetti, 1991), studies suggest that at least some level of phoneme awareness is necessary, but not sufficient, in early reading development (Ball, 1993; Gough & Juel, 1987; Tunmer & Nesdale, 1985).

These findings have important implications for instruction. Presenting a child with word families, or the two words *fat* and *bat*, for example, is not sufficient for the child to deduce that the letter f corresponds to the phoneme /f/ and the letter b to the phoneme /b/. Experiments show that children fail to deduce these associations for themselves (Byrne, 1991). Progress can only be made if information about both (a) how words are made up of separate sounds, and (b) how certain letters represent certain sounds, is provided.

Many studies have shown the value of direct, explicit instruction, particularly that which includes the teaching of letter-sound associations, and blending skills, in developing higher-order phonological skills (Cary & Verhaege, 1994; Foorman & Francis, 1994; Perfetti, Beck, Bell, & Hughes, 1987; Seymour & Evans, 1994). Ehri (1983) suggests that since it is the introduction of letters that provides children with concrete symbols with which to associate sounds, higher-order phonological skills develop only as a result of letter-sound teaching.

Once the alphabetic principle is grasped it is a robust and powerful tool. An initial understanding of the principle spreads, so that a minimal ability to decode leads to further insights about other sounds and letters in the developing reading vocabulary. With increasing practice, these effects quickly become widespread (Byrne & Fielding-Barnsley, 1990; Goswami & Bryant, 1990). Gough and Walsh (1991) found that children who are cipher readers learn to read and spell new exception words faster and more accurately than those who are not. Thus, even though training to improve *both* phoneme awareness *and* knowledge of letter-sound correspondences is crucial during the beginning stages of reading instruction, later it may only be necessary to teach a limited number of additional letter-sound correspondences, as this will be sufficient to spur the development of further phonological skills (Byrne, 1992).

Instructional Implications

These findings indicate that in order to promote early reading success, it is of critical importance that beginning-reading instruction is focused on:

1. developing phoneme awareness; and

2. developing knowledge about letter-sound associations.

Since research shows that children, even at the ages of 6 or 7 (Lundberg, Frost, & Petersen, 1988; Vellutino & Scanlon, 1987), lack the ability to hear separate sounds in words, and that they are also unable to deduce letter-sound associations for themselves (Byrne, 1991), appropriate instructional intervention is particularly important.

There are several ways in which a teacher can promote the development of these two forms of crucial knowledge, and dramatically improve reading progress. The teacher can: (a) begin instruction regardless of children's print concept understanding; (b) teach children to hear and identify phonemes; (c) teach the alphabetic code; (d) teach synthesis or blending skills explicitly; (e) develop children's knowledge of spelling patterns; and (f) promote fluent, automatic decoding through carefully arranged reading practice. A discussion of each of these follows.

(a) Developing an Understanding of Print Concepts

Before attending school, most children will have adequate knowledge of the various conventions of print: the correct way to hold a book, how to turn the pages, the direction in which print is read, and the concept that print symbols correspond to words and sentences that are read either silently or aloud. Pointing to words while reading to children, for example, helps them to understand that print represents spoken language (Adams & Bruck, 1993). If however, children have little or no understanding of these concepts, teaching children to read need not be delayed. Indeed, studies show that children from disadvantaged backgrounds can benefit early on from code-oriented instruction while learning about basic print concepts at the same time (Ball & Blachman, 1988; Ehri, 1989; Vellutino & Scanlon, 1987).

(b) Providing Direct Instruction in Awareness of Speech Sounds

Since the printed symbols of alphabetic languages represent speech sounds, having an awareness of these sounds (or phonemes), is particularly important in learning to read English (Liberman & Liberman, 1992). However, many children in the age range of 6-7 years are not able to hear the separate sounds in spoken words or to say what they are (Bowey & Francis, 1991; Wimmer, Landerl, Linortner, & Hummer, 1991). Unless specifically stimulated (either through direct training in hearing the separate sounds in spoken words, or through the explicit teaching of letter-sound correspondences), sensitivity to the phonemic structure of words does not develop (Badian, 1993). Simply being exposed to reading activities, of the type that does not provoke the specific awareness that words are composed of separate sounds, or does not make the links between sounds and spelling explicit, will not improve phonological awareness (Ellis, 1993).

26

Appropriate instruction, therefore, is vital if children are to be made aware of the existence of phonemes, and of how words in speech can be segmented (Gleitman & Rozin, 1977). Direct instruction to help children develop this sensitivity to phonemes during or before initial reading instruction can have dramatic effects, producing statistically significant advantages in reading achievement (Alegria, Pinot and Morais, 1982; Bradley & Bryant, 1985; Tunmer, Herriman, & Nesdale, 1988; Olofsson & Lundberg, 1985; Vellutino & Scanlon, 1987).

Although such instruction is best provided in the first year of school, such training can be accomplished at any age. Phoneme awareness training programmes are described by Ball and Blachman (1991), Blachman (1987), Camp et al., (1981), Liberman and Shankweiler (1991), Lie (1991), Lindamood and Lindamood(1975), and Rosner (1975).

The learning of songs and nursery rhymes, at home or nursery school, before attending primary school, will help to develop sensitivity to the sounds in language. Kindergarten children (5 years of age) exposed to such activities become significantly better readers and spellers in the primary grades than children without this experience (Lundberg, Frost, & Peterson, 1988).

As soon as possible, however, the more advanced skill of being able to identify individual sounds in words should be developed. In one study (Sawyer, 1992), 6-year-old children were given daily instruction in auditory segmentation (training to hear the separate sounds in spoken words), with the result that by the end of one year, the usual discrepancy between the below-average readers and average readers was narrowed, and after one more year, was eliminated.

Although early reading instruction often includes teaching letter recognition and letter-sound relationships, attention to phoneme segmenting skills (detecting the separate sounds within a *spoken* word) may rarely be given. This is a significant shortcoming because contrary to what many may believe to be the case, proficient reading is more dependent on auditory skills than it is on visual skills (Bakker et al., 1990; Brouininks, 1969; Hynd, 1992). Badian (1994) found evidence that compared to visual processing skills, auditory-analysis skills contribute almost twice as much to the variance in children's word reading. A recent study conducted over three years by Grogan (1995) found that once the less important factors of age and intelligence were partialed out of statistical analyses, auditory skills (related to memory for speech sound sequences) at age 4 were almost *three times more influential* on reading ability at age 7 than visual skills (related to memory for printed letter sequences).

It is thus absolutely critical that children be helped to develop this initial ability to hear the separate sounds in words, since it is also true that only a minimal amount of phonological awareness is required in order to facilitate the learning of letter-to-sound correspondences (Juel et al. 1986; Tunmer et al, 1988; Tunmer & Rohl, 1991), which will, in reciprocal fashion, promote further, higher-order phonological awareness skills. For all children, but particularly for children 'at risk' (those who will experience particular difficulty in learning how to read), ensuring that this sort of instruction is included may help boost their performance significantly at the start, as well as reduce the incidence of reading failure in primary schools later on (Mann, 1991a; Wagner, 1988).

(c) Providing Direct Teaching of the Alphabetic Code

Since there is some evidence that beginning readers may initially treat words as if they are pictures, rather than examine the letters in a left to right sequence (Byrne & Fielding-Barnsley, 1989; Ehri, 1992; Gough & Hillinger, 1980), instruction is required in order to give children a more productive strategy. Without instruction, the continued reliance on the visual appearance of words eventually leads to severe difficulties in learning to read (Gough & Juel, 1991; Snowling, 1987). Children must be helped to break away from a whole-word or logographic way of looking at words, in order to advance to an alphabetic stage where connections are made between spellings and sounds. This is a crucial step in learning to read (for reviews, see Adams, 1990; Adams & Bruck, 1993; Liberman & Shankweiler, 1991; Rieben & Perfetti, 1991; Stanovich, 1991; Sawyer & Fox, 1991).

The most effective route in helping children to establish the connections between letters and sounds is through direct instruction. A number of studies indicate that teaching letter shapes along with their corresponding speech sounds is more effective than teaching either letter recognition or phoneme awareness on its own (Ball & Blachman, 1991; Bradley &

Bryant, 1983; Byrne & Fielding-Barnsley, 1991; Cunningham, 1990; Ohnmacht, 1969); indeed, some researchers have found that phonological training by itself produces no significant effects, unless it is supplemented with training in letter-sound correspondences (Byrne, 1991; Defior & Tudela, 1994).

On the question of whether or not teaching letter names should be part of an early reading programme, researchers are divided (Adams, 1990; Hohn & Ehri, 1983). Although letter-name knowledge is an important predictor of later reading success, some researchers provide evidence that confusion between letter names and sounds can persist throughout primary school (Harrison, Zollner, & Magill, 1996), and others argue that the teaching of letter sounds is more profitable for developing blending and reading skills (Englemann & Bruner, 1983). However, a year-long study comparing two systematic phonological, code-oriented programmes, one which taught letter names along with letter sounds, and one which did not, found no significant differences in achievement (O'Connor, Jenkins, Cole, & Mills, 1993).

This issue aside, early code instruction should be systematic, structured, and sequenced, so that the skills to be learned are taught in progression from the simple to the more complex (Williams, 1985); for example, consonant, and short vowel sounds should be taught before digraphs and blends; simple, regularly spelled words should be introduced before irregularly spelled words (Felton, 1993).

(d) Helping Children to Blend Phonemes to Form Words

Many children require particular assistance in learning how to synthesise or combine separate phonemes together to form a word. What is the most effective way to accomplish this? Following the simple-to-complex rule, it has been found that if simple words containing *continuants* (sounds such as 'sss', 'mmm', 'fff', for example) are used first when modelling the blending process, children find the task much easier; 'sss' /a/ 'mmm' is an easier word to synthesise than 'buh' /a/ 'guh', since the latter consonant phonemes, if not pronounced carefully in isolation, produce the *schwa* ('uh' sound) (Byrne & Fielding-Barnsley, 1990).

Instruction that involves teaching the specific relationships between letters and sounds is found to help develop blending skills more effectively than instruction involving writing activities (Vellutino, 1991). Tunmer & Hoover (1993) found evidence that only letter-to-phoneme knowledge (required in reading) contributed to variability in reading real and nonsense words whereas phoneme-to-letter knowledge (required in spelling) did not. These findings are not unrelated to others which show that it is more difficult for young children to isolate or segment phonemes in a spoken word than to synthesise or blend individually presented spoken phonemes to form a word (Perfetti, Beck, Bell, & Hughes, 1987; Torgesen, Morgan, & Davis, 1992); similarly, segmenting a spoken word into its separate phonemes and then blending them in order to write a word (as is demanded in the task of spelling) is a more difficult task for young chldren to perform than simply blending individual letter sounds (presented visually) together to form a word (as is demanded in the task of reading).

However, if instead of asking children to spell a word by writing it, children are asked to 'make' a word using manipulative materials (letters printed on cards or blocks, or magnetic letters, etc.), this is a task found to be very effective in developing blending skills. The value of this technique should not be overlooked. It has been employed by a number of researchers and has resulted in significant effects compared to groups who did not receive this type of instruction (Ball & Blachman, 1991; Bradley & Bryant, 1983; Iversen & Tunmer, 1993). Uhry and Shepherd (1993), however, found that this particular type of segmentation/spelling training (where manipulative materials are used and no writing is involved) even produced significantly better blending and reading ability compared to a control group who were actually taught blending skills specifically (children simply listened to the teacher model blending). The segmentation aspect of the training is likely to improve memory for strings of phonemes, a factor in blending ability. Thus, the fact that this training produces better reading and blending is consistent with a great deal of research which shows that there is a relationship between verbal short-term memory, phonological awareness and reading (see Brady, 1986 for review).

O'Connor and Jenkins (1995) make the point that for some children, even if they succeed in learning letter-sound correspondences and a strategy for blending phonemes into words, the invitation to notice that spoken words can be decomposed into phonemes may go unheeded. Thus, a number of studies have found that supplementing letter-sound and synthesis instruction with related spelling activities (using manipulative materials and/or some writing) not only improves segmentation ability but also reading performance (Ehri, 1989 ; Foorman & Francis, 1994; O'Connor & Jenkins, 1995).

(e) Developing Knowledge of Spelling Patterns

Beginning readers are often insensitive to frequent spelling patterns (Bruck & Treiman, 1992; Ehri & Robbins, 1992), but with carefully arranged reading practice this knowledge develops very rapidly (Treiman, Goswami, & Bruck, 1990). Writing activities which closely parallel reading development (Cunningham & Stanovich, 1990) are also found to help children develop knowledge of spelling patterns. Some researchers argue, however, that writing activities should be kept to a minimum in the beginning, since for many 5- and 6-year-olds, the motor demands of writing may disrupt the transfer of alphabetic understanding from spelling to reading (Foorman, Francis, Novy, & Liberman, 1991). That is, for many children, more learning will take place if they are permitted to concentrate on mastering one skill at a time, without interference from the simultaneous demands of another (Bialystok & Niccols, 1989).

(f) Developing Reading Fluency, Automatic Decoding

Once spelling-to-sound relationships are established, fluent, efficient decoding is dependent upon practice and abundant exposure to text written at an appropriate level. The degree to which children are successful in their first efforts at decoding print will largely determine their inclination to read more (Juel & Roper-Schneider, 1985). Children will not enjoy reading if they experience initial difficulty with decoding, and they will miss out on the much needed practice. The importance of ensuring that children's first books contain liberally-repeated spelling patterns, sequenced in difficulty, and that the children themselves are sufficiently equipped to decode the first words they encounter with a high rate of success, is strongly supported by research evidence.

31

Summary

While learning to decipher words is only one part in the whole process of becoming a proficient reader, it is a vital part in the beginning. Early decoding fluency profoundly influences all other aspects of reading development (for reviews, see Adams, 1990; Liberman & Shankweiler, 1991; Stanovich, 1986, 1992). Children who quickly master the idea that spoken words are made-up of separate sounds, that printed letter symbols correspond to these sounds, and that reading involves the deciphering of these letter symbols into their corresponding speech sounds and then blending the sounds to form words, will progress faster and further than those who do not. To produce significantly superior reading achievement, these are the reading skills that need to be taught first.

Whether it is developed through direct instruction or otherwise, understanding the alphabetic principle is *the* crucial prerequisite in the early stages of learning to read, speeding the development of all other subsequent reading-related skills.

Part 2 Practice: The Eclectic Approach

Reading Methods in Use

What is the state of present reading practice? How do the teachers in the primary schools of England and Wales help children learn how to read? In one large survey, teachers, when asked to describe their predominant approach to teaching reading, responded as follows:

A mixture of methods	almost 85%
'Look-and-Say' (whole-word recognition) approach	less than 10%
'Real books' (use of non-scheme books)	5%
Phonics (code-emphasis) approach	3%

(HMI, 1990).

Fewer than 15% of teachers, according to this survey, concentrate on only one method of teaching reading, while a very large majority report using a combination of methods to teach children how to read. These findings were confirmed in a later survey which found that 83% of teachers reported using a combination of approaches to teach reading (Cato et al., 1992).

32

No Particular Focus or Reading Approach

Current practice does not reflect the fundamental conclusions of research discussed earlier in this chapter. Instead of an early focus on phonological learning and letter-sound associations, as research demonstrates is essential, a much less focused approach is adopted. Almost 85% of teachers describe their approach as a mixture of methods. That this idea is so popular among teachers is hardly surprising. The mixed methods or eclectic philosophy is supported and encouraged by:

School inspectors
'In most schools the eclectic requirements of the National Curriculum, which provide for a carefully considered combination of approaches, were well understood and observed' (HMI, 1989-90, p. 13).
'As in the previous survey, a policy of using a mix of teaching methods was evident in nearly all the schools' (HMI, 1992 para. 35).

National Curriculum Dictates
Pupils should 'be taught to use various approaches to word identification and recognition ...' (SCAA, 1994a).

Teacher Training
'No one approach works well for every child' (Redfern & Edwards, 1992, p. 4).
'Effective practice ... is characterised by ... a variety of different approaches' (Ackerman & Mont, 1991).

Publishers of graded reading schemes
'There is no one method or technique that is the ONLY way to learn to read. Children learn in a variety of ways' (Ladybird series, 1992).

Government-supported adult literacy publications
'Reading should involve a combination of skills – whole word recognition, prediction and phonics' (ALBSU, 1994).

Television programmes
One typical programme included: demonstrations of shared reading, attention to pictures, limited attention to initial consonant sounds, and praise for 'guessing well'! (Words and Pictures, BBC series, 1994).

The Influences Shaping Practice

One large contributing influence on the practice of the mixed-methods notion is teacher training. Students are taught that there is no single method of teaching reading that is suitable for all children. As one interviewee, in a National Foundation for Educational Research (NFER) survey, summarised it, 'eclecticism rules' (Brooks, Gorman, Kendall, & Tate, 1992).

However, while most teacher trainees appear to be well acquainted with the popular concept that only a mixture of methods should be used to teach reading, few may learn the actual details of how to teach a child to read. In fact, a recent survey conducted by the Office for Standards in Education (Ofsted, 1994) revealed that nearly half of primary school teachers do not feel adequately prepared to teach reading at all. In the NFER survey it was found that trainee teachers may receive as little as six hours of instruction in the teaching of reading. Researchers studied 181 teacher training courses in 92 institutions and questioned 400 graduates. High proportions of graduates reported receiving little or no teaching about reading, and admitted having little confidence in their ability to teach the subject.

The same NFER report found that new teachers' experience was heavily influenced by their individual school placements and by the methods they saw in use at first hand. According to school inspectors' reports from various educational authorities over the last few years, what is ostensibly being used to teach children to read is a mixture of methods. Whether the government's plans to make teacher training more school-based are implemented or not, there is then a very high probability that the eclectic approach will continue its reign.

The Mixed-Method Approach

As the eclectic view is currently so fashionable, it is important to examine more closely exactly what is meant by these 'almost 85%' of teachers, when they say they use a combination of approaches (HMI, 1990). In the NFER survey conducted by Cato and her colleagues (Cato et al., 1992), when asked to describe their approach to teaching reading, 83% of teachers said that they used an approach involving the combination of reading schemes and 'real books', 12%, an approach involving only reading schemes, and 5%, an approach involving only 'real books'. But these are not teaching methods. Reading schemes and 'real books' are types of reading materials. It is important, therefore, to examine the nature of the instructional *methods* used in conjunction with these materials.

In nearly all Key Stage 1 classrooms (ages 5-7) in England and Wales, graded reading-scheme materials, and the teaching methods advocated by them, are widely in use and form the basis for reading instruction (HMI Reports and Surveys, 1989-1994). In fact nearly all teachers make use of published reading schemes; they are used in 'more than 95%' of classes (HMI, 1990, p. 2).

Similarly, ordinary story books or 'real books' are materials widely used in primary classrooms. Although the HMI report of 1990 revealed that only 5% of teachers concentrate on a real books' approach, the later survey cited above (Cato et al., 1992) suggests that such materials, and the methods that accompany them, may be more widely used than would at first appear. If the 'almost 85%' (HMI, 1990) of teachers using a mixed-methods approach use these materials, along with the 5% of teachers who concentrate only on a 'real books' approach, approximately 90% of teachers may use such materials during reading instruction. In short, these figures suggest that the use of 'real books' may be almost as popular as the use of reading schemes.

There are thus two main components of the mixed-methods or eclectic approach. These are:

1. the use of the teaching methods that are dictated by the teacher manuals of current reading schemes;

2. the teaching methods that are implicit with the use of non-graded, ordinary story books, or 'real books'.

The teaching manuals of published reading schemes adopt a definite approach towards the teaching of reading. Crucial questions arise from this: Perhaps the teaching approach advocated by today's reading schemes consists of a mixture of methods? Perhaps there is some reading instruction advocated by these schemes, which has an emphasis on the alphabetic code? If this were the case, such instruction would in effect represent at least a partial implementation of relevant research findings. Do the reading schemes in use focus on different approaches at different stages of the reading process? Do they have an early focus, for example, on the development of phonological and alphabetic knowledge, as research suggests is essential? Or, do they adopt a mixed-methods approach to the teaching of reading right at the outset, and throughout the different stages of learning to read? These are questions examined in the next chapter, where we focus on teaching materials.

Summary

There appears to be no particular instructional focus given at different stages of the reading process. Teachers report using a mixture of methods to teach reading right from the beginning, and this eclectic philosophy is advocated very strongly by teacher training institutions. Materials in use include published reading schemes and ordinary story books or 'real books'.

Part 1 Research: What Kind of Reading Materials Promote Early Reading Development?

Schemes Cater to Popular Views

Publishers of reading schemes are careful to gauge the climate of educational theory so that their programmes will reflect the doctrine that teachers and educators currently endorse. Over the last twenty years, *whole-word, 'meaning-emphasis' methods* have been popular and most reading schemes currently on the market have attempted to cater to this view. With whole-word, 'meaning-emphasis' methods, children are encouraged to recognise whole words on the basis of their shape, the surrounding context, the accompanying pictures, or the syntax of sentences. Attention to the interior details of words is avoided; without any prior alphabetic instruction, children are to guess at unknown words, using any available clues, such as the other words that may be recognised, or simply knowing what the whole story is about as a result of hearing the teacher read the story many times.

It should be pointed out that although such methods are often said to focus on the meaning of stories, to refer to such approaches as 'meaning-emphasis' is misleading, since whatever the method of instruction being used, the main goal of reading is to derive meaning. It would be more accurate to think of such methods as memory-emphasis methods, methods that rely on memorisation of words and stories as the route to accessing meaning. To illustrate this point, the guide to the Oxford Reading Tree states that the scheme uses the 'story method', where the needs of the 'whole child' are addressed; 'children hear the stories, talk about the pictures and text, and re-tell the stories themselves, they ... gradually match and check what they are hearing and seeing [and come] to an ... appreciation of what reading is about'; teachers are further instructed, 'it is important not to worry too much ...

whether children are reading or *simply memorising* (Hunt et al., 1996, p. 6, emphasis added). In an earlier version of this text they labelled this method a 'whole language approach'.

However, progress in learning to read is largely determined by how early children are able to shift their attention from purely visual information (seeing words as whole visual shapes) to graphic or letter information (Biemiller, 1979). Research evidence consistently shows that adherence to whole-word methods, particularly during the early stages of learning to read, produces significantly inferior achievement on a number of reading measures (including reading comprehension), compared to methods with a code-emphasis approach (Becker & Gersten, 1982; Blachman, 1987; Calfee, et al., 1973; Chall, 1989; Enfield, 1987; Pflaum, et al., 1980; Wallach & Wallach, 1976; Williams, 1985). There may be several factors that contribute to this phenomenon.

The Vocabulary of Current Reading Schemes

One problem with these schemes concerns the vocabulary. Code-emphasis methods require a controlled vocabulary while whole-word methods demand that reading materials have 'natural-sounding' language, wide-ranging vocabularies, and/or predictable, easy-to-memorise text. As a result, today's reading schemes have turned into 'anthologies of children's literature' (Juel, 1995). Just as with the use of 'real books', the vocabulary contained in these books is not controlled or sequenced in difficulty. Even in the very first early reading books of current schemes, common, but irregularly spelled words, as well as uncommon longer words (the most unpredictable from context) occur frequently. Children cannot deduce letter-sound correspondences for themselves, but even if they have been taught and do possess such knowledge, they would find it extremely difficult to build on their knowledge of spelling patterns with such texts. These texts lack the carefully sequenced presentation of short, regularly spelled words. Indeed, even in a case where reading materials might contain many regularly spelled and simply decoded words, children learning to read are often insensitive to spelling patterns (Bruck & Treiman, 1992; Ehri & Robbins, 1992). Carefully sequenced materials and much practice are required to develop this knowledge (Treiman et al., 1990).

However, the use of the randomised, uncontrolled vocabularies evident in today's reading scheme books appears to be based on the false assumption that children are able to discover letter-phoneme relations quite readily for themselves, after being taught to memorise whole words based on their shape, words that are frequently irregular in their spelling or pronunciation.

The effects of word type on children's beginning-reading progress were investigated in a study by Juel and Roper-Schneider (1985). Children of similar entry ability drawn from 11 grade one classrooms were taught a strictly controlled programme of synthetic phonics instruction for thirty minutes a day, followed by reading activities using one of two scheme readers. The texts in one reading scheme stressed (and repeated more often) common, irregularly spelled words, while in the other, the texts stressed easily decoded, regularly spelled words. Assessment of children's skills at five different times during the year revealed that there were no differences between the two groups in their ability to read the core words of their particular reading scheme, and no differences between groups in their ability to make use of context cues. However, significant differences between groups did occur in their ability to read words with letter sounds that had *not yet been taught*. After as little as two months into the project, those children using the phonic-oriented readers were much better able to decode novel words and were found throughout the year to be making far greater use of phonological decoding strategies than those children using the whole-word-oriented readers. This study shows that, *even when the method of reading instruction is identical and phonic-oriented*, the type of texts young, beginning readers are first given to read will significantly influence the extent to which children develop either generative, alphabetic, or non-generative, whole-word reading strategies.

The type of words used in reading schemes also affects the level of text difficulty. Stories containing common, irregularly spelled words are more difficult to read than those written with short, regularly spelled words. Thus, in the whole-word-oriented schemes, in order to compensate for this problem, the common words to be learned may sometimes be repeated even more often than they occur in 'real books'. Whether or not they are repeated liberally, however, these irregularly spelled words will be difficult to 'read' initially and many adult-assisted readings will be required. Used as beginning reading

39

materials these texts (their difficult vocabularies, and their demand for adult involvement) encourage whole-word, memorisation strategies. If a child is constantly encouraged to memorise, the ability to *decode* novel words is effectively retarded; even if a child has learned the alphabetic principle, this knowledge will not be encouraged to spread in the same way as it would with the use of phonic-oriented texts.

Why is the level of text difficulty important? The high error rates, often accepted as part of the learning process with today's reading scheme books, are negatively correlated with growth (Rosenshine & Stevens, 1984). Studies have shown that for maximum reading progress the text a child is to read must be written at a level of difficulty that is neither too easy (can be independently read with 98% success) nor too difficult (can only be read with frustration where less than 90% of the words are read correctly). Thus, if a reader is to be matched with a text written at an appropriate instructional level, he or she should be able to read without any type of error at least 9 out of every 10 words (May, 1986).

Currently there is concern that books children are to read be interesting, appealing, colourfully illustrated, tell 'real' stories about everyday events and use 'natural' language; these are all laudable goals but there is little, if any, attention paid to the fact that the words appearing on the pages might be far too difficult for the children to read. While it is important that children be interested in the *idea* of reading, they will not like 'reading' very much if it means that the words on the page are largely a mystery, any attempts to read the words resulting in frustration and a sense of failure.

Attention to the Alphabetic Code

The type and amount of phonics instruction advocated by today's reading schemes is of particular concern when, unlike code-emphasis schemes, they carry the expectation that teachers will introduce children to such books at the very beginning of primary school without any prior alphabetic or phoneme training. At the same time, it has been noted that currently there are no reading schemes available that offer a code-emphasis approach (Cato et al., 1992). Whereas it was possible in the past for teachers to choose reading schemes that provided either a whole-word approach or a code-emphasis approach, this is now very difficult.

Approaches to teaching reading are sometimes referred to as *analytic* (involving *segmentation*), or *synthetic* (involving *blending*). Synthetic methods begin with the introduction of letter sounds and/or the sounds made by combinations of letters, and culminate with whole words (the sounds /s/, /u/, /n/ are blended to form the word *sun*). Such instruction is comprehensive, sequenced in difficulty, and *precedes* the reading of material that practises what has been taught. Analytic methods begin with the word, phrase, sentence, or story, and the whole is broken down or analysed into its separate components (the word *sun*, for example, is segmented into its three separate sounds – /s/, /u/, /n/ – or more commonly only one segment of the word is isolated and examined, the initial consonant, the medial vowel, or the final consonant). This sort of instruction usually occurs *after* reading, where the reading material itself furnishes the words chosen for particular instructional focus. The teaching, therefore, tends not to follow any specific sequence.

Letter-sound relationships are taught directly in synthetic methods, but, in analytic methods, these associations must often be inferred. Researchers have found that analysing sounds in words, or breaking words down into parts, appears to be a more difficult task than blending separate sounds together (Goldstein, 1976; Torgesen, Morgan, Davis, 1992). Perfetti and others (1987) concluded that high levels of synthesis or blending skills predicted better reading gains than analysis skills, and Fox and Routh (1984) found that training only in analysis skills failed to help children read new words. However, in the teaching manuals of current reading schemes, if there is any attention addressed to sounds and letters at all, activities suggested are invariably of the less effective, analytic type.

Of relevance here, five programmes that taught *phonics* synthetically (direct teaching of letter-sound correspondences and phonological skills, including blending sounds together to form words) were compared to another five that taught phonics analytically, in twenty classrooms of beginning readers (Bliesmer & Yarborough, 1965). After one year it was found that students being taught with one of the five synthetic reading schemes significantly outperformed students taught by the analytic programmes on a number of reading measures, including comprehension skills. Others have found similar results favouring the synthetic approach used in the first one to three years (Henderson, 1959; Shore & Marascuilo, 1974) and with retarded children (Vandever & Neville, 1976). Synthetic phonics teaching that does not include training children to detect the separate sounds in spoken words may not be so successful with learning-disabled children (Lovett, Ransby, Hardwick, Johns, & Donaldson, 1989; Lyon, 1985), but training in this area prior to synthetic phonics instruction has produced dramatic effects on such children's alphabetic reading skills (Alexander et al., 1991).

Training in Phonemes or Speech Sounds

Whole-word, 'meaning-emphasis' reading schemes also fail to recognise the importance of developing phonological awareness at the initial stages of learning to read, the inherent assumption of these schemes being that without any prior or simultaneous instruction, children can immediately tackle a reader. However, phonological awareness does not develop automatically as a consequence of learning to read. Direct evidence against this idea has come from many studies which show that the level of phonological awareness is not altered by reading activities alone (Bradley & Bryant, 1983; Tunmer et al., 1988; Vellutino & Scanlon, 1987). Training in phonological awareness, especially for at-risk children, results in better and faster reading progress (Ball & Blachman, 1988; Content, et al., 1986; Lundberg et al., 1988; Vellutino & Scanlon, 1987), their lead being maintained even after 4 years (Bradley, 1987).

Children who are exposed to a strictly whole-word setting when learning to read (as would be the case if taught entirely through the use of today's reading schemes) have no segmental awareness of speech; such an ability, without opportunity for use, is never developed (Morais, Alegria, & Content, 1987).

Although experiments show that giving direct instruction which points out shared sounds in words, for example, is an effective way to promote phonological awareness (Byrne & Fielding-Barnsley, 1993), most reading schemes include only a minimal amount of direct teaching. And, rather than attention to phonological awareness or letter-sound correspondences, the bulk of the teaching suggested is directed towards helping children to memorise stories so that they might use this knowledge to guess what the words on the pages are, perhaps eventually building a store of easily recognised words.

Illustrations

Large, colourful illustrations are a major feature of today's reading schemes. While the presence of pictures is unlikely to present a problem for the skilled reader, there is evidence that for the child who is in the very beginning stages of learning how to read, pictures may cause some difficulty. If one is skilled at both picture and print decoding, problems with the simultaneous processing of them do not arise; it is only when, as is the case for the beginning reader, he or she possesses limited skill with both tasks, that interference results (Wu & Solman, 1993). Under the principle of least effort, faced with both picture and text, the child will choose to concentrate on the picture. If the child is faced with such a combination when the words are unfamiliar and have not been encountered before in a non-picture setting, the presence of the picture will be particularly influential in diverting attention away from the print.

Many researchers have studied this phenomenon and reached the conclusion that while pictures may be helpful in some circumstances with skilled readers, they are detrimental in the context of beginning reading instruction (for review, Brigham, 1992; also McDowell, 1982; Rusted & Coltheart, 1979; Saunders & Solman, 1984; Willows, 1978). Recently two studies have suggested that the combination of written word with picture results in a learning deficit or blocking effect with young children, severely hindering word decoding (Singh & Solman, 1990; Solman, Singh, & Kehoe, 1992).

The Rhyme Element

Books that make use of rhyme or repetitive patterns are likely to be easier for children to memorise. Although this may be what has motivated the use of rhyme in reading scheme books in the past, a number of publishers have offered something new recently by introducing whole books of poetry to their schemes. Recent studies investigating both the use of rhyme, as well as *onset and rime* (in the word *cat*, the sound /c/ is the *onset*, and the sound /at/ is the *rime*) appear to have provoked this sudden inclusion. This innovation is misguided on two fronts.

First, if the poetry books are provided in response to the research on the usefulness of nursery rhymes, they are more appropriate materials for the preschool or nursery teacher. Research has shown that exposure to rhyming sounds in poetry is useful as a rudimentary form of phonological awareness training, alerting children to shared sounds in words, and encouraging the revelation that words are made up of separate sounds. But it has been shown that rhyming tasks are the easiest types of phonological tasks to perform (Yopp, 1988); the beginning reader must develop more advanced phonological skills. For the beginning reader, direct teacher instruction in how to identify the separate sounds of words would be more effective in developing the necessary prerequisite reading skills than simply listening to the teacher read these books. On the other hand, as these materials are written at a level appropriate for the already competent reader, for the older child who is able to read them independently, they could help to consolidate and expand a child's knowledge of spelling patterns.

Second, if the poetry books are provided in response to the onset-rime research as materials useful to the teacher during early reading instruction, they are also misguided. Onset-rime instruction has not been proven an effective method to teach children about individual letter-sound correspondences (Bruck & Treiman, 1992). If the poetry books are provided in order to encourage teachers to point out initial sounds (onsets) and common final chunks (rimes) of words to children, *before* they have developed any knowledge of individual letter-sound correspondences, such instruction will fail as a beginning reading method (see Chapter 3 for discussion of this topic). Similarly, assuming that children will deduce letter-sound correspondences for themselves, through the shared reading of such books, is not supported by research either (Byrne, 1991).

The Sight Word Foundation

Another disadvantage of many reading schemes is the emphasis given to whole-word learning and the building up of large sight vocabularies; this is a practice that reinforces the child's natural inclination, at an early stage, to see words purely as visual shapes. Byrne (1992) describes this natural tendency as the 'default acquisition procedure'; recognising words in a logographic way, as if they are pictures, occurs in the absence of guidance. The procedure eventually breaks down when the child is faced with too many words, and too many similar words (Ehri, 1991; Gough, Juel, & Griffith, 1992; Vellutino & Scanlon, 1991).

Evidence from a number of experiments suggests that reading failure may actually result from having too much success with this suboptimal strategy of word recognition, and that a substantial proportion of children with reading difficulties who have reached the limit of their memories do not abandon whole-word strategies (Boder, 1973; Johnston, 1985; Snowling, 1980).

Further support for this notion comes from neurological studies which indicate that encouraging sight word learning through whole-word or logographic strategies at the early stages of reading instruction reinforces visuospatial brain processing, the kind of cognitive operations which are performed in posterior regions of both hemispheres, but primarily within areas of the right hemisphere (Hynd, 1992; Iacoboni & Zaidel, 1996; Menard, Kosslyn, Thompson, Alpert, & Rauch, 1996; Pumfrey & Reason, 1991). This emphasis on the visuospatial aspects of words may make it more difficult for some children, research suggests (Bakker, 1992; Flynn, Deering, Goldstein, & Rahbar, 1992), to transfer to the sort of processing which occurs largely within language areas of the left hemisphere, to the sort of processing involved during phonological recoding or alphabetic reading (Flowers, 1993; Hynd, 1992; Ogden, 1996). This finding has particular relevance to the slower rates of reading progress observed in boys compared to girls. Boys, who initially spend longer than girls perfecting their right hemispheric visuospatial skills (Halpern, 1992; Harris & Sipay, 1990; Kail, 1992), may be particularly adept at memorising words as whole visual units. Their success with whole-word strategies may mislead teachers about their ability to decode.

Summary

Not unlike ordinary children's story books, today's reading schemes provide the child with very attractively illustrated books containing interesting, real-life stories that he or she can relate to. As books serving solely as practice reading materials, once the child has learned how to read, they are likely to be rather useful, but research suggests that published reading schemes may have many shortcomings as suitable tools for promoting the child's early acquisition of the alphabetic principle. These include: (a) the lack of regularly spelled, simple, short words in the children's readers, words that children are readily able to decode; (b) the lack of provision in the teacher's manuals for synthetic, code-emphasis instruction; (c) the absence in the teacher's manuals of a structured, systematic programme to teach letter-sound correspondences, where instruction is given *before*, and closely matched with what children are to read subsequently; (d) the failure to provide teachers with a systematic programme to develop phonological awareness skills; (e) the predominance of illustrations in the children's readers, a potentially distracting feature in the context of early reading instruction; (f) the limitations of using poetry books on their own in the absence of direct instruction as appropriate avenues to develop advanced phonological, letter-sound skills; and (g) the emphasis on encouraging memorisation and whole-word learning, thus training pupils to use suboptimal word-recognition strategies.

Part 2 Practice: The Wide Use of Reading Schemes

Universal Use of Schemes

According to a number of government reports (HMI, 1989-90; 1990; 1992), the use of published reading schemes is almost universal in the country's 19,000 primary schools; they are used by more than 95% of teachers. The two most popular schemes are *The Oxford Reading Tree*, used in about 50% of primary schools (approximately 10,000 schools), and Ginn 360, used in about 30% of schools. The *Ginn 360* 'meaning-oriented' reading scheme was widely adopted in British schools during the 1970s, while the 'whole language' *Oxford Reading Tree*, introduced in the 1980s has gradually infiltrated the market. Other schemes in use include *Story Chest* by Nelson Publishing, employing a 'shared reading', 'guessing game' approach (Nelson, 1991, p.8), and schemes from Heinemann, Longman, and Collins, all of which are meaning-oriented memory-emphasis, or non-alphabetic in their approaches.

The Vocabulary

An examination of the Ginn and Oxford schemes reveals that, rather than representing a mix of methods, these programmes stress only one way of teaching reading. In both of these schemes reading is taught by a whole-word or 'look-and-say' approach; children are to build up sight vocabularies (words automatically recognised, in this case because they are memorised by shape or idiosyncratic features). The vocabulary selected is not graded in difficulty, and key words are often common irregularly spelled words, or uncommon longer words. In the Oxford series, some of the words children are expected to read in their very first readers, after a series of wordless picture books, are: *couldn't, dragon, sleep, dreamed, nasty, fight, everyone, joined, pillow, hungry, shoes, laces.*

It is not clear how children are expected to read these words to begin with. What appears to be the goal is the eventual memorisation of the stories, and the gradual recognition of some of the words by sight, through many shared readings with the teacher. The Ginn series contains words which are repeated liberally throughout. Repetitions of common, often regular, but more difficult to spell words (such as *look, you, here)*, as well as common, irregularly spelled words (such as *said, the, was, come, where)* are prolific. In both schemes children are expected to learn to recognise words as whole visual units using any clues available such as shape or length of the word, accompanying illustrations, available context (derived mainly from knowing what the story is about after several 'readings'), and, only as a last resort, initial letters (whether or not children have been taught to recognise letters or associate them with sounds beforehand). The readers can be read in any order as there is no systematic, sequenced teaching of letter-sound correspondences, or spelling patterns.

Phonemes and the Alphabetic Code

Contrary to the scientific evidence of the efficacy of making children aware of the separate sounds in spoken words and of making sound/symbol correspondences explicit prior to giving children books to read, these schemes make no provision for prior training in this area. If there is any code instruction suggested at all, it is to occur primarily during reading activities and similar to any separate phonics activities described, it is of the discovery type. Unlike synthetic phonics instruction where letters and sounds are associated and then blended to form words, in these activities the teacher is instructed to read a word aloud and then select certain letters (initial consonants or medial vowels, for example) for children to guess what their corresponding sounds might be. Although research indicates that children are not able to perform this task (that is, they are not able to infer letter-sound relationships for themselves), this analytic phonics instruction is the type that schemes invariably model; synthetic phonics instruction, where letter-phoneme relationships are taught explicitly, is omitted.

The type of phonics instruction aside, the systematic and intensive coverage of sound-spelling associations in both the Ginn and the Oxford programmes is not possible because the text to be read is not sequenced in difficulty. Thus the words selected from the text drive a random, incidental approach to the teaching of the alphabetic code. Separate phonics instruction may be regarded as an optional extra. Indeed, in the case of the Oxford programme, until recently there was no phonics instruction of any kind offered until Level 3. In 1995, however, this scheme introduced an alphabet frieze, and card games for 5- to 7-year-olds. Despite the analytic approach taken, and the concentration on initial sounds of words and the ending chunks (or rimes) of words, these materials represent a significant improvement as they offer the opportunity for children to become sensitive to the separate sounds in words (initial consonants only), as well as to learn and practise some letter-sound correspondences.

Publishers' Concerns

When asked what determines the nature of their reading schemes, or the philosophy adopted, publishers agree that these are mainly driven by what teachers want. Sales directors list a number of elements which presumably teachers want and which contribute to the sale of their books (personal interviews, Birmingham Education Show, 1994). In contrast to the research findings indicating the rather dubious efficacy of the place of illustrations in beginning readers, all of those representatives interviewed agreed that the most important factor in selling their books was the quality of the illustrations.

Other current concerns included: stories with real language and everyday familiar events, provision for books of poetry to take advantage of the 'latest research about rhyme being helpful', and an abundance of different types of reading materials. None of these publishers mentioned provision for phonics, but when asked about it, they readily agreed that their schemes included that too. Several of these publishers pointed out that teachers now use a mixture of methods so it was important that their reading programmes catered to this need, and included 'a bit of everything'.

Seven new reading schemes were introduced in 1994. Accordingly, most of them include: attractive illustrations, stories about everyday events, books of poetry and rhyme, and a phonics element. But whether they are marketed as including 'everything' or not, the fact remains that the reading approach adopted is whole-word, with the emphasis on having children respond to printed words as if they are whole visual shapes, not as if they are symbols representing speech sounds, but as if they are symbols purely for meaning.

Illustrations

As illustrations are the most important feature teachers consider when buying reading schemes, early readers tend to be totally dominated by the illustrations. Both Oxford and Ginn offer a complete series of picture books for beginning reading that have no words in them at all. Thereafter the illustrations dominate the pages, with one or two words appearing insignificantly at the bottom of some of the pages. Instead of seeing the text as an important medium for interpreting the pictures, the new National Curriculum directs that reading materials should have 'illustrations that are visually stimulating and enhance the words of the text' (SCAA, 1994a, p. 6). Contrary to research evidence, illustrations are seen not as the distractors they are for many children, but as aids in learning how to read.

The Rhyme Bandwagon

The poetry books in the Oxford series are for older, accomplished readers beginning at Stages 3 and 4. Aside from this too-little-too-late attempt, until recently there was no provision for developing phonological awareness. Oxford's introduction in 1995 of the *Rhyme and Analogy* materials (edited by Goswami) do provide the kind of instruction which alerts beginning readers to shared sounds in words. In this sense, this addition to the Oxford Reading Tree is to be greatly applauded as it puts into practice what has been confirmed by hundreds of research studies. However, using analogy or rhyme to teach letter-sound correspondences, as some of the games attempt to do, is a strategy that research has shown to be ineffective (for a discussion of this research, see Chapter 3, part 1).

Do such reading schemes along with the supplementary activities employed by teachers constitute a mixed-method approach to teaching reading?

The Mixture of Methods

In general terms, the mixture of methods used by almost 85% of teachers consists of: (a) the liberal use of reading schemes and their methods, and (b) the supplementation of this instruction with other materials and approaches. A closer look at the elements making up the 'mixture' will throw light on the degree to which the approaches used actually do represent a combination of different approaches.

(a) Reading Schemes in the 'Mixture'

If most of the popular reading schemes now being sold are marketed as programmes which incorporate a wide variety of approaches, as claims among publishers would suggest, then it is likely that teachers view their main reliance on a published reading scheme as fitting the mould of a mixed-methods approach. However, in a recent survey of schools, the fallacy of assuming that today's reading schemes provide a mixture of teaching methods was acknowledged (Cato et al., 1992). All of the reading schemes in popular use today advocate *only one way* of teaching reading: whatever the terms used to describe the methods, these schemes are fundamentally whole-word, non-code, so-called 'meaning-oriented' in their approaches. They all encourage whole-word or whole-story recognition, they emphasise deriving meaning through the use of memorisation and guessing strategies, and they are further characterised by their lack of attention to the importance of the alphabetic code.

(b) Supplemental Materials and Approaches in the 'Mixture'

An HMI survey of 470 classes (1990) describes in more detail some of the reading activities that are in common practice. While most of children's reading is 'centred' on books from various reading schemes during Years 1 and 2, other 'non-scheme books to widen the choice' are also in use (HMI, 1990, p. 9). The 'non-scheme' books referred to here are often called 'real books'. These are ordinary story books, but they are whole-word materials in the sense that the vocabulary is non-graded and it is expected that children will gradually learn to memorise what the words on the pages are.

Accompanying the use of these non-graded materials is a whole-word method, 'shared reading', cited by inspectors as a supplementary activity (HMI, 1990, p.9). This teaching method is often known as the *apprenticeship approach*. The method involves an adult reader, who models the reading process, shares the reading of a book with the child, reading it over and over aloud until the child is able to join in with the occasional word, recognising some of the words on sight in a whole-word fashion (i.e. no attention is paid to the individual letters making up the words).

There are additional supplementary activities, or 'associated work' noted by inspectors. These include the use of 'workbooks', 'games', 'practice sheets', 'word banks', 'dictionaries', 'sentence building', and 'phonic work' (HMI, 1990, p. 9). The 'workbooks', 'games', 'practice sheets', and 'phonic work' represent some of the practice materials that accompany the whole-word-oriented published reading programmes. These supplementary materials are invariably focused on developing reading comprehension and/or analytic word-attack skills. Finally, the 'sentence building', 'word banks', and 'dictionaries' are all features of a teaching method known as *language experience*, an approach which integrates the teaching of reading and writing. Language-experience is a whole-word approach where children are encouraged to memorise by sight an increasingly large collection of words that they have used in dictating their own personal stories to the teacher; after dictating, they copy out the stories and are then required, through various activities, to learn their own sets of words. Because the children effectively choose the words themselves, the words to be learned vary greatly in difficulty.

Taken together, neither the reading schemes in popular use nor the activities used to supplement them embody a mixed-methods approach. There is one basic method being used to teach reading in all these situations. As has been seen, not only are the reading schemes in use completely whole-word in their approach, but the supplementary activities observed reflect whole-word practices as well.

The Real Picture: The Mix-of-Methods Illusion

If, as shown, almost 85% of teachers concentrate on a mixture of methods, centring their instruction around reading schemes in combination with the supplementary activities, and a further 15% of teachers primarily use either a look-and-say, or a 'real books', shared-reading approach, *the actual percentage of teachers emphasising whole-word methods of teaching reading could be greater than 95%.*

Rather than a mixture of different methods, the true state of practice is that what most teachers are currently using to teach reading is a mixture of whole-word methods, methods that are not different, but all very much the same. That this is very much the case is confirmed by a National Foundation for Educational Research (NFER) survey in which 90% of teachers reported that they used a method of teaching reading 'involving look-and-say' (Cato et al., 1992, p. 23). Once again, *look-and-say* is another term applied to a whole-word approach: children are taught to *look* at words, and *say* them, automatically recognising them as whole visual shapes; this is accomplished either through flashcard practice, or through the repeated exposure of the words in context.

Reading Schemes and the Alphabetic Principle

In short, the current reliance on the methods advocated by today's reading schemes is not supported by research as an effective way to teach reading at an early stage. There is little time spent on what children really need to know – the alphabetic principle. Progress towards a grasp of the alphabetic principle is hindered because:

1. the vocabulary presented is ungraded, irregular, and not sequenced in a way that facilitates the grasp of spelling-to-sound connections;

2. the type of phonics instruction, where provided, is infrequent, and analytic rather than synthetic, and therefore not systematic or explicit enough for most children;

3. the use of rhymes and poetry books is too late for promoting phonological awareness (most children will already possess phonological awareness at this rudimentary level by the age of 5);

4. there is no provision for early phonological training in hearing and identifying individual speech sounds, or for the systematic, sequenced, explicit teaching of letter-sound correspondences;

5. the whole-word emphasis encourages readers to remain stuck in a rudimentary pre-reading stage where words are perceived as visual wholes; unproductive reading strategies are encouraged to the point that for some children the 'reading' habits developed will be very difficult to break.

Thus, although present reading schemes may provide useful materials for later reading development, the current readers, and approaches advocated within these schemes, do not support *early* reading development, where acquisition of the alphabetic principle is key.

On the other hand, reading-scheme books that were to introduce regularly spelled words gradually in a structured, systematic, sequenced manner would provide the necessary practice; reading scheme books that were to introduce simply spelled words in parallel with the direct teaching of the letters and sounds needed to make up these words would provide the support needed for early reading progress. One research-based scheme that did provide such books was *Language in Action*. This scheme was based on the forty-four sounds of the English language and their degree of usage (Morris, 1974-1983) but unfortunately it is no longer in print.

The next chapter examines the research related to code-emphasis instruction, in order to gauge more clearly the impact that whole-word, 'meaning-emphasis' approaches have in dominating the current teaching of reading.

Summary

In spite of publishers' claims to the contrary, presently available reading schemes do not advocate a mixture-of-methods approach to teaching reading. The one universal approach adopted is to encourage the memorisation of whole words and whole stories. The importance of teaching the alphabetic code is neglected in favour of satisfying other more fashionable demands from teachers. The features that publishers see as most important to include in their reading schemes are: natural-sounding language, poetry and rhyme, and above all, attractive illustrations.

3 | The Code-Emphasis Method

Part 1   Research: What Teaching Approach – a Mixture of Methods or a More Efficient Route?

Dangers of the Mix-of-Methods Philosophy

There are a number of dangers in adopting a mix-of-methods philosophy, whether a real mix or not, most particularly at the beginning stages of reading, when a combination of reading methods is not appropriate. Because a child must grasp the alphabetic principle in order to learn to read, a code-emphasis approach is particularly relevant during the initial stages of instruction. Research shows that, whatever the methods of instruction used, 75% of children will eventually discover the alphabetic principle and learn to read, but unless they receive the appropriate instruction at an early stage, at least 25% of children may not learn how to read at all (Liberman & Shankweiler, 1991).

What Is in the Mixture?

One of the dangers of adopting a philosophy that advocates a mixture of methods is that it obscures the need to examine exactly what is in the mixture. There is a tendency to accept such a philosophy as reasonable and 'balanced' (National Curriculum, SCAA, 1994a, p.7). To question such a concept would be, by implication, an unbalanced thing to do. However, in the light of research findings, there is a need to question whether the methods being delivered are those most appropriate to the particular stages of reading development.

Research evidence, for example, shows that children taught by phonics methods early on progress faster and further than children taught by whole-word methods (see Jorm & Share for reviews that support this claim, 1983). There is a danger that the reading progress of even those lucky 75% who do learn to read, regardless of method, will not be as fast as it could be. Seymour and Elder (1986) have found, for example, that after three years of whole-word instruction, readers were decoding phonologically (no longer 'reading' words as whole units or shapes), and had discovered the alphabetic principle, but their performance was much poorer than that of a comparison group taught by phonics. Much research (where I.Q. and reading levels have been controlled) shows that cipher readers learn to read faster and more accurately than whole-word readers (Gough & Walsh, 1991; Stanovich, 1984, 1992; Vellutino & Scanlon, 1991). A recent study reported by Foorman and Francis (1994) found that all beginning readers move through the same response patterns when learning how to read and spell. The pattern progresses from non-phonetic to phonetic to correct response. However, the reading progress of children who receive more code-emphasis instruction is significantly faster than that of those who receive less of this type of instruction.

At-Risk Readers Overlooked

Another danger of the adoption of a variety of approaches is that it overlooks the at-risk reader where a mix of methods will not work. The children who do learn to read regardless of method are those that have reasonable levels of phonological awareness. The at-risk reader is one who, in spite of normal mental development, fails to read; these children have been found to be deficient or delayed in phonological awareness. They have great trouble identifying the separate sounds in spoken words. Without some level of rudimentary phonological skills, which promotes the learning of letter-sound correspondences, they have difficulty acquiring the necessary alphabetic insights. Calfee (1983) suggests, in fact, that the majority of children identified as dyslexic reflect an instructional dysfunction rather than a constitutional disability. Indeed, others point out that the primary cause of dyslexics' reading problems are due to the limits imposed by inadequate instruction, which usually provides only limited attention to the development of phonological awareness and spelling-to-sound knowledge (Ehri, 1989).

Importance of Sequence Ignored

A third danger of the mix-of-methods approach is that it obscures the need to address the issue of sequence, the possibility that certain instructional approaches need emphasis at different stages of reading development. Reading achievement may be influenced not only by the type of mix, but also by the order of presentation or the emphasis given at different stages. Of interest in this context is a study conducted by Brown and Felton (1990) which avoids many of the shortcomings found in the studies concerned with disabled students. (Many studies suffer from small sample size, limited instructional time, cross-sectionality of design rather than a longitudinal design, and no control of the instruction already received.)

In this American study, two groups of 5-year-old children identified as at risk were taught for two years using one of two graded reading schemes. These children were selected from a larger population of children and identified as at risk on the basis of large discrepancies between their mental ability and scores on phonological awareness measures. One reading scheme was Houghton-Mifflin, a programme that emphasises meaning, context use, sight word learning and basic phonics elements. The other was Lippincott, a structured-phonics, code-emphasis programme. It is important to note that both programmes included phonics instruction.

Children were tested at the end of Year 1 and Year 2, with the code-emphasis or structured-phonics group earning higher scores on all measures in both years. Statistically significant differences in favour of the code-emphasis group were found on measures of word identification, spelling, and decoding of real and nonsense words. These results are striking because they show that crucial differences were not due to the presence or absence of phonics but to differences in how presentations were structured, in the attention paid to careful sequencing of material, and in the intensity or amount of code instruction given. This study and many others illustrate that for at-risk children early, well-structured, systematic teaching that explains how the writing system works should be the prime goal of beginning instruction if reading failure among those with poor phonological skills is to be overcome (Ball, 1993).

Other research has shown that among the practices of effective teachers are: (a) teaching in small, sequential steps, (b) maintaining a relatively fast teaching pace but avoiding large mental leaps, and (c) providing practice at graduated levels of difficulty in order to ensure relatively error-free experiences (Yates & Yates, 1993).

Why Phonics Has Something to Offer

To become a successful reader, the child must master the cipher (Gough et al., 1992). Because of the critical importance of decoding, phonics instruction may have something to offer all children at the beginning stages of learning to read. The most basic skill in learning to read is word identification. Experiments show that universally for all readers, including Chinese readers, skilled word identification is dependent on retrieving the phonological form of a word (Perfetti, 1995b). Fluent, fast, word recognition, which is not dependent on context or whole-word memorisation, is the foundation supporting skilful reading comprehension (Gough & Tunmer, 1986; Perfetti, 1985; Vellutino, 1991), spelling (Cunningham & Stanovich, 1993), and vocabulary acquisition (Aguiar & Brady, 1991; Stuart, 1995). Recent reading models now reflect this thinking as they are interactive, recognising the reciprocal relationships between decoding and comprehension), but with a heavy bottom-up, or decoding emphasis (Stanovich, 1991).

In order to be able to decode alphabetically, there are, as stated previously, two requirements: the child must be phonologically aware (be able to detect and identify separate sounds in spoken words), and the child must be able to make connections between these speech sounds and the letters used to represent them. Research suggests that phonological development is influenced by the type of instruction children receive (Foorman et al., 1991; Uhry & Shepherd, 1993). In addition, it also shows that phonics-taught children develop better phonological skills. Alegria et al. (1982) found that beginning readers who received instruction based on a phonics approach developed phonological awareness very rapidly over four months; the whole-word taught children, however, did not make any gains in phonological skills.

In fact, phonics instruction, itself, constitutes a form of phonological training (Tunmer & Rohl, 1991). By helping the reader attend to the sequences of letters and their correspondences to speech patterns (Adams & Bruck, 1993), it forces attention to the interior details of words. Phonics instruction focuses directly on the alphabetic code; that is, it makes explicit the sound/symbol correspondences (Ball, 1993). Both the requirements for promoting the grasp of the alphabetic principle, then, are components of phonics instruction. It is perhaps not surprising, therefore, that explicit, systematic phonics teaching is the most efficient method to ensure that the beginning reader acquires the crucial decoding skills necessary to read (Liberman & Liberman, 1990).

Components of High Quality Phonics Instruction

A great deal of research has important implications for designing an effective programme of phonics instruction. The following topics have relevance here: (a) rudimentary phonological awareness; (b) more advanced phonological awareness; (c) onset and rime; (d) irrelevance of onset and rime; (e) training in letter-phoneme correspondences; (f) phonological and letter-sound training in combination; and (g) practice.

(a) Rudimentary Phonological Awareness

It has been found that children as young as 3 years of age can appreciate rhyme, and knowledge of nursery rhymes corresponds significantly with subsequent development of phonological awareness (Maclean et al., 1987). Of ten tests designed to test phonological awareness, the three tasks that involve rhyme are the easiest and produce the best performance (Stanovich, 1984; Yopp, 1988). Thus, instruction which develops an early appreciation of poetry and nursery rhymes, before formal school instruction, may constitute an early form of phonological awareness training.

(b) More Advanced Phonological Awareness

A more advanced form of phonological awareness, *phonemic awareness*, involving the sensitivity to the separate sounds in spoken words, is needed in learning how to read. Unlike the awareness of rhyme, which develops relatively easily (Maclean et al., 1987), the insight that words are composed of separate sounds *does not develop* in the absence of either explicit training of this knowledge, or code-emphasis reading instruction (Adams, 1990; Blachman, 1987; Bruck & Treiman, 1992; Byrne, 1991; Tunmer & Nesdale, 1985).

Without specific training in this area, children with weak phonological skills at the beginning of primary school will struggle with reading years later. In fact, it has been shown that those with poor phonological skills at the start of school are poor readers four years later, with decoding skills only as good as those achieved by average to good readers almost three years earlier (Juel, 1988). It has been found that even when IQ, gender, school, and sight word knowledge are held constant, very small differences in initial phonological ability result in increasingly large differences in reading achievement (Jorm, Share, Maclean, & Matthews, 1984); this particular study found that after one year the group of children superior in phonological skills differed by four months in reading achievement, but by the end of a second year of schooling the difference had increased to nine months.

In one longitudinal study, it was found that the disparity between two groups of English children classified as either phonologically aware or unaware at age four, grew from a six-months' difference in reading age at the age of 5, to a difference of three years in reading age at age 11 (Stuart, 1995; Stuart & Masterson, 1992). Furthermore, as shown in Figure 1, an investigation of the reading attainment of these children at age 10 showed that it continued to be significantly correlated with the prereading phonological awareness scores obtained at age 4.

Finally, in another study, evaluating a phonological assessment battery, it was found that between the ages of 6 and 10, increasing differences in phonological awareness ability contributed to growing differences in reading ability. As shown in Figure 2, the gap between good and poor readers widened from a difference of just under twelve months at age six to a difference of more than two years at age 8, with finally, a difference of more than four years appearing at age 10 (Gallagher & Frederickson, 1995).

However, a number of studies have demonstrated the startling long-term effects of training in phonemic skills. Blachman and others (1994) found that eleven weeks of training in these skills to 5-year-old children (who did not differ from the control group in age, sex, race, socioeconomic status, phoneme awareness, letter/name knowledge, or letter/sound knowledge) resulted in significant reading achievement advantages which were still apparent after two years. Others have found that phonological training can have lasting and increasingly positive effects on reading achievement after one year (Lundberg et al., 1988), and even after 4 years (Bradley, 1987). Byrne & Fielding-Barnsley (1995) found that twelve weeks (one thirty minute lesson per

Figure 1: Effect of Either Good or Poor Pre-Reading Phonological Awareness Scores at Age 5 on Reading and Spelling Scores at Age 11

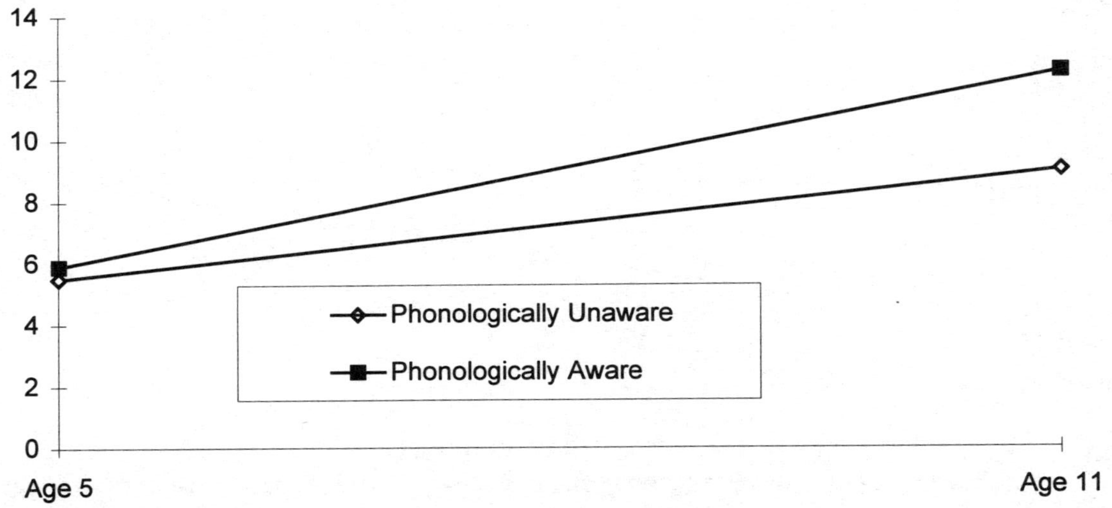

Phonologically Unaware
Phonologically Aware

Age 5

Age 11

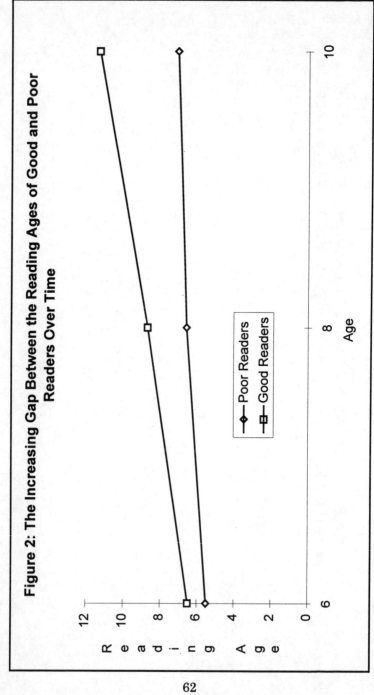

Figure 2: The Increasing Gap Between the Reading Ages of Good and Poor Readers Over Time

week) of experimental phoneme-identity instruction given to 5-year-olds resulted in significantly improved reading (of regular, irregular, and pseudo-words) and reading comprehension scores compared to a control group; significant differences were not only found at the end of the first year, but also at the end of the second and third year of schooling. These studies and other similar investigations (e.g. Hurford, Schauf, Bunce, Blaich, & Moore, 1994) reinforce the value of early screening of children's phonological skills in order to identify as early as possible those children who will require more intensive instruction.

There has been some dispute as to what constitutes the best training in this area. Some have found that segmentation training (isolating the separate sounds in words), or segmenting-plus-blending (isolating the separate sounds and then joining them together to make a word), and then naming are more effective than instruction in blending alone (Davidson & Jenkins, 1994; Torgesen et al., 1992), while Wagner and Torgesen (1987), and Perfetti and others (1987) have argued that being able to segment words is a consequence of learning to read, and only blending skills affect reading acquisition.

It has been suggested that a phonics programme that provides training in all three of the following areas will be of benefit to all children, while at-risk children should receive more intense and prolonged teaching of these skills (Blachman, 1994). (These tasks are all conducted orally.)

1. *Identification* – (identify sounds in words): Is there a /s/ sound in snake? or, which word does not sound the same? at the beginning? at the end?

2. *Blending* – (blend separate phonemes together): Here are some sounds: /f/, /i/, /n/; can you say them quickly?

3. *Segmentation* – (isolate or count sounds in words): What sounds are in this word? or, how many sounds do you hear in this word?

Is there one of these three phoneme skills which, when taught, will lead to more potent reading gains than the others? Pertinent to this particular issue, Byrne and Fielding-Barnsley conducted a number of experiments (1989, 1990, 1991, 1993) which led them to conclude that being able to *identify* or recognise a single sound in a word is not only easier for children than breaking words down into all of their separate sounds (segmentation), but also 'provides a firmer foundation for discovering the alphabetic principle than (does) segmentation ability' (1991, p. 83). (Asking a child, 'Is there an /s/ sound in this word?' or, 'Do *cat* and *cow* start with the same sound?' is a task requiring phoneme *identity*, whereas asking; 'How many sounds do you hear in *bat*?' requires phoneme *segmentation* or *counting*.) These researchers found that only those children whose segmentation training had included phoneme identity succeeded in a decoding test; children who could successfully segment but who failed to notice phoneme identity failed in decoding (Byrne & Fielding-Barnsley, 1990).

A recent research study involving more than 1,500 beginning readers in Norway found results which strongly support the findings of Byrne and Fielding-Barnsley; among the three phoneme tasks of identifying, blending, or counting sounds in words, it was found that being able to identify sounds in spoken words was the most powerful predictor of reading ability (Hoien, Lundberg, Stanovich and Bjaalid, 1995). In terms of designing effective reading instruction, these research findings taken together indicate that teaching children to hear and identify the individual sounds in spoken words is the type of phoneme instruction which will produce the most benefit.

(c) Onset and Rime

In addition to the finding that phoneme-related skills are important in predicting reading ability, Goswami and Bryant (1990) have found some evidence that a child's ability to perform rhyme-related tasks is associated with subsequent reading ability. Consistent with their findings are the results found in the large Norwegian study (Hoien et al., 1995) mentioned above. Hoein and others were able to isolate three separate phonological factors which each make independent contributions to learning to read: these were a syllable, a rhyme, and a phoneme factor. However, *by far the most important of these was the phoneme factor*. Their findings reveal that performance on phoneme identity tasks alone is twice as powerful in predicting reading ability as performance on rhyme tasks, while performance on combined phoneme tasks (identity, counting, and blending) is *four times more important* than rhyme task performance. Performance on rhyme and syllable tasks were found to make only very small contributions in predicting subsequent reading ability.

In investigating the possible contribution rhyme knowledge makes towards learning to read, it has further been proposed that training in onset (initial letter) and rime (remaining phonogram), or in analogy (noticing that *book*, *cook*, and *hook* end in the same way as *look*) may have some value in beginning-reading instruction before attention to individual sounds and letters, and before children can read (Goswami, 1988; Goswami & Bryant, 1990). These researchers point out that it is difficult for children to break words down into individual phonemes. In much the same way that it is *easier* for children to recognise words as whole visual units, it is easier for children to break words into onset and rimes.

However, simply because it is easier for children to memorise whole words or parts of words, does it follow that instruction, therefore, should avoid focusing on single letters and phonemes?

The research of Ehri & Robbins (1992) sheds light on this question. They report that children are only able to use analogy if they have some letter-sound knowledge, phoneme segmentation ability, and blending skills. Without these skills, children are not able to perform the necessary requisite operations to read words by analogy. To further illustrate this, in another study, training in rhyme and alliteration over a two-year period did not result in statistical differences compared to a control group; another experimental group, however, in the same experiments, taught about letter-to-sound relationships *as well as* rhyme, outperformed all other groups (Bradley & Bryant, 1985). Goswami (1994a) is forced to conclude that analogy training is only of benefit if grapheme-phoneme training is included as well; in addition she admits that it is not an approach to reading that helps 'children to learn spelling-sound correspondences' (Goswami, 1995, p. 138).

In relation to the three stages of reading development proposed by Frith (1985) (logographic, alphabetic, and orthographic), or to the four stages proposed by Ehri (1991; 1992) (non-alphabetic, pre-alphabetic, full alphabetic, consolidated alphabetic) there are a number of possible explanations for the fact that analogy is only of use if a child possesses some decoding skill. One possibility is that the development of onset and rime knowledge belongs to Frith's or Ehri's third or fourth stage of reading, the orthographic or consolidated alphabetic stage, where knowledge of spelling patterns is developed only after some alphabetic knowledge is gained, where readers begin to make use of multiletter units such as morphemes, syllables, or subsyllabic units such as onsets and rimes. The possibility that onset-rime use belongs to a pre-alphabetic stage where only partial connections are being made between some letters and sounds does not seem viable since children would not possess a sufficient amount of alphabetic knowledge to make use of onset and rimes beyond the level of initial letters (onsets). Information about rimes (phonograms) could not be retained and could not be made use of subsequently because pre-alphabetic children are unable to deduce the spelling-to-sound connections contained within rimes. Another possibility proposed is that logographic (whole-word) and alphabetic reading emerge in parallel, contributing independently to orthographic development (knowledge of spelling patterns) (Seymour, 1990; Seymour & Evans, 1994), in which case, alphabetic knowledge would still have to be sufficiently advanced to enable a child to capitalise on onset-rime training. Further evidence that rime is helpful only to older readers comes from a study which showed that 10-year-olds were able to read words faster that contained letter patterns shared by many other words, but this factor made little difference to 7-year-olds' reading speed (Juel, 1983).

Consistent with these explanations is the finding that onset and rime knowledge does not develop ahead of alphabetic reading (involving individual sounds and letters) or whole-word reading, *unless* the instructional setting explicitly emphasises this spelling-related knowledge. In comparing the reading strategies used by German and English children, Wimmer and Goswami (1994) acknowledge that it is the different instructional régimes in the two countries, phonics in Germany and whole-word in England, that account for differences.

(d) Irrelevance of Onset and Rime

Training in analogy or rimes during the *beginning* stages of reading instruction may have little if any practical use. It has been found that children fail to retain this information over the long term. As little as one day after training, it was found that children trained in single letter-sound correspondences (vowels) were the only ones to show significant benefit compared to those trained in analogy or 'cv' (consonant + vowel) (Bruck & Treiman, 1992). This finding is similar to that of Wise et al., (1990) who found that significant effects disappeared only thirty minutes after training.

Contrary to Goswami's suggestion that a child is able to make use of onset and rime in order to read words before developing the ability to segment and identify individual phonemes, Seymour and Evans (1994) have recently found evidence that 5- and 6-year-old children demonstrate an earlier ability to separate words into individual sounds than to separate words into onset and rime. In contrast to Goswami's proposal that children learn to read by progressing from the recognition of larger chunks (whole words) to medium chunks (onset and rime) to smaller segments (individual letter sounds), Seymour and Evans have demonstrated that the opposite order of development is true. Over a period of two years of initial reading instruction (combining phonics and whole-word), the phonological awareness skills that developed in 5- and 6-year-old children favoured small-unit segmentation over larger unit segmentation; the sequence of development observed was: first, the ability to manipulate single units (phonemes), followed by the ability to make use of two units (consonant/vowel, vowel/consonant, or onset/rime), and finally, the ability to recognise and manipulate three units (initial consonant, vowel, final consonant). Thus, over a two-year period, children's ability to perform certain phonological tasks proceeds in the following order:

1. Ability to segment a word into individual phonemes;
2. Ability to segment words into two units, e.g., onset + rime;
3. Ability to segment words into three units, e.g., consonant(s) + vowel + consonant(s).

Furthermore, and significantly, it has been found that instruction in letter-sound correspondences promotes knowledge at the rhyme and syllable level, whereas instruction at the rhyme and syllable level fails to result in any alphabetic insights (Cary & Verhaeghe, 1994). This research means that training in onset and rime as a way to develop letter-sound knowledge is misguided. It will not work. And, since such training would only create delay in gaining alphabetic knowledge, it is therefore irrelevant to the purpose of promoting early and efficient reading progress.

Evidence confirming that training to develop an awareness of syllables and rhyme does not induce or promote phoneme awareness has been found by Morais and Kolinsky (1994). These researchers have found that Chinese non-alphabetic readers and adult illiterates are able to manipulate syllables and appreciate rhyme, and (unlike adults taught to read later in life) they completely lack any awareness of individual phonemes. Their research, involving findings from brain imaging, reveals that there appears to be a unique region of the brain that deals with phoneme awareness tasks, separate from adjacent regions that deal with a number of other phonological tasks. Morais and Kolinsky conclude that there is a basic *discontinuity* between awareness of rhyme, or syllables, and the phoneme. The awareness of individual phonemes simply does not spontaneously arise from this other phonological knowledge related to larger units; a specific type of intervention – alphabetic intervention – is required. Some of this research is summarised in Table 1.

(e) Training in Letter/Phoneme Correspondences

A general finding is that explicit teaching of spelling-to-sound correspondences, a component of phonics teaching, facilitates reading acquisition (Anderson et al., 1985; Chall, 1983; Share & Jorm, 1987). Related to the positive effects that arise from the training of letter-sound associations, research also demonstrates the consistent finding that the skilful reader attends to every letter in each word in a left to right order (Just & Carpenter, 1987; Patterson & Coltheart, 1987; Perfetti, 1995a; 1995b). In one study, subjects read text while a computer masked one letter in the centre of their span of visual focus; the loss of this *single letter* reduced reading speed by 50% (Rayner & Bertera, 1979). During one eye fixation (a period of time between eye movements when the eyes are relatively still) the area of visual focus of adult skilled readers extends three to four letter spaces to the left of fixation to about fifteen letter spaces to the right of fixation (Rayner, 1995). However, in children of 6-7 years of age, the span extends to only about eleven letters (Rayner, 1993).

TABLE 1
Summary of Research Findings in Onset-Rime Training Studies

Author	Findings
Hoien et al. (1995)	ability on phoneme tasks, especially involving phoneme identity, are by far the most important predictors of reading achievement – 4 times more important than ability to perform rhyme or syllable tasks
Ehri & Robbins (1992)	children cannot make use of analogy to identify words without phonological recoding skills (letter-sound knowledge, segmentation, and blending)
Bradley & Bryant (1985)	rhyme and alliteration training over 2 years produced no effects compared to control group; only training to produce significantly better spelling and reading performance was rhyme PLUS letter-sound instruction
Bruck & Treiman (1992)	one day after, rime-based analogy training produced no positive effects compared to consonant-vowel and vowel training; only vowel training resulted in significant long-term effects on word reading
Seymour & Evans (1994)	over 2 years, the order of reading development found to emerge was: first, the ability to segment individual phonemes, then, 2 units (onset/rime), and finally, 3 units (initial consonants, vowel, terminal consonants)
Cary & Verhaeghe (1994)	phoneme instruction produced insights about rhyme and syllables, but instruction in rhyme and syllable produced no gains in phonemic awareness tasks
Morais & Kolinsky (1994)	brain imagery detected a unique area of the brain used for performing phoneme awareness tasks distinct from areas used in performing rhyme and syllable tasks; also, failure of illiterates is restricted to the phoneme

More recently, a team of researchers at Glasgow University have used an electronic eye-tracker which was developed for the US space programme. Their findings confirm that, far from skimming, readers fixate on a very narrow text window, focusing on the individual letters of one word and a few letters of the next (Glasgow University, 1994).

Further evidence that readers pay attention to individual letters, and to groups of letters, not to word shapes, comes from neuropsychological research (Bishop, 1993). Individual letters or groups of letters are attended to because of the speech sounds they represent. The results obtained from a study involving brain scans (using positron emission tomography) showed that the brain is almost instantly able to tell if a string of letters composes a word or not, but the different areas of the brain that are stimulated by the presentation of words and non-words shows that it is not the shapes of the letters or words that the brain pays attention to in reading, but the particular spelling patterns (those that can be translated into speech sounds) that the letters make.

In light of these findings it is not surprising that the best phonics instruction, producing significantly larger gains compared to many other methods including phonics-related methods, is that which teaches children about letters and phonemes (letter sounds), at first separately, and then blended together (large survey by Pflaum and others, 1980). Foorman and others (1991) compared two groups of 6-year-old children over a one-year period: both groups were taught using a graded reading scheme supplemented by either more, or less, letter-sound instruction. It is important to note that groups did not differ in IQ or in levels of phonological awareness. The group receiving less letter-sound instruction were taught phonics in context, in an incidental fashion, with the emphasis on meaning-oriented instruction. Results showed that the children who had received more letter-sound instruction improved in their ability to spell and read words correctly at a significantly faster rate than the group who had received less letter-sound instruction.

In fact, the amount of letter-sound instruction children receive in their first year at school will determine whether they attend to words in an alphabetic or a whole-word fashion. It has been found that children taught by whole-word methods, in their first year at school, use only whole-word strategies while reading, whereas those taught by mixed methods, with some phonics, use both whole-word and phonological reading strategies (Sowden & Stevenson, 1994). At the same time, children who receive some phonics teaching develop phonological awareness earlier than those who are taught in strictly whole-word, 'real books' settings (Alegria et al., 1982).

(f) Phonological and letter-sound training in combination

Instruction which includes both phoneme awareness and letter/sound training has been shown to produce significant long-term effects on a variety of different reading-related measures (Ball & Blachman, 1988; Byrne, 1991; Hatcher, Hulme, & Ellis, 1994; Ellis, 1993; Foorman et al., 1991). Gersten & Keating (1987), for example, found that children given systematic instruction in phonological and cipher skills at age 6, still outperform their comparison group at age 17, not just in reading achievement but also on general measures of school success.

In a study conducted over five years (Bradley, 1987; Bradley & Bryant, 1983, 1985), just seven hours of training involving plastic letters and sounds given to 6-year-old children resulted in profound long-term effects: at age 8, the children trained with letters and sounds had reading levels six months better than another treatment group of children taught how to categorise sounds only, ten months better than a group of control children taught how to categorise words conceptually, and fourteen months better than another control group who received no training at all. (The group trained with letters *and* sounds, that is, letter-sound correspondences *and* phonemic awareness, was the *only* group to demonstrate significant effects.) By the age of 12 or 13, the control groups had still not made up the difference in their reading ability in spite of receiving extra remedial instruction. The fact that in this study the remedial instruction given later to the control groups did not enable them to catch up to the treatment groups in their reading performance highlights the crucial importance of early intervention.

(g) Practice

It has been found that even when children know that spoken words are composed of separate sounds and that those sounds are represented by letters of the alphabet, it does not guarantee that they will make functional use of the alphabetic principle (Byrne & Fielding-Barnsley, 1991); a phonics programme needs to provide ample opportunity to practise the skills taught by relating these directly to reading experiences.

Children who have not been taught how to tackle text by breaking the spelling to sound code are likely to be exposed to much less text than their peers (Stanovich, 1981), since often the reading materials they encounter will be too difficult for them to read (Allington, 1983; Bristow, 1985; Forell, 1985). If a child, weak in alphabetic decoding skills, is faced with a difficult text and relies on whole-word (guess - by shape, by context, or by picture - strategies), the text will have to be 'read' and re-read many times before the child is able to recognise and remember all the words by this approach. Eventually, such unrewarding and frustrating reading experiences may result in a child avoiding reading practice altogether (Stanovich, 1992). Some studies have found that after five or six months of school the poorest readers will have had less than half the exposure to text than that of the average readers and only a fifth the exposure gained by the best readers (Biemiller, 1977-8). Others have estimated that average and good readers are exposed to as much as ten to a hundred times more words than poorer readers in the middle grades (Nagy & Anderson, 1984).

In contrast, those children who have grasped the alphabetic principle and learned to read will immediately begin to differ from struggling readers in the amount of practice they receive and begin to benefit from. This is where code-oriented methods, producing faster early reading progress, have a distinct advantage over whole-word, slower-progress methods.

Once a child can read independently, the growth of many other skills is promoted; demonstrated by many research studies, some of these include enriched vocabulary development (Hayes, 1988; Sternberg, 1985; Vellutino & Scanlon, 1987) growth of syntactic knowledge (Mann, 1986; Perfetti, 1985), increased general knowledge (Tunmer & Rohl, 1991), better verbal processing skills and improved working memory (Ellis, 1990a; Tunmer & Rohl, 1991), improved reading comprehension ability (Juel et al., 1986; Sawyer, 1992; Share & Silva, 1987), the development of more advanced phonological skills (Ehri, 1985; Ehri et al., 1987), and increased knowledge of spelling patterns (Ehri & Robbins, 1992; Foorman et al, 1991; Rohl & Tunmer, 1988). With regard to spelling, Lennox and Siegel (1996) found that poor spellers were more likely than good spellers to use a whole-word rather than a phonological approach. Finally, skilled reading encourages more reading, and the act of reading itself, a form of self-tutoring, leads to a myriad of further gains.

Studies Which Support Effectiveness of Phonics

Despite the criticism levelled at studies comparing different methods of reading instruction, numerous reviews of this research firmly support the general conclusion that code-emphasis methods are more effective than meaning-emphasis programmes for beginning reading instruction (e.g. Adams & Bruck, 1993; Beck, 1981; Chall, 1967, 1979; Jorm & Share, 1983; Johnson & Baumann, 1984; Schickedanz, 1990; Vellutino, 1991; Williams, 1979).

Some research investigations showing the superior effects of code-oriented instruction compared to other methods are summarised in Table 2. It has been found that explicit, direct attention to phonics supports reading progress better than instruction in spelling with incidental attention to phonics while reading (Foorman et al., 1991). Phonics instruction results in better reading performance compared to a control group (Williams, 1980), and in spite of maths scores remaining the same (Wallach & Wallach, 1976). Tunmer and Hoover (1993) found that systematic phonics instruction is more effective than incidental phonics instruction, or a reliance on writing activities as the primary means of developing knowledge of the alphabetic code, while Stoner (1991) found that systematic, sequential teaching of phonics compared to teaching based on a meaning-oriented published reading scheme produced significantly better reading achievement. Finally, Brown and Felton (1990) studied children at risk for reading disability and found that systematic, structured phonics teaching compared to whole-word, context-oriented instruction, produced significantly better effects over two years on reading and spelling measures.

Schools that Use Phonics

Evidence from school practice shows that any shift of emphasis in the early years away from meaning and towards the mastery of the alphabetic code brings positive results. A

TABLE 2
Summary of Some Research Investigations Demonstrating Superior Effects of Code-Emphasis Approaches

Author	Comparison of	Age	N	Time-Span	Significant Effects On
Seymour & Elder, (1986)	whole-word (1) vs phonics-taught (2)	5-7	26	after 3 years	reading performance for group (2)
Foorman & Francis (1994)	some letter-sound (1) vs more letter-sound instruction (2)	6	40	6 months	reading achievement for group (2)
Brown & Felton (1990)	two reading schemes, one with less phonics (1), one with synthetic phonics (2)	6-7	48	over 2- year period	word reading, word attack, spelling, rdg. comprehension for group (2)
Evans & Carr (1985)	individualised language experience(1) vs code-oriented rdg. scheme (2)	6-8	~ 500	one-year period	basic reading skill for group (2)
Defior & Tudela, (1994)	5 groups: conceptual training (1) or phoneme training (2) with (A) or without (B) manipulative materials, and a control group (C)	6	55	6 months	reading and writing achievement for group (2A) only
Stoner, (1991)	control (reading scheme) (1) vs systematic phonics group (2)	6, 7, 8	190	one year	word reading, reading comprehension, word study skills for group (2)

study undertaken for the Plowden Committee suggested that urban schools that used phonics, in a systematic and structured fashion, had better reading results than similar schools that did not (Bald, 1994). A similar observation by HMI (1990) of a 'clear link between higher standards and systematic phonics teaching' (p. 7), was confirmed in a report on Suffolk schools in 1991, which found that the ten most successful schools (based on standardised reading scores) all used systematic phonics. A school with a high proportion of second-language speakers, St Clare's School in Handsworth, won the Jerwood Award in 1992 for teaching reading effectively using systematic, explicit teaching of phonics (Bald, 1994).

Since discontinuing the 'real books method' and adopting early phonics teaching, the reading performance of children in Kensington and Chelsea has improved steadily since 1989, and by 1994 was above the average for inner London. Scores have continued to improve regardless of ethnic background and socioeconomic standards (Smith, 1994a).

In 1987, in Raglan School, South London, a third of 7-year-olds were found to be two years behind in reading achievement. Reading standards six years later in 1993 were approaching the best among state schools, since the head directed that children be 'almost indoctrinated' with phonics. The average reading age of 7-year-olds in 1993 was two years ahead with the top 10% reading at a level expected of a 10- or 11-year-old (Hymas, 1993).

The methods of teaching reading at Woods Loke Primary School were developed over seventeen years. Lloyd (1993) reported that two major innovations over this period resulted in dramatic improvements in age 7+ standardised reading scores, or reading quotients: first, after teaching letter-sound correspondences in the first few weeks of school, the average reading quotient improved from 102 to 108 (quotients or standard scores have a mean of 100, and a standard deviation of 15) and secondly, after training children to hear all the sounds in spoken words as a prerequisite to the other teaching, scores jumped even further to 110-116 (as one point of standard score is equivalent to roughly two months of reading development, this means that children were now reading at a level twenty to thirty months above their chronological ages). Whether these two changes are regarded as phonics instruction or not, the two kinds of instruction given match exactly what hundreds of research studies have indicated as the most effective means of improving reading performance.

In Downham Montessori School in Norfolk, where phonics methods are used to teach reading, the average 7+ reading quotient is 125 (four years advanced from chronological age), and in Holland House School in Edgware, where phonics methods are also in use, the average 7+ reading quotient is a remarkable 135 (almost six years advanced). These scores are very high in comparison to a national average 7+ reading quotient of 100, and an inner London average reading quotient of 89 (almost one year behind) (Tizard, Blatchford, Burke, Farquhar, & Plewis, 1988).

Finally, on a larger scale, Scottish primary schools have remained more traditional and structured in their teaching methods. In Scotland, phonics methods are widely used to teach children how to read (Johnston, 1995; Scottish Education Department, Edinburgh, 1995; Scottish Education Department, Fife, 1995; Maxwell, 1977).

Results obtained on the standardised Edinburgh Reading Test for large samples of 7- to 9-year-old children drawn from England and Scotland show that in 1975 and, among 11-year-olds in 1992, Scottish children significantly outperform English children; very large differences of more than a year of reading age occurred between the countries (average reading quotient in Scotland of 107-108 versus 100 in England), and particularly large differences are apparent when comparing those children who are either poor or average in reading (University of Edinburgh, 1994).

Summary

There are a number of dangers in adopting a mixture-of-methods approach during early reading instruction. These include the danger that: what is in the 'mixture' will not be examined and that the quality of instruction will not be monitored carefully, at-risk readers will not receive the concentrated code-emphasis instruction they need in order to learn how to read, the reading progress of other readers will be considerably slowed if there is little phonics instruction in the mixture; and the reading progress of all readers will suffer if the emphasis is on delivering a mixed approach rather than on scientifically sequencing instruction so that it produces the maximum reading gains. Both in research studies and in primary schools, code-emphasis or phonics instruction given at the beginning stages of learning to read has been shown to speed a child's grasp of the alphabetic principle and to result in superior reading progress compared to other forms of instruction. Training in onset and rime represents an unnecessary detour en route to developing the two necessary alphabetic requirements: phonological awareness and knowledge of letter-sound correspondences.

Part 2 Practice: A Recognition Problem

Contrary to the research which shows that, during the early stages of learning to read, children need code-emphasis instruction (instruction which will promote the acquisition of the alphabetic principle), in practice, this may not be the emphasis that is given by a large proportion of teachers. Since almost all teachers use published reading schemes, and almost 85% of teachers describe their approach to teaching reading as a mixture of methods, there may be a widespread lack of recognition that the phonics instruction that is given is not only minimal but lacks progression and systematic coverage.

What Does Phonics Instruction Consist Of?

Two surveys indicate that nearly all teachers teach phonics (HMI, 1991; Cato et al., 1992). The difficulty is in determining what 'teaching phonics' actually consists of. Are teachers teaching phonics when they: draw attention to phonic elements during a child's reading, conduct the phonics exercises suggested by the reading scheme in use, or supplement the core reading activities with phonics activities? Do inspectors conclude that phonics is being taught when, contrary to the research indicating that skilful readers attend to each letter of every word, they observe a teacher drawing a child's attention to initial letters of a word as a last-resort decoding strategy? Is there an early emphasis on teaching phonics, when as research indicates, this is exactly the time children could most benefit from systematic, intensive, phonics instruction?

Phonics Instruction Is Minimal

Evidence suggests that phonics instruction is minimal during the early primary school years. According to the HMI survey conducted in 120 schools, *The Teaching and Learning of Reading in Primary Schools* (1990), 10% of teachers do not teach phonics. It is also stated that in two-thirds of classes the phonics teaching is satisfactory or good; that is, phonics teaching is poor or unsatisfactory in 33% of classrooms. The results of this survey are purported to be consistent with those of 3,000 recent inspection visits to primary schools. This means it is likely that almost half of teachers currently either do not teach phonics or do not teach it effectively (10% + 33% = 43%).

Government officials have stated that there should be a 'balance between real books and published teaching materials' (House of Commons, 1990-91a, p.xii), revealing the common failure to recognise that these two types of materials are very much the same in the sense that both are currently used in a similar fashion, encouraging children to read by memorising words as whole visual shapes. Also noted (HMI, 1990, p.7) was that some 'schools adopted popular published schemes for teaching phonic skills', further evidence of inadequate phonics instruction. Far from an emphasis on phonics instruction, or even a balance between phonics instruction and whole-word approaches, there is a clear imbalance.

Further evidence that phonics teaching may be quite minimal comes from a report from Suffolk (HMI, 1991). This report showed that as many as 18% of teachers thought children did not need phonics, and those that did use phonics concentrated on initial letters of words only. For those children who were, later on, non-readers, teachers may fail to teach them phonics even at this stage because of time constraints (Cato et al., 1992).

In contrast to the research which indicates that all children, particularly those at risk, benefit from explicit, structured, phonics teaching compared to incidental or opportunistic phonics instruction, inspectors view as appropriate the teaching of phonics merely as an adjunct to meaning-based instruction. Even though one report notes that 'the teaching of phonics was more prominent when children showed signs of reading failure', and that 'a concentration on phonics was seen as the last resort when all else had failed' (HMI, 1990, p. 7), this same report also states with regard to phonics skills that: 'It was clear that these skills were best learned when they were embedded in activities that were relevant and enjoyable and, particularly, where children were helped to put them to use in writing and making sense of texts they wanted to read' (HMI, 1990, p. 7).

That phonics is not the approach given emphasis during beginning-reading instruction is evidenced by teachers reporting recently that what they used, instead, and, 'for beginning readers only', was look-and-say methods (Cato et al., 1992, p. 24). In the same survey, it was found that the amount of phonics instruction teachers gave varied widely: some teachers taught phonic points to children only as the need arose, others taught phonics to small groups experiencing problems, and others taught one sound a week to the whole class (Cato et al., 1992).

The recent inspectors' study of forty-five London primary schools drew a number of conclusions with regard to the amount of phonics teaching observed: (a) phonics teaching was 'relatively rare'; (b) if it occurred, it was usually limited to focusing on initial letter sounds; (c) there was no systematic teaching of phonic knowledge; phonics activities were 'often superficial and ill-planned'; (d) too often phonics teaching made its appearance as a last resort attempt to help children with reading difficulties; and (e) teachers lacked adequate training in how to teach phonics (Ofsted, 1996).

The lack of attention given to phonics teaching in schools may, indeed, be traced to the training teachers have received. A NFER survey in ninety-two teacher-training centres found that while tutors reported that they taught their students about the traditional phonic method, as well as real-books, apprenticeship, or paired-reading method, there was a contradiction between their claims and those of their former students (Brooks et al., 1992). More than half of the students said they had been taught little or nothing about phonics and would have liked more help in learning about the approach.

Phonics is Unpopular

In practice, phonics teaching is unpopular. One can sympathise with teachers who choose not to teach phonics, if they do not feel confident to teach it effectively. It is the so-called meaning-emphasis approaches, which require less direct teaching, less structure, and less training, that are regarded with favour. Although the publication of the 'LINC materials' (1990) was banned by the government, these materials have nevertheless been distributed widely and have influenced practice. These materials are dismissive of phonics teaching and promote the anti-phonics, whole-word theories of Frank Smith and Kenneth Goodman.

The anti-phonics stance and the irrational prejudice against phonics that is displayed so strongly in some people, has been termed 'phonicsphobia' by Morris (1993). She offers a comprehensive list of explanations for the phenomenon: early personal trauma with phonics teaching that ignored the importance of phoneme awareness, the appeal of the progressive, child-centred, teacher-as-facilitator view, the lack of necessary knowledge about the English orthographic system, inadequacies of teacher training, experiencing failure after only teaching enough phonics to fit the accepted 'mix-of-methods' concept, ineffective teaching in general, resulting in withdrawal from phonics teaching since it is difficult to conduct in noisy, uncontrolled classrooms, and fear of reprisal if one publicly supports the teaching of phonics.

That 'phonicsphobia' is widespread is evidenced by the recent teacher reaction to the National Curriculum Proposals for Key Stage 1, English. As a result of vociferous teacher protests that there was too much phonics in the Order, the final draft has now been altered so that there is a watering down of the phonics element so that children must now only be taught to identify 'initial and final sounds in words' (SCAA, 1994a, p. 7). In spite of this, teacher trainers continue to protest against the orders that 'expectations...have been raised to an unrealistic degree, as children are expected to "use their knowledge of letters and sound-symbol relationships in order to read words..."' (Dombey, 1994a).

That phonics is unpopular is also reflected in the details of classroom observations (HMI, 1990) where the real books approach is much in evidence and described by inspectors in glowing terms as an approach that 'attempts to move away from published reading schemes in favour of motivating children to understand and take a strong interest in reading by teaching them from an early stage from attractively presented children's literature' (HMI, 1990, p. 6). The bulk of the reading activities observed by inspectors constitute either look-and-say, language experience, or 'real books', *all* whole-word memory approaches, none of which are supported by research as effective ways to teach beginning reading.

The fact that currently available reading-schemes are all similar in nature also reflects teachers' disregard for phonics. Teachers' views have directly shaped publishers' views with the result that there are no reading schemes available at the moment which are capable of supporting early reading development. This is a very serious shortcoming, a state of affairs which has the potential to produce far-reaching deleterious effects.

Popularity of Onset and Rime

More recently, there has been a considerable amount of attention paid to Goswami and Bryant's work on rimes. University professors are prepared to assert that the 'onset-rime concept ... has revolutionised our understanding of children's phonological awareness' (Wray, 1994, p. 19). The idea is not new, however; in the past, teaching of phonograms (e.g. words ending in *ake, ight, ate*) has been used to enrich children's orthographic knowledge at later stages in a reading programme, but as research evidence shows, there is no justification for using phonograms or rimes as an initial reading approach. Although children can be *more easily trained* to break words into onset and rimes (perhaps accounting for the confusion in understanding this research) than to separate words into individual sounds, studies have shown that letter-sound knowledge is necessary in order to make effective use of onset/rime knowledge, and that training in single letter-sound correspondences is retained whereas training in analogy or rimes is not.

Furthermore, research shows that training in onset and rime does not give rise to an ability to detect individual phonemes in words, a skill which is necessary in learning how to read. Children must be taught to detect individual sounds in words; analogy or rhyme training will not help children to discover them. If, however, children are taught specific letter-sound correspondences and how to blend separate sounds together to form words, this ability to spell words (in effect) leads rapidly to the ability to read them (Calfee, 1995; Share & Stanovich, 1995a). Drawing attention to common spelling patterns at this point would help to enrich and consolidate developing awareness of these phenomena.

It should be stressed, however, that teaching children about onset and rime as a route to discovering individual phonemes is similar logic to thinking that a person can be taught how to read music by memorising chords on, say, a guitar or piano. Although it may be relatively easy for a person to learn the names of some musical chords and how to play them, there is little possibility that this knowledge will lead to the ability to read musical notation, to the ability to play individual notes on these instruments in response to the corresponding written symbols. (In the same way as skills in letter/phoneme translation are crucial to the child learning to read, skills in symbol/note translation are crucial to the person learning to read music.) Although it may be quite easy for a person to learn to play chords, is it logical to focus on such instruction with only the very remote possibility that the learner will discover how to read music as a result? Learning how to read music will simply be delayed and likely never accomplished unless the learner receives some direct instruction in symbol-to-sound translation.

Teaching children about onset and rime will simply not help them learn how to read. Yet the eagerness with which onset-rime research has been misinterpreted and seized upon as a route to discovering the individual phoneme is unfortunate and quite startling. Unfortunately, Goswami herself has confused the issue by advocating that in teaching children to read, onsets *and rimes* should be introduced before teaching children to identify single phonemes in spoken words, and before teaching children letter/sound correspondences systematically (Goswami, 1995), a recommendation which her research findings do not justify, and which is at variance with a great deal of other research demonstrating the common stages all children must inevitably pass through if they are to learn to read. So popular has the general concept become, however, that teaching about onset and rime is now sometimes referred to as 'the new phonics'.

Government officials have voiced their concern over alphabetic phonics in favour of a 'syllabic approach' (House of Commons, 1990-91b), and now such misconceptions have been duly incorporated not only within the 1995 National Curriculum Orders, but also within the national curriculum reading assessment procedures. Children at Key Stage 1 are to be given opportunities for: 'recognising... sound patterns and rhyme, and relating these to patterns in letters', and for 'considering syllables' (National Curriculum Orders, SCAA, 1994a, p. 7). The procedures for the national curriculum assessment of reading instruct teachers to judge whether a child has reached Level 1 by, among other criteria, looking for evidence that 'the child is using knowledge of rhyme' (DfEE, 1996c, p. 13).

There is nothing wrong with developing this sort of knowledge in order to help children *consolidate* their alphabetic knowledge. But for the purposes of teaching a child to read in the beginning, these are procedures according to research that are not any more effective than teaching a child to recognise whole words by attending to their shapes or to their context within a sentence. Neither the ability to recognise whole words nor the ability to recognise chunks of words is helpful in gaining the reading prerequisite: the ability to identify single phonemes.

In contrast, that children should be (a) made aware of the separate sounds of spoken words, and (b) 'taught how symbols correspond to those sounds' are two concepts that clearly reflect experimental research findings. This first concept, however, never has appeared in the government's Curriculum Orders, and the second concept, embodied in the words quoted, was removed from the earlier Curriculum draft proposals and does not appear in the final 1994 draft Orders (SCAA, 1994a).

Summary

One of the reasons given against phonics teaching is that over-attention to it might marginalise other aspects of reading (Brooks et al., 1992). In practice, however, the opposite appears to be the case. Whole-word, context-emphasis methods predominate to the almost total exclusion of code-emphasis instruction. To examine further why this has happened, and why this trend should be of concern, it is necessary to look at the empirical evidence related to context-emphasis approaches, the subject of the next chapter.

4 | The Whole-Word Method

Part 1 Research: Searching for the Foundations of the Whole-Word Method

Whole-word methods of learning to read are not new. The idea of teaching children to recognise words as whole visual units on the basis of their shape or a few selected features was invented by Thomas Gallaudet in 1830, as a method of teaching deaf children to read (Blumenfeld, 1990). In England such methods were popularised by the Americans, Frank Smith, who promoted his book *Understanding Reading* (1971) in 1978, a work entirely devoid of scientific evidence, and Kenneth Goodman, the past president of the International Reading Association. In America, whole-word methods are known as *whole language*, so that Kenneth Goodman observes, 'The basic concepts of whole language (largely without the term) have become institutionalized in British schools, and parents like what their kids are doing in school' (Goodman, 1992a).

Whole-Word Methods:
A Case of *The Emperor's New Clothes?*

In spite of claims from Goodman that whole language is founded on a 'comprehensive knowledge base' (1994, p. 346), a number of critics have argued that whole-language advocates have failed to support their position with research (Adams & Bruck, 1993; Chall, 1989; Ellis, 1993; Felton, 1993; Liberman & Liberman, 1992; McKenna, Robinson & Miller, 1990; Stahl, 1990; Stanovich, 1991; Vellutino, 1991). One may look very hard for some supporting facts, but just like the Emperor's new clothes, they do not actually exist. Others have pointed out that the current research base clearly contradicts the whole language position (for example, Adams, 1990). This means that, although one would like to appear even-handed in presenting data for and against whole-word instruction as a beginning method to teach reading, there is a difficulty.

(There is, however, some evidence to support the use of such methods in preschool or nursery programmes, introducing children to the pleasures and rewards of reading, and to the idea that reading is a process of communication [Stahl & Miller, 1989]).

Thus despite the lack of evidence in support of whole-word methods to teach reading, at the beginning of formal instruction in the primary school, there are a number of such approaches advocated for just this purpose, although the terminology varies. The following are some of the whole-word, 'meaning-emphasis' (or non-code) approaches recommended to teach a child to read:

1. *Whole-word, look-and-say, sight word learning* (at the beginning of instruction) approaches (all of which involve the memorisation of *words* as whole visual units);

2. *Language experience, integrated reading/writing* approaches (which involve the memorisation of personal *sets of words* used in individualised writing activities);

3. *Shared book reading, paired reading, apprenticeship,* and *whole-language* methods, either with the use of 'real books' (ordinary story books) or reading scheme books (all of which involve the memorisation of whole *books*).

All of these approaches have in common an aversion to teaching a child how to read. Although what the child does is called 'reading', these approaches all teach a child to memorise. All of these approaches fail to draw attention to the fact that the English language is an alphabetic system, based on a code or a cipher representing speech sounds. All assume that children will discover the alphabetic principle for themselves.

Recently, Chall (1995) observes that large analyses and syntheses of research, by Share and Stanovich (1995a), for example, have led to the conclusion that learning to read is a two-stage process concerned with letters and sounds, as well as with meaning. All of the foregoing meaning-emphasis approaches view reading as one single process concerned with getting meaning from print. Reading is defined by these methods as solely making connections between print and ideas, and it is little concerned with making connections between print and sound. Code-emphasis approaches, however, view reading as a two-stage process, concerned with decoding print *and* obtaining meaning from print.

All of these whole-word, 'meaning-emphasis' approaches hold common assumptions that have surprisingly little, if any, scientific evidence to support them. What are some of these assumptions and what is wrong with them?

'Reading Is a Natural Process Like Learning to Speak'

One of the most serious flaws of the whole language or whole-word approach is the assumption that learning to read is a natural process, much like learning to speak. It is assumed that as long as someone can speak, and written language is not broken down into abstract, meaningless bits, but kept whole and 'meaningful' in sentences, and in books, the child will spontaneously and naturally learn to read. This idea is simply not true. Learning to speak is a biological process and virtually universal. Learning to read is a cultural invention (about 4,000 years old) which not everyone learns; it is a cognitive intellectual achievement in a way that speech is not (see Liberman & Liberman, 1992 for a discussion).

Something more than learning how to speak is required in order to learn how to read in an alphabetic language. What is required is the awareness that speech is made up of separate sounds or phonemes, those abstract, little bite-size pieces that Goodman and other whole-word proponents object to. The difficulty is that speech articulation is so rapid that the internal structure of words is obscured, and neither knowing how to speak, nor even cognitive maturation, is enough to produce this phonemic insight. There is nothing in speech to produce this awareness: a word like 'sun', for example, is a single seamless piece of sound. A child does not understand why the word should be represented by three letters.

Contrary to Goodman's assertion that the child does not have to be a linguist, the child does need to be enough of a linguist to recognise that all words have an internal structure. Studies have shown that this awareness does not come naturally (Liberman, Shankweiler, Fischer, & Carter, 1974). Alegria and Morais (1991) found that children in a strictly whole-word setting have no segmental awareness of speech because they have not been confronted with a situation requiring such awareness. As mentioned earlier, research has also shown that adult illiterates do not have this awareness.

Rather than assuming that this awareness is not needed, or will arise spontaneously, as whole-word advocates appear to do, research suggests that developing this awareness directly should be of primary concern.

In fact, it has been proposed that learning to read, rather than being a natural process, is an 'unnatural act' (Gough & Hillinger, 1980). During an early stage the child is naturally inclined to recognise words as visual wholes, or in a logographic fashion (note that such an approach is visual memorisation, not reading). It is perhaps not surprising, therefore, that between this type of initial stage and the next alphabetic or cipher stage (where entirely different processes are involved), research evidence demonstrates that there is a basic discontinuity. In order for the child to progress to the second stage, intervention is nearly always required. Research shows that later stages of learning to read are not natural, continuous extensions of a first logographic stage (Byrne, 1991; Cary & Verhaeghe, 1994; Masonheimer et al., 1984; Morais & Kolinsky, 1994; Seymour & Evans, 1994; Vellutino & Scanlon, 1991). The assumption made by the whole word-approach that children will deduce what they need to know simply by being immersed in meaningful language activities is unsupported by research (Byrne, 1991). Instead, research findings underline the importance of providing children with training in phonological awareness and letter-phoneme relations, knowledge which must be acquired in order to read in an alphabetic language, knowledge that is needed to make the major necessary leap from a logographic (actually non-reading) way of looking at words to a real reading alphabetic stage.

'Individual Letters Are not Important'

Another tenet of the whole-word approach is the assumption that children and adults read by recognising whole words as visual shapes, and by sampling whole groups of words, recognising some of the words and skipping others. This idea is not supported by research either. While children in the very earliest stages of learning to read *may* 'read' logographically, recognising whole words simply by shape or other features, later all people must learn to attend to every letter in every word if they are to read fluently.

Because adult skilled readers' decoding skills are so automatic and effortless, it may appear as if readers are instantly recognising words or groups of words in whole chunks. Eye-movement studies, however, have proven quite categorically that this is not true. Skilful adult readers attend to every letter in each word, instantly recognising familiar spelling patterns in the process; they read alphabetically, not logographically (Perfetti & Lesgold, 1979; Perfetti, 1995a; Rayner & Pollatsek, 1989; Rayner, 1995). Recall that the loss of a single letter in a small window of text reduces reading speed by 50% (Rayner & Bertera, 1979).

Evidence from many studies suggests that there are possibly three stages in the reading process. Frith (1985) describes these three stages more formally as: (a) a logographic stage, where visual cues only are used, and there are no alphabetic insights; (b) an alphabetic stage, where children discover letter/phoneme relations and use them to read; and (c) an orthographic stage, where children use letter groups, or spelling patterns to identify words.

Some researchers have pointed out, however, that children do not necessarily pass through an initial stage of logographic reading (Morais, 1991); in fact it is argued that recognising words purely as if they are pictures is not actually reading. Children who possess some phonological awareness and a minimal amount of letter-sound knowledge before formal instruction do not pass through a logographic stage. In the complete absence of any such skills, however, some children may be inclined to read logographically, and if they are denied access to phonological and alphabetic information through a lack of appropriate instruction, there is a danger they will remain stuck at this stage by default. Interestingly, one study has shown, for example, that children with a history of reading problems in English were rapidly able to learn to read some words in Chinese (Rozin, Poritsky, & Sotsky, 1971), suggesting a continued and engrained reliance on whole-word reading strategies.

'Direct Alphabetic Instruction Is Not Required'

A third whole-language assumption is that no particular instruction which explains the point of the alphabet needs to be given. This is partially true, since no matter how unhelpful the instruction, 75% of children, given enough time, will discover for themselves the principle of how speech is encoded alphabetically and will eventually learn to read. However they gain this insight, all children must understand that units of print correspond to units of sound if they are going to learn how to read. That phonological recoding is the *'main mechanism'* of early reading development is supported not only by the vast amount of research on the importance of letter sounds, but also by the fact that pseudo-word reading (which tests the ability to decode alphabetically) accounts for *most* of the word recognition variance among beginning readers (Share & Stanovich, 1995b, p. 106).

Although the majority of children will eventually discover the alphabetic principle even in the absence of direct instruction, avoiding delay in learning how to read is a serious issue. The instructional setting plays a critical rôle. The longer a child's reliance on the use of partial visual cues (as encouraged under whole-word approaches) the greater the delay in learning to read, and for some, the continued reliance on such strategies will lead to severe difficulties in learning to read (Gough & Juel, 1991; Snowling, 1987). On the other hand, much evidence shows that the amount of time children are involved with alphabetic or phonic instruction in the early grades is found to be highly correlated with their reading achievement (Fisher & Berliner, 1985). Research has shown also that an overemphasis on context, at the expense of instruction in decoding strategies, will result in a slower rate of reading progress (Evans & Carr, 1985; Nicholson, 1991).

One of the problems with whole-word learning is that there is a lack of real engagement with the print, depth of processing, or what Ehri (1991) calls 'press'; there is little desire to look beyond the cues that are the easiest, and most obvious to discern. Why should the child attend to letters, when all the information needed can be derived from non-alphabetic sources? In fact, several investigators have suggested that the reason phonics instruction is so effective is because it forces attention to the interior details of words, it involves more work, more fine-grained processing than whole-word strategies; thus, more thinking and learning take place. Phonics instruction facilitates the development of the very processes that characterise real reading. It facilitates, unlike whole-word learning, the rapid development of alphabetic decoding skills typical of the skilled reader (Perfetti, 1995a; Rayner, 1995), including the development of orthographic knowledge (Adams, 1990; Stanovich, 1992; Vellutino &

89

Scanlon, 1984), and an efficient verbal memory (Tunmer & Rohl, 1991).

Further research has pointed out another related problem with whole-word learning: this is the difficulty a whole-word reader encounters in trying to decode a novel word. Such children simply lack any effective mechanism for deciphering unfamiliar words. Seymour and Elder (1986) conducted a study in a Scottish primary school where Year 1 children were taught for two terms using sight vocabulary and whole-word methods. After this period of time, none of the children were able to recognise new words, unfamiliar to them. Others, too, have found this lack of transfer phenomenon, or the inability to read novel words in children trained in whole-word methods (Vellutino & Scanlon, 1991), or even in children trained in a combination of whole-word and phonics methods (Juel & Roper-Schneider, 1985). Although experimental studies have shown that the repeated presentation of whole words (often a major feature of whole-word reading methods) may result in faster recognition of the trained words (Reitsma, 1988), studies have failed to demonstrate a transfer effect from trained to untrained words, or even from trained words in one context to the *same* words in another context (Adams, 1990; Ehri & Wilce, 1983: Fleisher, Jenkins, & Pany, 1979). Such findings reduce the value of teaching children to recognise whole words.

Repeated presentation of words as whole shapes to be learned either in the context of reading material or in isolation as sight words on flashcards is of limited value, especially for poor readers, for three reasons: (a) poor readers evade phonological decoding if context is available to help them guess at words (Stanovich, 1980); (b) children taught by whole-word methods will still try to bypass the phonological decoding route even with words presented in isolation (Stanovich, 1980); and (c) poor readers' slow decoding skills are not speeded by methods that allow unlimited exposure time (van den Bosch, van Bon, & Schreuder, 1995) (as is the case in whole-word methods where the same words and stories are repeatedly presented).

It should be explained that not all forms of 'sight word learning' have nothing to do with letter-sound correspondences. The type of sight word learning which has been referred to here, usually involving irregular spelled words, is characterised by the memorisation of words based on their shape or selected features; it occurs in young children who lack alphabetic decoding ability. However, research shows that 'mature forms of sight word learning are alphabetic and phonological at root' (Ehri, 1995, p. 117), where words (irregularly and regularly spelled words) that readers have encountered many times, phonologically recoding them over and over, are eventually stored in memory. The sight of the word (*not its shape*, but the sequence of *letters* and the familiar *spelling patterns* within it) immediately activates that word in memory along with all the connections previously made about its spelling, pronunciation and meaning.

What, then, are the instructional implications of the research pertaining to this early non-alphabetic (memorising shapes and features) form of sight word learning? Teaching to improve decoding skills, particularly for poorer readers, will be much more effective if: (a) words are first presented in isolation, not in context; (b) pseudo- or nonsense words, instead of real words, are used in order to compel readers to decode phonologically and to abandon their fixation with lexical features such as shape or length as a means to recognise words, and (c) words are presented very quickly with unlimited response time allowed (a procedure found to be the optimum method for improving the slow decoding skills of poor readers) (van den Bosch, van Bon, & Shreuder, 1995).

'The English Language Is Too Irregular'

One of the arguments of whole-word advocates against the use of phonics is the irregularity of the English language. While it is true that English is one of the most irregular of alphabetic orthographies, it is not as irregular as one might think. Because common words, spelled irregularly, occur frequently there is a tendency to overestimate the percentage of total words they occupy in everyday English usage. While Morris (1990) found that less than 10% of English words are spelled irregularly, a major computer study of 17,000 words (from Charlton, 1989) found no less than 84% of the words were spelled according to a regular pattern, and only 3% were so unpredictable that they would have to be learned by memorisation.

With this 3% in mind, it is clear that the English language is certainly not irregular enough to prevent one reading by using knowledge of spelling-to-sound connections. The emphasis on irregularities is misleading in a number of other ways: (a) first of all, spelling-to-sound relationships (the letter f = the sound /f/), which are needed for reading, are much more regular than sound-to-spelling relationships (the sound /f/ = f, ff, ph, gh); (b) nearly all consonants have regular letter-to-sound correspondences; (c) it is the vowels which are the most irregular, but one is able t- r--d w-th--t th-m; (d) English is more regular than one might think, if the position of letters in words is also taken into account; and (e) the systematic regularity of groups of letters makes English even more regular. Furthermore, once a child has mastered a limited number of spelling-to-sound correspondences, this knowledge appears to spread rather efficiently (see Stanovich, [1991] for a discussion of this topic).

The alphabetic route certainly represents a very easy task in comparison with the whole-word approach where it is expected that thousands of words will be memorised based on their shape. It is far easier to learn the seventy ways to spell the forty-four sounds made by the twenty-six letters of the alphabet than to memorise thousands and thousands of words in an arbitrary fashion.

Indeed, one of the shortcomings of a whole-word approach is that the child is not provided with a structure or filing system that promotes memory storage. Instead, remembering the spellings of words is completely randomised. Whole-word readers find the task of remembering more and more words on the basis of their shape or peculiar features an increasingly more difficult and frustrating task, and it is a system that inevitably breaks down (Gough & Juel, 1991). On the other hand, the utilisation of letter-sound correspondences provides the child with a systematic way of storing spellings in memory. Memory research shows that it is far easier to remember a structured set of information than one that is a random collection (Gough et al., 1992; Sawyer & Fox, 1991). Ehri (1991), for example, points out that children in Japan, given a similar task to whole-word taught children, are asked to learn fewer than 200 kanji characters per year.

'Words Are Identified Using Context, Guesses, Predictions'

Whole-word proponents actually promote procedures designed, not to reveal the alphabetic principle and assist meaning, but to obscure it. In the twenty years since Frank Smith promoted his book *Understanding Reading* (1971), science has consistently, firmly, and indisputably refuted his claims that skilful readers use context to guess at the words on the page. This is one of most problematic of whole-word notions. In fact, research shows that exactly the opposite is the case. It is only poor readers who rely on context to assist with their poor decoding ability (Bruck, 1990; Nicholson, 1991; Perfetti, Goldman, Hogaboam, 1979; Schwantes, 1991; Stanovich, 1992). Good readers' word-recognition skills are so accurate and fluent that they don't need to use context to guess at words. Goodman's assertion that reading is a 'psycholinguistic guessing game' is not true. Eye-movement research proves, beyond all shadow of doubt, that skilled readers do not use context as a decoding strategy to guess at words (Perfetti, 1995a; Rayner, 1995).

Yet teachers using whole-word or whole-language approaches base much of their teaching on this false premise. Teachers using these approaches actually teach children, as a decoding strategy, to guess. Thus, when children encounter a difficult word, they are encouraged to guess what the word might be, to look at the accompanying pictures and guess, to read through to the end of the sentence and guess, or to look at the first letter and guess.

There is absolutely no data either from empirical research or from whole language studies to support guessing. Research does show that guessing from context leads to the most astonishing and frequent errors. Even skilled adult readers are only able to guess correctly one content word out of ten (Gough, 1983). Content words are more important than function words because they convey virtually all the meaning of a text but such words are also the least predictable. Context will help the child to recognise short, familiar function words, but as these words are more likely to be recognised by the child, context will let the child down precisely where he needs help the most with longer, less frequently occurring content words (Gough & Juel, 1991).

Whole-word supporters profess to be interested in ensuring that reading is a meaningful exercise; but it is precisely such practices as the use of context and guessing which prevent the child from acquiring the sort of strategies which will assist the access to meaning. Research has shown that for effective comprehension a whole clause or sentence must be read quickly enough to be in the reader's memory, ready for interpretation. If word recognition is too slow, meaning will be lost. In support of these findings, many studies have illustrated that poor decoding results in poor comprehension (Perfetti, 1985; Rack, Snowling, & Olson, 1992; Stanovich, 1991; Stuart, 1995; Vellutino, 1991). Fluent, fast word recognition, unassisted by context, facilitates reading comprehension.

Although whole-word advocates often criticise code-emphasis methods of reading instruction for failing to develop reading comprehension, many studies have demonstrated that phonological and alphabetic instruction given to young children not only produces significantly superior word-recognition skills, but also results in better achievement on measures of reading comprehension as well (Brown & Felton, 1990; Hatcher et al., 1994; Iversen & Tunmer, 1993; Juel, 1994; Lie, 1991).

Whole-language instruction, however, offers the following advice for the reader who encounters difficulty with a word: don't sound it out, don't look for familiar word parts within the word because these activities will divert attention from meaning, do skip it, use prior information, read ahead, reread, or put in another word that makes sense (Goodman, 1988). These are practices used by all those who adhere to whole-word emphasis methods of reading instruction and who profess to be interested in helping children understand what they read. (These methods include: shared reading of real books, apprenticeship reading, look-and-say, language experience, story-book methods of reading schemes.) According to research findings which are now beyond debate, however, *all* of these instructions are diametrically *opposed* to practices that will facilitate comprehension of text.

'Good Readers Rely on a Variety of Cues to Extract Meaning'

Part of the whole-word approach is to praise children for 'making sense of print', using a variety of cues, such as context, syntax, semantics, or illustrations. Research shows, however, that good readers use these strategies to *confirm* meaning, not to extract it in the first place. Research also demonstrates that the encouragement of such strategies may result in harmful effects.

First, information gained from more than thirty years of eye-movement studies indicates that accomplished readers make use of contextual, syntactic, or grammatical cues only where there is some doubt about the meaning of the text (Garrod, 1995; Perfetti, 1995a; Rayner, 1995). During reading there is an initial activation of the connections between letters and sounds, and as each new word is decoded, comprehension is automatic and incremental, the word being incorporated into the interpretation of the sentence or passage thus far. Comprehension is automatic because, in most cases, words that are read will be in the reader's speaking vocabulary. Ambiguous words or phrases, however, produce longer-duration-eye fixations, and greater frequency of regressions (where the eyes move back over the text). In this case a reader may momentarily entertain a number of meanings for a word, but use of context resolves the issue. As Garrod (1995) explains: 'the input proposes interpretations and the context disposes them'. Thus, while in most cases decoding unlocks meaning automatically, other features of the text are used as confirmation or checks on meaning when the initial decoding processes put the meaning in doubt.

Secondly, as mentioned previously, experiments have demonstrated that young children learn to read in the very beginning stages much more easily in the absence of accompanying illustrations (Levy, 1981; Rusted & Coltheart, 1979; Solman et al., 1992; Wu & Solman, 1993). Evidence suggests that illustrations hinder the young beginning reader's attempts to deal with print. Picture processing involves right-brain processes, which may interfere with the left-brain processing required for decoding sequential print. Heavy use of pictures as context cues and the constant demands on attention made by large and colourful illustrations act to force right-brain engagement when it is the left side of the brain which is especially suited to deciphering print. Boys are particularly susceptible to this danger since they do not specialise in using the left side of their brains for language tasks as early as girls do (Bakker & Moerland, 1981; Buffery & Gray, 1972; Halpern, 1992).

Thirdly, while it might be accepted whole-word practice to encourage approximate meanings (for example, if a child guesses 'horse' instead of 'donkey'), there is evidence to suggest that encouraging such practices will lead a child to develop the wrong idea about what reading actually is. Byrne (1992) notes that the origins of reading disability seem to be in the early conception that reading is largely remembering; he points out that one adult dyslexic's memory of standing up in class and being praised for 'reading' via memorisation is likely to be a common experience among dyslexics. Research has shown that whole-word learning may impede reading performance by preventing children from seeing any other alternative to the use of global strategies, and rote memorisation (Vellutino & Scanlon, 1991).

Summary

To summarise, research indicates that look-and-say or whole-word methods, which assume that the child will assimilate the alphabetic code intuitively, are potentially damaging, and especially so for the at-risk child (Ackerman, Anhalt, & Dykman, 1986; Brown & Felton, 1990). While Goodman asserts that whole-language methods are founded on a 'comprehensive knowledge base', findings from empirical research suggest that this particular 'knowledge base' is unreliable. Scientific research demonstrates that learning to read is not a naturally occurring process but a skill that must be taught, skilled readers attend to all the letters in every word, and direct instruction in the alphabetic code is required to assist children out of a logographic stage of 'reading' to a stage where more productive, more memory-efficient reading strategies are used. Scientific evidence also shows that context is not used by skilled readers as a decoding strategy; nor can context be used by beginning readers as an effective decoding strategy. Finally, teaching children to use a variety of cues may result in their having a distorted view of what reading actually is.

Part 2   Practice: Context-Emphasis Approaches In Use

Contrary to Goodman's assertion, many parents may *not* like what their children are doing in school. When their child fails to learn to read at school, parents write to newspapers or government officials in despair of methods which assume that children will learn to read by 'osmosis' (Speed, 1994), or by 'some mystical process' (Graham, 1993). Far from being happy with what is happening in primary schools, when polled by MORI and Gallop, almost 90% of parents (parents unconnected with the educational establishment) were anxious that more emphasis be given to the teaching of reading (Moller, 1994). Alarmed at the state of current practice, parents' most common request was for a change to more structured, traditional teaching methods (SCAA, 1994b).

Although research has demonstrated that many of the tenets of whole-word teaching are in error, practice generally does not reflect an awareness of this knowledge. In practice, both the use of whole-word materials and whole-word methods are much in evidence. Most teachers use a combination of reading schemes and 'real books' (HMI, 1991; Cato et al., 1992; Gorman & Fernandes, 1992). Both materials are alike in that the vocabulary is ungraded (making it extremely difficult for children to discover the alphabetic principle), and illustrations dominate the pages (distracting children from the already too-difficult-to-read print). Reading scheme books and 'real books' may differ to the extent that, in schemes, certain key words (Oxford) or common words (Ginn) are repeated, whereas in 'real books', there may or may not be words and phrases that are repeated.

With both the current reading schemes and the ordinary story books certain methods are adopted. These methods require that children memorise words, phrases, sentences, and/or whole books, remembering them through the use of sight word recognition or picture, context, syntactic or phonic (initial letter) cues.

There is a curious belief that reading schemes and ordinary story-books, or real books, are vastly different. Some believe that reading schemes provide more structure than real books (House of Commons, 1990-91b, p. xii); others are of the opinion that only real books are interesting to children and have natural-sounding language (Dombey, 1994b). How different are these materials? As reading schemes do suggest procedures for teachers to follow, it is possible they might provide more structure; and, as storybooks are not normally designed to teach a sight vocabulary of common words, their language may sound more natural. On the other hand, storybooks with patterned language, or with vocabulary matched to the child's reading level, may provide more structure than a scheme book, and reading-scheme stories may often be more interesting and natural-sounding to a child than a number of repetitious storybooks. Finally, in the case of both materials, any stories that must be read over and over, no matter how interesting, must lose some of their charm. In effect, differences between the two materials become negligible, particularly when one considers the common teaching practices or philosophies that are applied to both.

Reading Is Erroneously Viewed as a Natural Process

In direct contradiction to the most solid research findings that learning to read is not a natural process, there is much evidence in practice that teachers, teacher trainers and government inspectors support the notion that 'children learn to read by reading', in a natural, effortless way, much in the manner claimed by Smith, where 'the better reader barely looks at the words on the page' (1973, p. 190). Teacher organisations, teacher training centres, and government inspectors advocate the use of 'phonics in context', where the systematic direct teaching of phonics, decoding, spelling, and vocabulary skills are abolished in favour of teaching these elements incidentally and individually to each child, if and when they crop up. In doing so, they reveal their bias in favour of meaning-emphasis methods, where reading is viewed as a process as natural as learning how to speak, as a process that will simply and spontaneously emerge at each child's own individual rate.

At a recent United Kingdom Reading Association (UKRA) conference, held at the Institute of Education, Cambridge, the theme was shared reading, and the natural 'emergence' of literacy. Involving parents with reading to their children, the speakers suggested, would result in spontaneous, effortless, learning to read (UKRA, March, 1994). At the same time, however, because direct, structured teaching is not advocated, this approach does require the unnatural practice of constantly reading and rereading stories over and over, in order for children to begin to 'read' (guess at and memorise) the stories for themselves.

In Liz Waterland's *Read With Me* (1985), a variant of this approach, the apprenticeship approach, is described. This text has become the most recommended text on the teaching of reading in initial teacher training courses in England, Wales, and Northern Ireland, appearing on almost 70% of all reading lists at teacher training centres. This approach is described as the new orthodoxy in education (Brooks et al., 1992). Waterland sees reading as a process that can simply be picked up, and caught 'like a cough', through the use of guessing strategies: 'The reader reads a text by making informed guesses as to the likelihood of what that text will mean' (Waterland, p. 9). Many staff in training colleges also hold the view that reading is a naturally occurring process, and see phonics methods as unnatural, and too mechanistic (Brooks et al., 1992).

Other popular texts in use at many teacher training colleges include those by Meek and Smith which encourage the appealing, but erroneous, idea that all children will naturally and spontaneously learn how to read if they read with, or are read to by adults. Meek, for example, is a strong proponent of the view, 'to learn to read, children need the attention of one patient adult...for long enough to read something that pleases them both' (p. 9). According to Meek, children 'teach themselves to read... by turning the pages of books and looking at the pictures' (from *Learning to Read*, 1982, p. 11, a text compulsory or recommended in more than half of teacher training centres, the third most popular text). Her views have a powerful influence since there are three texts by Meek which appear on teacher college reading lists, two of which appear approximately half the time, and one a fifth of the time.

An examination of the top thirty most recommended teacher training texts (Brooks et al., 1992) reveals that there is not a single text among these that presents an objective up-to-date review of the experimental research on beginning-reading instruction. All of the texts and government documents listed espouse a 'meaning-emphasis', whole-word method of teaching reading in one form or another. A careful examination of these materials exposes the staggering bias in current teacher training, a bias that amounts to nothing short of indoctrination on a very wide scale. All of these texts, without exception, promote whole-word, 'natural' or discovery methods of reading instruction to some degree, either just one or a mixture of these, along with the child-centred, progressive philosophies that accompany them, none of which are supported by empirical research as effective ways to teach beginning reading.

Government inspectors, informed as they are by the professionals, are inclined to lend their support to the idea that reading is a natural process. The use of non-graded, non-sequenced, ordinary 'real books', which children select for themselves and 'read' with an adult or partner are seen by inspectors as an appropriate way to promote beginning reading: '"Real books" ...(motivate) children to understand and take a strong interest in reading by teaching them from an early stage from attractively presented children's literature' (HMI, 1990, p. 6).

Although current reading scheme books are really no different from 'real books' in the lack of code-emphasis support provided, they are held in disfavour, and reference to them as suitable materials for beginning-reading instruction has been removed from the National Curriculum proposals (SCAA, 1994c, p. 25) so that they are not referred to in the final draft orders (National Curriculum Orders, SCAA 1994a). Although the natural-sounding language and attractive illustrations that ordinary story books are supposed to be unique in having are just as much in evidence in reading-scheme books, almost the entire first page of the Orders for English Key Stage 1, Reading, is devoted to the wholesale endorsement of 'real books', books with 'illustrations that are visually stimulating', have 'interesting subject matter and settings', and that have 'language that benefits from being read aloud and reread' (SCAA, 1994a, p. 6).

The books described may be excellent for adult readers to read to children (just as are the current reading-scheme books); indeed, reading *to* children in order to pique their curiosity and interest in books and develop their listening skills should unarguably form a part of the English curriculum. These books and these procedures, however, will not teach *children themselves how to read*. It is unfortunate that the sort of reading materials that are suitable for supporting children in their first independent efforts to read are not described. There is no mention that for the purposes of reading instruction, as opposed to literature appreciation or listening comprehension, there should be books provided that are especially designed for children to practise their early reading skills; missing is a description of the sort of difficult-to-find books that have graded, sequenced vocabularies, books that arrange for practice of specific skills and knowledge taught beforehand by the teacher, and books that allow children to experience high rates of success in their first efforts to decode and understand print.

It Is Falsely Assumed That Adults Are Whole-Word Readers

As the research on eye movements show, skilled readers focus on each letter of every word although it may not appear that this is the case because processes are so automatic. Unfortunately, in practice it is commonly believed that readers see words as visual shapes, sample words here and there, and guess at others from context. Teacher trainers admit that this is one of the first concepts they teach their students (Dombey, 1990-91). Teachers in turn encourage children to use whole-word, guessing and sampling strategies when trying to decode print based on the false premise that this is what adult readers do.

Indeed, a survey of teaching practice in 234 primary schools found, as previously stated, that nearly all teachers employ a whole-word, look-and-say, sight word approach in the initial stage of teaching a child how to read (Cato et al., 1992). As the research clearly indicates, however, encouraging beginning readers to read in a whole-word or logographic fashion is precisely the kind of training that they do not need, as there is a natural inclination, early on, to read in this manner anyway. What they do need is a strategy that will help them decipher novel words, so that HMI inspectors will not find themselves making the following sort of observations: 'Year 1 children were unable to work out words that were new to them' (HMI, 1991), or 'the majority of pupils can read when they leave primary schools, although comparatively few have yet become independent readers' (HMI 1989, p. 2).

Yet not only do the National Curriculum Orders support the learning of a 'sight vocabulary' (words recognised automatically by shape, context, or visual cues) (SCAA, 1994a, p. 7), the National Curriculum assessment instructions also state that when reading a story passage children should not be penalised for making sensible guesses at words if they use 'word-shape' (SCAA, 1994d, p. 8).

There is much evidence in practice that children are viewed as apprentices, encouraged to mimic the way adults read, erroneously assuming that adults read in a whole-word fashion. As observed in 1990-91 (HMI), 'Since the introduction of the national curriculum, there has been a steady growth of interest in paired reading, linking of younger and older pupils' (p. 13). Teacher trainers, seemingly ignorant of the research, misguidedly promote this approach: 'Children can and do learn much about reading from listening to and watching skilled adults who show them how it is done' (Dombey, 1992, p.18). The government-funded Adult Literacy and Basic Skills Unit also advocates 'natural', whole-word methods. Such statements as, 'The shape of the word is an aid to the reading of words' (ALBSU, 1994, p.3) reveal their bias.

Belief That No Direct Alphabetic Instruction Is Required

Because of the commonly held belief that children will learn to read by reading, it is widely assumed, in sharp contrast to the research, that no direct instruction is required. The UK Reading Association gives advice accordingly: the parent or teacher must read with the child and follow the 'PPP' procedure – pause, prompt, praise (UKRA, 1994). Practices such as 'shared reading', 'paired reading', or 'apprenticeship reading' mean that a child is perpetually dependent on another person who is a competent reader. It was found in one study that only 51% of children surveyed liked reading on their own because, as various children described it, 'Every time I don't know a word and I feel sad', or 'I don't like reading 'cos sometimes you need a teacher to tell what you don't know, and she is talking to someone else, and she says "wait a minute"' (Tizard et al., 1988, p. 144).

Evidence from inspectors' reports suggests that such frustrating experiences may not be uncommon for young children, exposed as they are to apprenticeship or shared-reading methods, methods where parental help is especially important. As a telling indicator of current practices, encouraging parental involvement is becoming a significant feature. Government officials report: 'it would be hard to overstate the value of the active involvement of parents in "paired reading"' (House of Commons, 1990-91a, p. xi), and a third of children at the end of Year 3 still need 'adult support when they read' (HMI, 1990, p. 5). These observations attest to the widespread use of shared-reading methods.

Of course, in the absence of direct teaching, such practice entails introducing parents to the current doctrine (i.e. reading is nothing more than memorising the story), so that they may share in the large and relatively fruitless task. Parents who intuitively sense that productive strategies are needed, and try to teach letter-sound knowledge directly, are actively discouraged from such efforts, encouraged instead to teach their children to memorise print. As one illustration of current attitudes, at the UKRA conference in Cambridge LEA, (March 1994), one speaker urged: 'We must get parents to understand what we are trying to do. When you show them, they *all do it*. "See if you can remember this word, now this one, now this one!"' (Pearce, 1994).

The fourth most popular teacher training text in use, *Reading*, is written by Frank Smith (1978). It appears on 52% of teacher training reading lists of the most recommended texts. Like Waterland, and Meek, Smith proposes that 'children learn to read by reading' (Smith, p. 7) and they do not need to be taught 'since a large part of what we expect them to learn – including reading – cannot in fact be the subject of formal instruction' (Smith, p. 8). These views contrast sharply with experimental research studies that show, if all children are to succeed, or make an acceptable rate of progress in learning to read, they *must be taught*; the necessary phonological awareness and letter-sound knowledge do not spontaneously arise.

Phonics, a Structured System Enhancing Memory Storage, Is Rejected

In practice it is evident that systematic phonics instruction is rejected as being too difficult. As already stated, many teachers have not been trained to teach phonics and do not feel confident to try. Instead, random attention to initial letters while reading may be all that is offered. A careful examination of spelling-to-sound relationships in the English language reveals that it is certainly regular enough to support reading by making these connections. Yet a common excuse given by teacher trainers, and commonly believed by teachers is that the English language is too irregular and there are too many exceptions to the rules.

Teacher training professionals help to consolidate this view with such statements as 'a phonic method ... is very abstract for little children. It means nothing to them and they usually find it boring' (Root, 1989, p. 42), and 'the well-known irregularity of English spelling means that `phonic rules' are only an approximate guide to a limited number of words' (Fox, 1991). Phonics is accused of being dull and tedious, too abstract or mechanistic, and divorced from meaningful activities. However, phonics instruction does not demand that any of these unappealing conditions be met; it is quite possible for phonics instruction to be fascinating to children, easy to grasp, very much enjoyed and deeply rewarding. Nor does the use of a code-emphasis or phonics approach preclude the parallel use of amusing, interesting or otherwise appealing reading material once children have learned enough letter/phoneme and blending skills to experience a high rate of success in their first efforts to read them. Other teaching approaches have equal downside potential. For a parent to read the same text over and over to a child until the child begins to memorise it (as advocated in whole-word methods), must be an exercise not only prone to tedium, but rather lacking in the 'rewarding meaningful activity' department as well.

In contrast to research demonstrating the need to give children useful, generative, memory-enhancing strategies for decoding novel words, children are encouraged to read, instead, by stumbling along with their small store of sight words, hoping to recognise words they know, guessing at most of the rest, and as a last resort, using the initial letter or two. The most popular teacher training text in teacher colleges today asserts (in contrast to eye-movement research) that 'efficient readers ... use little more than the initial letter to check out their expectations of the word' (Waterland, 1985). Similarly, Smith (1986) asserts that the only point of the alphabet is that it provides 'a means of memorising written words' (p. 8).

Parents, too, are instructed; a BBC publication directs them to help their children to make sensible guesses at words by, among other ploys, looking at initial letters of a word only (Body, 1990). More recent, lavishly illustrated materials from the government-funded Adult Literacy and Basic Skills Unit

(1995), published in collaboration with the BBC, continue to instruct parents that a code approach is far too difficult for children as the orthography of the English language is too irregular: 'The English language doesn't have simple phonic rules. Try reading 'cough' by sounding it out' (ALBSU, 1995).

Use of Context and Guessing Is Encouraged

As has been pointed out, the use of guessing from context or picture 'cues' is simply not supported by research as an effective approach to beginning reading instruction. Evidence of its use, however, suggests that it is almost universal. For example, there is the look-and-guess technique, 'Encourage the child to guess any words he or she can't read' (Doncaster LEA, 1983, p. 18), or the read-the-pictures technique, 'The reader can use illustrations as a clue to the text' (ALBSU, 1994, p. 3), or the picture-plus-context strategy, a statement of attainment in the National Curriculum assessments: 'use picture and context cues...' (SCAA, 1994d, p. 7). An ALBSU publication (1991, p. 8) entitled *Extending Reading Skills* advises how to help pupils with unfamiliar words: 'skip the word', 'read on', 'read back over', 'ask what he thinks the word might be' (i.e. ask him to guess), 'draw attention to helpful characteristics', such as 'initial sound/letter', or word 'length'. The reader may find these instructions familiar; they reproduce Kenneth Goodman's advice, detailed in the first part of this chapter, almost word for word. ALBSU is a charity-funded organisation supported by the government.

Because of the widespread encouragement of such strategies, there is evidence that many children do not understand what reading is. Some children are suffering from the misconception that reading is nothing more than memorisation. One child, discussing a book that was difficult to read at first, reported that 'I cracked it in the end by reading and reading and reading' (DFE, 1989, p. 4). A BBC publication for parents instructs parents to 'help' by operating in a manner directly opposed to research findings. When encountering unknown words, parents are instructed: (a) to say 'Let's miss it out and read on to the end of the sentence...now can you guess what the word is?'; and (b) 'Don't ask or expect your child to build up or sound out words... this is hard, it often doesn't work', and as further justification for such advice 'this way is no longer used in most schools' (Body,

1990, section 3). For some other children, reading means telling a story using the large and colourful, often dominant, accompanying illustrations. Tizard and others (1988) found that at the end of nursery school, *more than half* the children surveyed thought that when one reads a book, it is not the print that is read, *but the pictures*.

Summary

In conclusion, then, the following practices, none of which is supported by experimental research, are in widespread use among primary school teachers: (a) encouraging children to read by gradually memorising, and guessing at text; (b) neglecting explicit, systematic, intensive code instruction that forces attention to every letter of every word (in favour of incidental attention, and/or the use of initial letter cues only); (c) providing little, if any, direct instruction (assuming that children will eventually catch on if they read with an adult often enough); and (d) encouraging children to recognise words by their shape, or through the use of context, syntactic, or picture cues. These practices produce a substantial number of children who fail to learn how to read at the crucial, beginning stage, and who, later on, may or may not receive help through appropriate code-emphasis instruction.

5 | Pupils: Similarities versus Differences

Part 1   Research: Individual Differences

One very popular assumption made by teachers and other professionals is that a mixed-method approach is required in order to meet the needs of *individual* children. It has already been seen, however, that in reality the mixture of methods now in use represent largely just one way of teaching reading, the whole-word, 'meaning-emphasis' (memory-emphasis) approach. These methods of teaching are also viewed as child-centred. Children are permitted to learn at their own pace often working individually on their own projects and activities, they are encouraged to choose their own books and write about what interests them personally. Teacher-directed activities are regarded as less important than individual enquiry, which allegedly results in more meaningful learning experiences.

Propounding a mixed-method philosophy, however, achieves the goal of shifting emphasis away from children's similarities and common needs to their differences. Instead of concentrating on similar ways in which all children can be taught to read, it is, instead, deemed necessary to find different methods to suit individual children. This attitude also effectively shifts blame from the possibility of flaws in the instructional setting to flaws in the child. When explaining poor reading standards, apart from blaming the government for overloading the curriculum, various child factors are named as likely contributing influences. Since there is supposedly no one method of reading instruction being used to teach reading, there is no one method of instruction that can be blamed. The quality of teaching escapes critical examination, and the individual characteristics of children become the focus. Child factors blamed include: individual learning styles (visual or auditory), individual differences (psychological and ability), socioeconomic differences, particular reading disabilities and gender differences.

But to what extent are these factors to blame, when the shortcomings of the instructional setting are recognised and taken into account?

The Myth of Individual Learning Styles

It is often assumed that whole-word methods are good for the visual learner, while a code-emphasis approach is good for the auditorially attuned. Although there have been many empirical studies addressing this issue, there is absolutely no evidence of an interaction between method and preferred learning style (Arter & Jenkins, 1977; Groff, 1979; Liberman & Liberman, 1992; Stahl, 1988). If the notion that children have individual styles of learning is not an issue then, both whole-word (supposedly catering to visual learners) or code-emphasis (supposedly catering to auditory learners) approaches should be suitable for early reading instruction. This, however, is not the case.

As pointed out in earlier chapters, compared to whole-word methods, code-emphasis approaches result in faster and superior reading progress. Among the reasons why code-emphasis approaches are more effective is the fact that certain types of linguistic skills, *both* visual and auditory, are required in learning how to read. Whole-word methods assume that learning to read is a visual process. However, as is shown by the research on the importance of being phonologically aware or being able to *detect speech sounds*, and the importance of *relating speech sounds* to printed symbols (letters), the process of learning to read is much more reliant on the skills of *hearing* than seeing.

Code-emphasis or phonics instruction specifically addresses the fundamental nature of the reading process; such instruction focuses attention not only on the development of a child's speech sound awareness, but also on the development of a child's ability to relate the alphabetical symbols to speech sounds. Whole-word methods, on the other hand, do neither. Whole-word methods concentrate on the learning of words as whole visual shapes, as if they were pictures; but visual skills are not extended to examining the interior details of words such as the shapes of individual letters or familiar spelling patterns. While the emphasis is on remembering visual shapes, some auditory skills are developed; these involve listening comprehension of stories read by the teacher, and recall of whole words pronounced by an adult reader. But whole-word methods both ignore the elemental importance of developing phoneme awareness as a requisite reading skill as well as fail to teach children the specifics of how letters and speech sounds are related.

Although studies show that a strong reliance on the visual mode is often detrimental to the process of learning to read (McGuinness, 1981), research has also demonstrated that what is required is not merely the ability to learn across both auditory and visual domains, but the ability to learn *a particular type* of auditory response (to do with speech sounds), as well as *a particular type* of visual response (involving letters *and* speech sounds) (Stevenson, Parker, & Wilkinson, 1976). These findings help to explain why investigations have found that, regardless of children's auditory or visual capacities, higher reading achievement is produced by phonics-emphasis programmes than through the use of whole-word, meaning-emphasis schemes (Harris, Serwer, Gold, & Morrison, 1967).

Individual Differences Augmented by Classroom Setting

It is commonly believed that child-centred approaches where children direct their own learning are merited on the basis that children will learn more and be happier in an environment where their individual differences in ability, in their own particular interests, or in their levels of emotional development are taken into account and catered to.

However, where efficiency of learning is the aim, direct instruction results in superior effects in comparison to discovery or learner-centred methods of teaching. Teacher-led activities are found to be strongly associated with higher levels of pupil concentration and engagement, which, in turn, are directly related to the learning that results (Rosenshine & Stevens, 1984; Yates & Yates, 1993). In fact, there is a great deal of evidence that teaching methods whereby the teacher sets the pace, sets the standards and teaches the class as a whole tend to achieve better results than teaching methods that emphasise pupil-directed learning and/or individual consultations with children (Gutierrez & Slavin, 1992).

Children's reading achievement is better, for example, when they receive direct group, or whole class code-emphasis teaching, regardless of their ability, simply because they are receiving more systematic and comprehensive instruction from the teacher (of the kind that is needed) than is possible under individualised, whole-word teaching régimes. Many studies have shown this to be the case (for reviews, see Adams & Bruck, 1993; Jorm & Share, 1983; Schickedanz, 1990). Even if the instruction received is not tailored perfectly to suit the needs of each individual child, if a pupil is exposed to more direct teaching, it is likely that more learning will result.

Two further factors help to explain the superior achievement produced by code-emphasis instruction. First, children in code-oriented classrooms become independent readers sooner than those in whole-word classrooms and the sooner a child is able to read independently the sooner he or she will begin to benefit from the many positive spin-off effects that reading practice brings.

Second, differences in reading methods mean that those in code-oriented classrooms are given more opportunity for teacher-directed reading practice than those in whole-word classrooms. Every child in a 'real books' or whole-word classroom is likely to be 'reading' a different book, whereas those in a code-oriented classroom are likely to be reading either the same book as many others in a group or the same book as the rest of the class. These differences in teaching method mean that a teacher in a whole-word or 'real books' classroom is faced with the difficulty of having to 'hear' children read on a very time-consuming, individualised basis, and, at the same time, constantly trying to arrange the most appropriate practice for each child; in a code-oriented classroom, however, the teacher is able to hear a group of six to eight children read all at once. (Children in a group taking turns to read are in effect all reading at once because they are all reading silently as they follow what is read orally.) Thus, children in a whole-word setting, having to rely on one-to-one adult help for reading practice (which is necessarily limited in availability), not only suffer the effects of a slower start in reading but they also make very slow progress towards becoming better readers once they do begin to grasp the alphabetic principle.

A survey undertaken by Reading University explored the effects of traditional classroom organisation versus progressive methods where 'for the past twenty years most classes have had pupils sitting in groups for much of their work' (Hastings & Schwieso, 1995). The results showed that traditional seating of pupils in rows led to increased time on task, ranging from as much as one-third to double the amount of time spent working productively. Seated in groups, children were found to talk to each other more, have difficulty seeing the blackboard, become easily distracted and more often behave disruptively. Seated in rows, pupils concentrated better, could see the blackboard more easily, were less distracted and were better behaved.

Boys, compared to girls, are at a disadvantage in noisy, whole-word, meaning-emphasis classrooms. Boys are at greater risk of dyslexia and it has been shown that dyslexics' performance is particularly, and adversely, affected by noise (Nicholson & Fawcett, 1990). It has been documented that in whole-language, child-centred classrooms there is far more talking and generally higher noise levels than in code-emphasis, teacher-directed classrooms (Stahl & Miller, 1989). It is extraneous speech in particular that disrupts working memory in dyslexics (Ackerman & Dykman, 1993), so that children working in small groups, or the teacher's speaking with another group, television or radio in the background, are noted as situations that will have deleterious interference effects on dyslexics' reading ability.

On the other hand, it has been suggested that boys may perform badly in relation to girls in child-centred, whole language classrooms because girls are better at the language and communication skills being emphasised. However, among cognitive sex differences, the magnitude of the sex difference in verbal ability is very small; in fact, it is estimated that it is probably the smallest among the cognitive sex differences (Halpern, 1992). Additionally, the chances are that it is the boys who are practising their language and communication skills far more than girls since some studies find that boys dominate teachers' time in nearly all classroom situations (for reviews, Reid & Stratta, 1989). Thus when considering what factors may contribute to early sex differences in reading, the amount of time communication skills are being practised by each sex may be a factor to be discounted, whereas the differences between the sexes in their distractibility due to noise, and in particular extraneous speech, may be important.

As far as the individual emotional welfare of children is concerned, there is no evidence that children are happier or have more positive attitudes towards reading in a whole-language, individualised setting (McKenna, Stratton, Grindler, & Jenkins, 1995; Stahl, McKenna, & Pagnucco, 1994). In fact, studies show that self-esteem is related more to levels of achievement. In a study involving 9,000 children aged 6 to 8 years, the relationship between academic performance and self-esteem was investigated; it was found that the teaching approaches that produce the highest achievement scores on basic skills, also produced the highest scores on self-esteem (Moeller, 1993, 1994). In classrooms where children receive little direct teaching, the reading performance of many will suffer; poor reading achievement is found to be associated with poor self-esteem, low motivation, apathy or anger (Brunner, 1993; Kline, 1994; Stuart, 1995).

Socio-economic Differences

The current debate about school league tables centres on the unfairness of comparing achievement of children from different social backgrounds, and of comparing children who start off with very different skills and levels of knowledge upon entering school. The assumption that expectations of achievement should be lower for socially disadvantaged children is challenged by several researchers. A NFER report (Cato & Whetton, 1991) which examined the test results of 7-year-olds in England and Wales found that there was no evidence that the decline, occurring in 73% of the twenty-six LEAs' reading scores, was an inner-city phenomenon. In another study, an analysis of the GCSE results of almost 12,000 state school students revealed that socioeconomic factors did not play a rôle, except in a very few schools where there were a high proportion of disadvantaged students (Sammons, Thomas, Mortimore, Owen, Pennell, 1994).

What researchers have found, however, is that differences in results are related to whether students are taught in the most effective or least effective schools. Another report found, for example, that while pupils entitled to free school meals are likely to do less well in their GCSEs, the particular school attended has an even greater impact on GCSE attainment (Thomas, Pau, & Goldstein, 1994). In one study examining school and pupil factors it was found that effective schools raise reading attainment between the ages of 7 and 10 for all pupils regardless of background factors or prior attainment, while less effective schools appear to depress later reading attainment for all pupils (Sammons, Nuttall, & Cuttance, 1993). Others have found that while only 2% of the variance in third-year reading attainment is due to background factors once initial attainment is accounted for, just over 9% of the variance in reading attainment can be attributed to the influence of the particular school (Mortimore, Sammons, Stoll, Ecob, & Lewis, 1988).

Tizard and others (1988) found no relationship between reading progress and social background, and no relationship between frequency of reading at home with parents and reading achievement. Others have concluded after reviewing a substantial amount of research in this area that there is no convincing evidence that parental help with reading at home results in better reading progress at school (White, Taylor, & Moss, 1992).[*]

Schools that provide effective reading instruction can be powerful in mitigating the effects of social disadvantage. A report from Suffolk (HMI, 1991) showed falls in reading scores of both disadvantaged and other groups of primary children, and warned against schools using social factors as the only explanation of reading performance. It was concluded, for example, in a study conducted in Canada in thirty-six classrooms of 5- and 6-year-old children, that none of the factors such as poverty, unemployment, single-parent families, English as a second language, or lack of books at home had inevitably to result in low reading attainment (Willows, 1996). The schools involved in this study were selected because they were attended by children from homes characterised by many of the disadvantages listed. After one group of children was taught using a British-designed phonics programme, and a control group of children was taught using the unstructured, whole-word based methods already in place, there were dramatic differences in the way each group could

---

[*] One curious exception to such conclusions was found in an Israeli study. Look-and-say methods were adopted in the schools with the result that most of the children learnt to read well, but some did not. Upon investigation, it was discovered that parents of the good readers were literate in Hebrew, and worried about their children's poor reading progress at school, had helped them overcome their initial reading difficulties with substantial amounts of letter-phoneme teaching at home; parents of failing readers, however, were new immigrants, not literate in Hebrew, and were unable to intervene in the schooling process (Feitelson, 1973).

read and spell. The results of this study were so convincing that three large education authorities in Toronto decided to use the phonics programme in all their schools.

This research provides evidence that there is simply no justification for assuming an inevitable link must always arise between social factors and educational attainment. Researchers who have conducted studies addressing this issue have warned against attributing reading difficulties to family or social background (Blachman, 1987; Read & Ruyter, 1985), and failing to recognise the importance of the instructional setting; in relation to reading progress, the type, the sequence, and the quality of instruction are crucial.

What of the possibility that a child's phonological skills, the most significant predictor of reading success, might be influenced by social background? Even in considering this possibility, studies have failed to find a convincing relationship between social background variables and the development of phonological skills in preschool children (Maclean et al., 1987; Tunmer, 1991). Jorm and others (1984) found no significant differences in phonological abilities between children of differing socioeconomic status. Once formal schooling begins, those children who do have poor phonological awareness can be trained so that initial differences in this area can be largely overcome. Research demonstrates, for example, that reading programmes which develop phonological awareness and which are found to be superior with one group of children tend to be superior with all groups of children, regardless of their intelligence or prior reading-related experiences (Alegria et al., 1982; Blachman et al., 1994). As Ehri (1989) points out, individual differences in phonological awareness ability influence reading development only when 'the instructional method is inadequate' (p. 361).

What influence do economic factors have on reading standards? Lack of funding is widely held to influence academic standards. In the years during which the Conservative government has been in power in England, educational expenditure has increased 50% per pupil (DES, 1992a), class sizes have decreased overall, and the teacher/pupil ratio in primary schools is relatively stable, an average of 22·7 in 1980 compared to 22·4 in 1993 (Government Statistical Service, 1994a). Reading standards among 7-year-olds, however, have not improved during this period, as we noted in the introduction they have significantly declined.

Particular Reading Disabilities

(a) Reading Failure and Remediation

If some children fail to learn how to read while others succeed, does this not indicate that children are indeed very different and need to be taught in different ways? Research investigating reading methods clearly indicates that failure can be avoided; if, instead of focusing on individual differences, children's common needs are taken into account, virtually all children can be taught to read within the first few months of school.

In fact, one study shows that instructional methods which are concerned primarily with children's individual differences result, paradoxically, in a substantial *increase* in the range of differences; within a class the overall spread in reading abilities, for example, becomes noticeably larger. Burkard (1996) found that such methods result in a greater proportion of very poor readers, lengthening the tail of under-achievers who trail far behind the average. In Suffolk primary schools where such methods are in use standardised testing reveals that the average proportion of children whose reading attainment is more than a year and a half behind is 15%; this is large in contrast to one school in Suffolk (Woods Loke) where common needs are the focus and systematic phonics is taught to the whole class in the first few weeks of school. At this school the average proportion of children in this category is only 1%. Furthermore, within the tail of under-achievers, 35% of children in Suffolk schools are six months retarded in their reading compared to only 8% at Woods Loke school.

On the other hand, children who fail to make reading progress in their first year at school will begin a downward cycle, falling further and further behind. Indeed, these children may struggle all their school lives to make up for this very serious initial delay.

Even if specialist help is eventually secured, it is more difficult to teach a child to read as the time passes, as ineffective habits and negative attitudes become more and more ingrained. These are the children who may have had a long history of using inefficient, whole-word strategies to tackle print. Difficulty may arise weaning these children from their heavy reliance on context and sight word reading.

One study, where children were identified as 'Chinese' (whole-word readers) or 'Phoenicians' (alphabetic decoders), monitored this problem (Byrne et al., 1992). Results showed that over a three-year period, Phoenicians improve while Chinese decline in their ability to read both regular (easily decodable) as well as irregular words (the kind of words best suited to whole-word readers). These findings illustrate how whole-word or visual cue reading might serve a child adequately until the age of 7, but still result in inferior reading progress over the long term.

Timing of instruction may be critical in helping children through the sequence of necessary reading stages. It has been suggested that phonological awareness may have 'a maturational component', or a critical period (Mann, 1991b; Silver & Hagin, 1990). Some children are aware of phonemes before they learn to read and before being exposed to alphabetic knowledge, whereas illiterate adults do not have this awareness (Mann, 1991b; Morais et al., 1987; Wagner & Torgesen, 1987). Exposure to an alphabetic system and to phonics methods, in particular, facilitates the development of phonological awareness (Alegria & Morais, 1991; Ellis, 1993; Jorm et al., 1984; Juel, 1988; Lundberg et al., 1988), but children, compared to adults, appear to have a 'window' of opportunity where it is easier for them to acquire and make use of the necessary phonological skills.

Indeed, waiting until children are in trouble is a serious mistake. Many remedial reading programmes produce only slow progress, and gains achieved in the short term may not be retained over the long term. In the case of the Reading Recovery programme, for example, measurements taken twelve months after intervention revealed no significant differences between groups (Glynn et al, 1989); any effects found initially were not maintained.

(b) Reading Recovery Programme

A vivid warning of the political dangers of assuming there will be individual differences in learning to read - and in particular, that some children will later need remedial help - comes from the example of Reading Recovery. Not only is Reading Recovery expensive, evidence suggests that it is limited in its effectiveness. Reading Recovery costs £800 to £1000 per child for the individual tutoring, and there are additional costs as well. Teachers are trained for a year before they become tutors and others are trained and hired to integrate and administer the programme.

An early intervention programme for children who have failed to make reading progress after one year in school, Reading Recovery was designed originally for use in New Zealand schools where whole-language methods are widely adopted. Its use has since spread to a number of other countries. The programme involves the use of 'real books', writing activities, and some phonics of the incidental and opportunistic variety. It differs little from the 'mixture' of methods most children are currently experiencing except that since the instruction is given privately on a one-to-one basis it exerts less pressure on the teacher. That is, the teacher does not have to be in 25 different places at once trying to deliver it. However, its effectiveness has not been adequately evaluated under conditions of stringent empirical research.

Studies which have attempted to establish its effectiveness have been criticised by a number of researchers for their flawed methodology (Center et al., 1992; Chapman & Tunmer, 1991; Nicholson, 1989; Shanahan, 1987). Although all criticisms do not apply to all studies, some of these criticisms include:

1. In most cases, only the Clay battery of tests was used to measure results, and no standardised measures, which would allow generalisations about reading skills, were used.

2. In isolated cases where standardised measures were used (Burt Graded Word Reading Test used in England), the *non reading recovery* children scored significantly higher in spite of there being no differences between groups on this test at the start (Hall, 1994). In one case, where another test outside the Clay battery of tests was used (a measure of syntactic awareness), there was no difference between groups on the post-test.

3. The use of the Clay battery of tests to assess reading ability has been questioned since they simply measure the specific skills taught in the programme; none of these tests measure knowledge that is significantly correlated with the ability to read connected text; a non-word or pseudo-word reading test, regarded as the most accurate measure in the research literature (Iversen & Tunmer, 1993), is not used.

117

4. Positive gain in text level has often been reported for the Reading Recovery children. However, comparison of gain scores is inappropriate. The comparison groups began with books containing much more text than the simple picture books of the RR children, and as a result, the average gain for those on the higher level texts was much lower than the average gain for those beginning on the lower-level texts.

5. Reading Recovery results have been inflated since they have been based only on those children who were successful in the programme, and the 25-30% of children who failed to benefit and were withdrawn during the studies were excluded from the data analyses.

6. *Serious* failure to assign children randomly to experimental or control group has been criticised; groups being compared were not equivalent. Groups were not equal in terms of quality of instruction: the RR teachers were more experienced and better trained, and individual instruction was compared with group instruction.

7. Statistical measures used were not as stringent or appropriate as they should have been.

8. Claims that children had achieved the target reading level of 'average' among their peers at completion of the programme are questioned since the comparison children referred to were not the average readers but the poorer readers.

Children who are having problems learning how to read are particularly deficient in decoding skills, and programmes which emphasise these skills achieve better and/or quicker results (Adams & Bruck, 1993; Iversen & Tunmer, 1993). Contrary to expressed opinion (Wright, 1994a; Beard, 1994), that Reading Recovery is the only suitable programme available, there are a number of alternative programmes available with proven effectiveness. Some of these programmes are better alternatives, not only in terms of cost, but because, in line with experimental research, they focus primarily on developing phonological awareness and decoding skills, skills that Reading Recovery has been criticised for failing to address (Adams, 1990; Center et al., 1992; Glynn et al., 1989).

Available programmes include: Williams' programme for learning-disabled children (1979, 1980); Wallach and

Wallach's tutoring programme (1976); the highly successful Distar programmes, *Reading Mastery* and *Corrective Reading*, which were originally aimed at disadvantaged children and which achieve extremely impressive long-term results (Engelmann & Bruner, 1983), and the *Units of Sound* (Dyslexia Institute, 1996), *Phonics 44* (Morris, 1983), *Alpha to Omega* (Hornsby & Shear, 1980), *Step by Step* (McNee, 1990), *Butterfly* (Tyk, 1993), *THRASS* (Davies & Ritchie, 1996), *Toe by Toe* (Cowling, 1994), and *SoundWorks* (Open School, 1995) programmes, each of which has a proven record for helping backward or dyslexic readers. Other useful resources include the *Morris-Montessori Word List* (Morris, 1990, 1994), and *The Phonics Handbook* (Lloyd, 1992).

The reading levels of 8-year-old Scottish children, taught by phonics, were compared with those of children in New Zealand, taught by whole-language methods (Johnston & Thompson, 1989). New Zealand is a country where Marie Clay expects that '30 to 50 percent' of children will need Reading Recovery (extra whole-language) treatment (Clay, 1985, p. 18). Among the Scottish children, there were fewer poor readers and the average reading level was six months higher than that attained by the New Zealand children. The results of this study suggest that there would be many fewer children in need of remedial teaching in England if at the beginning of primary school a *Phonic Prevention* programme were to be adopted by all schools.

Since all children must acquire the alphabetic principle when learning how to read, it is perhaps not surprising that programmes which address this issue are the most effective.

Indeed, one danger of remedial programmes is that they may masquerade as mixed or eclectic in approach, when in fact the instruction merely represents an increased diet of context and whole words. Clay (1985, 1991), for example, argues in defence of the Reading Recovery programme (in direct contrast to research findings) that it is unnecessary to teach alphabetic coding skills directly and that such knowledge can be developed effectively through writing activities as children try to spell words.

However, Iversen and Tunmer (1993) have shown that such an assumption is in error. They found that a modified Reading Recovery programme (which provided systematic letter-sound instruction) was almost 40% more effective than the standard

Reading Recovery programme (which provided only incidental phonics instruction in combination with writing activities). Those in the modified programme reached the same levels of achievement much earlier than those in the standard programme, within an average of forty-one lessons as opposed to fifty-seven lessons. Iversen and Tunmer suggest that even greater efficiency would result if alphabetic training were introduced at the start of the programme rather than delaying for ten or more lessons (a standard procedure adopted in Reading Recovery, where no instruction takes place for the initial two weeks while the teacher spends time 'roaming around the known').

(c) Dyslexia

Some children, approximately 4% of the population in the United Kingdom, are dyslexic (Brooks, 1994; Peer, 1994).* This 4% translates to only one dyslexic child per classroom, and even dyslexics can learn to read with the appropriate instruction. Ehri (1989) goes so far as to state: 'Inadequate instruction spawning limited reading and spelling development and limited phonological awareness is the primary cause of the dyslexics' reading disability' (p. 356).

Badian (1994) defines two types of poor readers: dyslexics, or those who have a discrepancy between their IQ and reading level (IQ can range from high to low but does not match reading level), and poor, backward readers, or slow learners (those that have below average intelligence and poor reading skills to match). Researchers investigating reading disabilities have convincingly argued, with over twenty years of research to support their view, that phonological processing deficiencies are the hallmark of both of these types of disabled readers (for reviews, see Hurford et al., 1994; Pennington, 1991; Snowling, 1995; Wagner & Torgesen, 1987). Research using non-word or pseudo-word tests to measure reading ability shows that both these types of disabled readers share an insensitivity to speech sounds and to sound/symbol relationships (Badian, 1994; Liberman & Shankweiler, 1991; Stanovich, 1988; Vellutino, 1979).

---

* The term dyslexia, derived from Greek origins, strictly means difficulty with speech; it is often confused, however, with the Latin term to read, and has therefore come to mean difficulty with reading (Brown, The New Shorter Oxford English Dictionary, 1993).

Dyslexics, however, do differ from ordinary backward readers. As well as suffering from more severe phonological deficits, dyslexics are poorer in other tasks which involve primarily left-hemisphere language processing, or the integration of right- and left-brain processing: for example, tasks such as automatic word recognition or naming speed (which involve linking visual information with phonological information retrieved from short-term memory), or orthographic processing (which involves recognising and then naming which letters in a sequence are reversed) (Badian, 1994; Bowers & Swanson, 1991; Felton & Brown, 1990; Holmes, 1994; Snowling, 1995). Dyslexics are also found to be impaired on tasks requiring long-term memory, such as remembering the months of the year or multiplication tables. Thus, although dyslexics' three areas of weakness are phonological awareness, naming, and verbal memory, the last two are not unrelated to the first since they both involve retrieving phonological information (usually stored in language areas within the left hemisphere) from memory.

Dyslexics' difficulties in these areas are related to the findings of other studies which involve the use of sophisticated equipment to investigate how the brain behaves during various processing tasks. Although research in this area is constantly changing and at this point inconclusive, to date a number of studies have produced evidence which suggests that dyslexics have difficulty shifting from right- to left-hemisphere processing, once the right side of the brain has been activated. If a letter or a numeral is shown to the subject, areas in both the right and the left posterior parietal-occipital regions of the brain are activated along with other areas in the right hemisphere (Hynd, 1992; Harter, 1991; Kershner & Micallef, 1991; Pumfrey & Reason, 1991), but naming requires processing which occurs in central language areas of the left hemisphere. Speed of shift appears to be affected in dyslexics. It is suggested that dyslexics may be susceptible to 'an exuberance of right hemisphere activation which, in turn, interferes specifically with the development of phonological skills by the left hemisphere' (Kershner & Micallef, 1991, p. 408).

Results of further investigations in this area (reviewed by Obrzut, 1991) support the view that dyslexic children appear to experience an 'attentional dysfunction' which interferes with left-hemisphere language processing. In one investigation, Rumsey and others (1992) found that, in contrast to non-dyslexic control subjects, severely disabled males with dyslexia failed to activate a region in the left hemisphere while performing a rhyme detection task. Another investigation found that unlike normal readers, dyslexics responded to linguistic stimuli as if they were non-linguistic stimuli (with right-hemisphere activity) (Landwehrmeyer, Gerling, and Wallesch, 1990). These findings coincide with the evidence that dyslexics have difficulties with short-term memory tasks, finding is easier, for example, to remember a short word than a longer word, or finding that their performance on one task is adversely affected if asked to perform another task at the same time (Nicholson & Fawcett, 1990).

In further support of this research, investigations comparing the neuroanatomy of dyslexics' brains with the brains of normal subjects (both at autopsy and in live subjects) have found evidence that dyslexics' brains may differ in a number of respects (for review, see Gallaburda, 1994; Flowers, 1993; Obrzut, 1991; Pennington, 1991), and in various aspects that would help to explain the speed-of-shift difficulties, and weak or unstable left-hemisphere processing that dyslexics appear to suffer from.

Finally, it would appear that boys have more difficulty with this problem. Estimates of the ratio of boys to girls who are dyslexic range from 5 or 6:1 in remedial settings (Finucci & Childs, 1981; Halpern, 1992) to 2 or 3:1 in school populations (for review, see Stevenson, 1992). In some research populations, the ratio of males to females with dyslexia may approach equality, but Feldman and others (1995) explain why this finding is unusual. They conclude from the evidence that female compared to male dyslexics are better able to overcome their reading impairment, they exhibit different patterns of reading skills, and their impairments are usually less severe. Thus, to some degree at least, the method of instruction used to teach beginners to read may be especially critical for boys, since it is suggested that being female acts as a 'protective factor' while being male is a 'potential liability' (Feldman et al., 1995, p. 160).

(d) Instructional Implications for At-Risk Readers

These findings have significant implications for instruction. First, if all types of poorer readers suffer from phonological deficiencies, and as pointed out earlier are unable to gain alphabetic insights for themselves, instruction which develops these skills should be stressed. This means that the sort of instruction which draws attention to speech sounds and the explicit connections between these sounds and letters in a structured, systematic, and intensive manner would be of benefit. Indeed a great deal of research has shown precisely this to be the case; all of the at-risk children in these studies were successfully taught to read using code-emphasis instruction (Ball & Blachman, 1988; Johnston & Holligan, 1991; Stoner, 1991).

It has been suggested that whole-word instruction is not particularly appropriate for disabled readers (Henry, 1991; Liberman & Liberman, 1990; Lyon, 1992; Mather, 1992); in fact, poorer readers appear to be relatively competent with top-down, meaning-emphasis processes (Stanovich, 1991). Some studies have demonstrated, for instance, that poor readers lacking in phonological skills achieve surprisingly high levels of performance on tests of right hemisphere visuospatial skills (Harter, 1991; Mann, 1991a). Kershner & Micallef (1991) found that dyslexic children who were better at recalling information presented to their left ear (and therefore, to their right hemisphere) were more disabled in pseudoword reading (a task performed by the left hemisphere). Structured, systematic, phonics instruction, which provides disabled readers with training in the area of their weakness (phonological skills), has been shown to produce superior reading performance with at-risk children compared to context-emphasis instruction (Brown & Felton, 1990).

Secondly, if dyslexics suffer from particular difficulties shifting their attention from visual to phonological stimuli, then instruction which plays down the visuospatial and concentrates on the phonological aspects should help to avoid these problems. Whole-word instruction (emphasising visual shapes), along with the guess-the-word-by-looking-at-the-picture strategy (activating visuospatial processing) is precisely the sort of instruction that one would expect to worsen this particular problem in dyslexics; as the research evidence suggests, overactivation of visuospatial processing in dyslexics can interfere with their ability to perform phonological tasks. And indeed, other research evidence

123

confirms that educational practices such as these may contribute to the development of reading problems (Brown & Felton, 1990; Calfee, 1983).

To help these children avoid the danger of becoming mired in the use of logographic strategies, recognising words purely by selective association, or by their visual peculiarities (Gough, 1993), it is important, in particular for these at risk children, that systematic and intensive code-emphasis instruction is provided. Researchers caution that some children, especially those poor in rapid naming ability as well as phonological skills, will need long-term intensive treatment (Blachman, 1994). The danger is that these children may not get the help they need when they do not respond as quickly as others to instruction.

Gender Differences

Are there differences between the sexes which imply that instruction should be designed differently to meet their individual needs? There are a number of differences between girls and boys that relate to reading instruction.

First, as outlined above, boys are more at risk of developing dyslexia than girls; it is frequently noted in the literature reviewing sex differences in reading that boys are more likely than girls to have problems learning to read (Halpern, 1992; Kail, 1992). Thus, boys more than girls, may be susceptible to some of the further ramifications associated with dyslexia: they may be more distracted by extraneous noise, particularly speech, during learning tasks, they may be more susceptible to picture effects, the wide range of bright and colourful illustrations in their readers distracting their attention from the decoding task. They may be more vulnerable to an over-exuberance of right-hemisphere processing in response to instruction which emphasises the shape or length of words and thus, the development of left-hemispheric phonological skills may be more at risk of interference.

Second, developmental differences between girls and boys may put boys more at risk of reading problems. Cerebral lateralisation for language-related, left-hemispheric tasks is present in girls at 5 years, but begins to develop later in boys, around age 6 (Buffery, 1976; Knights & Bakker, 1979; Halpern, 1992). A study in Australia, for example, found that up until the age of 7·5 years males are about eight months behind females in their visual attention span (VAS) level; VAS is defined as the number of visual elements a child can process at a glance (Harrison et al., 1996).

These findings are in line with research evidence that boys develop greater specialisation of spatial skills in the right hemisphere and language skills in the left-hemisphere than girls do, but they also demonstrate slower maturation in this development than girls. Girls not only pass through the successive laterality stages faster than boys, but they also show greater bihemispheric participation in both verbal and spatial processing (Harris & Sipay, 1990).

What implications do these sex differences have for instruction? Boys and girls have the same teaching requirements when it comes to learning how to read. The reading achievement of all children can be enhanced with the appropriate instruction; without it, the reading progress of all children will be curbed. However, since the factors described above may make boys more susceptible to developing reading problems than girls, it seems likely that the lack of appropriate instruction will take more of a toll on the reading attainment of boys.

Furthermore, since differences in phonological awareness ability contribute more than any other factor to reading development among all children, instruction which fails to address this aspect of reading is likely to aggravate initial sex differences in reading. In addition, in the absence of early, systematic code-emphasis instruction, the sort of instruction which has been found to encourage the development of left-hemisphere sequential processing abilities (Bakker, 1992), there is the risk that boys may become stuck in the early reading strategies (memorising visual shapes) primarily undertaken in bilateral posterior, and right hemisphere regions of the brain. Thus, in the absence of appropriate teaching, it is possible that early sex differences in reading ability are exacerbated, with the danger that these disparities, instead of narrowing over time, may instead grow worse.

Summary

When the instructional setting is considered, and designed to cater to the common needs of all beginning readers, individual difference factors such as learning style, academic ability, emotional maturity, socioeconomic background, and reading-related disabilities can be largely overcome.

Shifting the focus away from individual differences to the common requirements that research indicates all children have when learning how to read can also avoid the need for remediation later.

Part 2   Practice: Catering to Individual Differences

In practice, there is widespread agreement on the need to cater to individual differences. Examples of the popular adoption of this myth abound:

1. 'Individual children succeed best by different routes' (House of Commons, 1990-91a, p. 56).
2. 'Teachers should ... meet the needs of individual children.' (government curriculum proposals, SCAA, 1994c, p. 10).
3. 'Children also bring to school different styles of learning' (teacher trainer, Dombey, 1992, p. 20).
4. 'No one method works with every child' (teacher trainee, Brooks et al., 1992, p. 57).

It is on the basis of the individual-differences concept that teachers justify the use of a mixture of different methods to teach reading. However, as has been seen, this mixture of methods is invariably a mixture of meaning-emphasis approaches, all essentially the same. Common to all these methods as well, children are frequently involved in individual activities and receive very little direct whole-class teaching.

The Misguided Focus on the Individual Learner

Despite the lack of evidence that individual learning styles exist, or that children's learning or emotional welfare will be negatively affected if taught directly as a whole class, the use of a combination of approaches tailored to suit the individual needs of children is a stance that is widely accepted as appropriate. The almost universal adoption of this view is useful for a number of reasons.

Firstly, the assumption that the mixed approach adopted does in fact cater to the needs of all children helps to divert attention away from instructional factors, and avoids a careful monitoring of the constituents of the 'mix'. Since there is supposedly widespread use of different reading methods, one does not have to entertain the possibility that declining reading standards might have something to do with any particular teaching method. Although a decline in reading standards has been confirmed by Cato and Whetton (1991), they note that since all 'schools had similar mixed approaches to the teaching of reading, using a balance of reading schemes, 'real' books, 'phonic', and 'look-and-say' instruction, it was not possible for comparison of different approaches to the teaching of reading to be made' (p. 66).

Similarly, the debate over whole-class teaching versus individualised instruction has been labelled a non-existent problem, an instance of 'standard election-year scapegoating' (Kane, 1996. p. 7). Just as teacher trainers and teachers are quick to point out that they 'already do' teach phonics, they also point out that they 'already do' include whole-class teaching, and it is therefore considered impossible to make comparisons between the two forms of instruction, or to establish whether one might be preferable to another.

Thus, in spite of the fact that primary school inspectors note that the teaching of phonics is 'rare' (Ofsted, 1996, p.14), and the fact that according to inspectors' reports, whole-class teaching only occurs about 20-25% of the time in early primary classrooms (Woodhead, 1996a), these imbalances in the mixture of reading approaches and teaching styles tend to be obscured, and furthermore, they are safe from scrutiny or change as it is judged impossible to compare elements within the mixtures on their relative effectiveness.

Secondly, the combination of approaches, or 'no one method' stance, is convenient for publishers and some teacher trainers. Publishers of reading schemes who demonstrate that their schemes include something of every approach (even if only a token gesture in some cases) are able to appeal to a wide range of teacher preferences, and in this way, increase their chance of profit. (Teachers who have decided to use different methods of instruction to meet the needs of individual children, will also want to ensure that they have a wide variety of reading materials for the same sort of reasons.) The current cost of placing a reading scheme in a school can range from £2,000 to £7,000 per year. The popularity of the 'real books' approach represents another substantial opportunity for publishers. An abundance of ordinary story books are necessary, and these are now much in demand not only by schools but also by parents. As for teacher trainers, some have formed alliances with publishers, relationships that are undoubtedly mutually beneficial.

Thirdly, the 'balanced' multiple-methods view allows some educators, educational bureaucrats, or people in the public eye to agree with all views and thereby appear eminently reasonable. As the following cases illustrate, under this all-embracing philosophy, educationists may lend their support to such a wide selection of views that they may be led inadvertently to contradict themselves:

(a) *Waterland*:
'Reading cannot be taught' (1985, p. 10).
'I didn't make clear enough .... the need to continue technique teaching' (quoted by Gold, 1994, p. 2).

(b) *Dombey*:
'Phonics teaching can ... disable children' (1992, p.19).
'Children need to develop an awareness of phonemes and their relations with letters' (1992, p. 18).

(c) *Smith*:
'Such ability' (i.e. reading) 'is not taught'; 'decoding is not only futile but unnecessary' (1978, p. 2).
'The final strategy may be trying to work out what the word is from its spelling' (1988, p. 143).

Sending out mixed messages such as these reduces others to a state of confusion. It is an effective mechanism for establishing the perpetrators in their position as 'experts' (since others have difficulty in divining their message), and effective too, in bolstering the multiple-methods view as the widely accepted, correct view (since this is one message that can be grasped with some certainty). Many parents, however, may find the reality of dealing with the consequence of these views a frustrating experience. Instead of having their child practise reading, they are expected to teach reading. As one parent admits, 'it's hard work ... all this stuff about when you're both feeling in the mood ... I don't do it because what actually happens is you're saying 'What's that word, you know that word, you've seen it three times,' and it all goes wrong on you' (*Times Educational Supplement*, 1996, p.16).

Nevertheless, as long as the mixed-methods view remains firmly established, change is unlikely. The details and implications of important research are overlooked. As a result, important questions are not asked. For example, does the research indicate that there are specific types of instruction that will suit the needs of *all* children at different stages in the process of learning to read?

How Classroom Management Exacerbates Individual Differences

As research shows, direct teaching at an early stage is important, with the amount of direct teaching clearly linked with levels of achievement; in simple terms, more teaching equals more learning. In practice, however, it is the absence of direct teaching to the whole class, and the favouring of progressive practices such as topic work, group projects and individualised, child-centred activities (characteristic of whole-word methods) that is noticeable. Ofsted report that in approximately a third of unsatisfactory lessons (resulting in low student achievement), teachers engage in little or no direct teaching but act 'largely as servicers or supervisors of the pupil's tasks' (Ofsted, 1994, p. 3). This observation was confirmed in a survey of 175 high school and university teachers who displayed a similar attitude towards didactic methods: the statement 'teachers are facilitators of learning' elicited 100% agreement (Walker & Newman, 1995).

Some research suggests that teachers divide their type of instruction into thirds: a third of the time is spent in whole-class teaching, a third of the time is allotted to group work, and a third of the time is allowed for individual work (Alexander et al., 1994). However, in another survey, when asked what approach would ensure the highest standards of achievement, even though 90% of teachers indicated that a mixture of whole-class and group teaching would be best, at the same time, only 20% of teachers favoured whole-class teaching (Taylor & Miller, 1994). Another survey found that fewer than 2% of teachers use whole-class teaching as their main strategy (Cato et al., 1992).

One recent report (based on observations in forty-five inner London schools) reveals the emphasis placed on individualised classroom management which invariably accompanies whole language, or 'real books' methods. Inspectors noted that 'listening to individual pupils read was the principal strategy used by most teachers ... [which often became] ... an unproductive routine exercise of such short duration that very little actual teaching took place. The effective teaching of pupils in groups, and expecially as a whole class, about specific aspects of reading was uncommon' (Ofsted, 1996, p. 5).

Reflecting teacher concern with the learning context, or processes of learning, rather than the teaching of subject content or knowledge, 83% of teachers indicate that effective teaching consists first in relating to children, whereas parents feel it is more important for teachers to explain work, and know their subject well (Taylor & Miller, 1994).

The results of a more recent teacher survey support Taylor and Miller's finding that teachers are most concerned with creating a caring and happy environment. The results of this survey also confirm Ofsted's observation that there is a lack of direct teaching in primary school classrooms; investigators discovered that there is 'an avoidance of direct teaching', teachers seeing their rôle as a 'facilitator', someone to provide encouragement, a warm atmosphere and an attractive supply of materials (Blatchford et al., 1994; Ireson et al., 1995).

Between 1985 and 1989, the Leeds Local Education Authority was concerned with low standards, and spent £14 million implementing widespread changes in their primary schools. These changes fit the progressive, 'good practice' mould, with the emphasis on reorganisation of classroom seating (groups instead of rows); learning of topics (rather than knowledge in sequence); and discovery learning (instead of direct teaching). The main concern was to attend to the *context* in which learning should take place, rather than the *content* to be learned.

A report on this research revealed that the project in Leeds had resulted in no improvement in pupils' progress in any subject, and in reading, by 1987, scores for 7- and 9-year-olds began to decline (Alexander, 1992). By 1989, at the end of the six-year project, reading scores for 7- and 9-year-olds were lower than at the start of the project, with a 'disturbing' increase in the proportion of 7-year-old children at least one and a half years behind in their reading (Alexander, 1992, p. 52). The report criticised the commitment to discovery learning, where teachers were supposed to let children discover things for themselves, and the low targets and expectations set for pupils' learning. Professor Alexander's research examining the results of this project so alarmed Kenneth Clarke, who was then Secretary of State for

Education, that he commissioned a report on the project for wide circulation (Alexander, Rose, & Woodhead, 1994).

An embarrassing illustration of these practices was brought to the attention of John Patten (Patten, 1994a) when he was the Secretary of State for Education. A mother had written to a local newspaper. She was in despair because her son, after being in school for six months, had not learned how to write his name. Instead, he had spent his time 'stapling pieces of brown paper together' (Patten, 1994a, p. 2).

Nevertheless, in spite of such reports the current orthodoxy in England, promoted in most teacher training centres, and bolstered by powerful teacher unions, still continues in favour of child-centred learning; and, in spite of the government's attempts to reorganise education over the last six years, much of classroom practice has not been radically altered (Webster et al., 1996; Walker & Newman, 1995). Ofsted reports note that, particularly at Key Stage 1 (age 5-7), group work on topics and themes is widely practised and there is a resulting 'lack of subject progression...both within any one topic and between successive topics'; furthermore, the poor management and use of time result in 'a slow pace of learning and a drift of attention from the task in hand' (Ofsted, 1994. p. 3).

In order to facilitate individualised learning and discovery methods, teacher unions demand smaller class sizes, more teachers and increased parental involvement. Parents' help is increasingly enlisted to provide an additional support structure for such methods: it has been stated, for example, 'Parents too need educating...they are pulling pupils in a direction that we do not endorse and which may subvert our aims' (LINC, 1990). Programmes are set up to train parents in the specifics of how to encourage their children to view words as symbols of meaning rather than symbols for sounds; the goal appears to be the eradication of parents' intuitive, and usually correct, beliefs about how reading should be taught, in favour of training parents, instead, how to make the learning of the alphabetic principle as obscure as possible for their children.

Finally, are children happier in child-centred classrooms? As far as children's emotional welfare is concerned, to foster an enjoyment of reading is the most frequently expressed, top-priority aim of many teachers (Blatchford et al, 1994; Cato et al., 1992, Taylor & Miller, 1994), teacher trainers (Brooks et al., 1992), and inspectors. For example, in one of these studies, although a few teachers thought it important that they develop the constituent skills of reading, five times as many teachers thought it was important that they encourage positive affective responses in children (Blatchford et al, 1994).

The apprenticeship, or sharing of 'real books' method of teaching reading has gained enormous popularity because of the appeal of the simple belief that the 'sharing' of a wide range of interesting, colourfully illustrated, non-graded story books with natural-sounding language or 'real' (but difficult-to-read) words will result in spontaneous, effortless, 'emergent literacy', or learning to read. The theory is that – as long as the materials are attractive enough, personally interesting, and easy to guess at, as long as children are permitted to choose them themselves, are not pressured to read them, and are allowed instead to focus on the pictures while ignoring the print – then children will enjoy reading. Unfortunately, no matter how attractive the reading materials, or pleasurable or undemanding the teacher tries to make the reading environment, children will not enjoy 'reading' if they cannot read.

Reflecting research in this area, school inspectors have observed that 'lower attaining pupils [are] the least keen readers', and that 'girls' attitudes to reading are usually more positive than boys" (HMI, 1989, p. 3). Teachers almost invariably claim that their children love reading, but this claim is not borne out by researchers' observations (Cato et al., 1992). Perhaps whole-word advocates sense the frustration and lack of enjoyment some children feel when they experience reading problems; perhaps this is why these methods emphasise that accuracy in reading should not be demanded, that children's 'miscues' (not errors) should be accepted without correction.

Socio-economic Factors

Frequently socioeconomic factors are cited as contributing factors in the increasingly noted decline in reading standards. A connection between instructional methods and poor reading standards is regularly dismissed on the basis that most teachers employ a mixture of methods. Currently coming to light, however, are a number of examples where educational intervention has made a difference in socioeconomically depressed areas. Clayton Middle School in Bradford, with a working- to lower-class intake, has pupils who arrive with a reading age often one year below average. A change to phonics methods has resulted in children leaving the school after four years with reading ages usually a year above average (Hetherington, 1994). Information about declining reading scores in Essex has not been made public because, according to one spokesman, instead of being able to point to socioeconomic causes, there would have been 'a call for a change in teaching methods'.

Particular Reading Disabilities

(a) Remediation and Low Teacher Expectations

It is likely that many teachers accept the notion that a certain proportion of children will inevitably have difficulty with, need specialist help with, or will fail in learning how to read, in spite of the research indicating quite convincingly that this need not be the case. A recent study illustrates teachers' attitudes. A sample of 121 teachers from twenty primary schools were asked what factors were most important in contributing to children learning to read. Approximately 85% of these teachers thought that factors other than teaching (to do with the home or the child) were the most important (Blatchford, Ireson, Joscelyne, 1994). Contrary to the research-verified view that any child 'with an IQ of 70 can be taught to read at age 5' (Engelmann, 1993), others believe that it takes up to four years for a child to become a fluent reader (Clay, 1993). Clay believes that up to half of all children will fail to learn how to read after spending a year in school so that the need for intervention is 'probably unavoidable' (Clay, 1992, p. 70). One prominent, whole-word advocate maintains that some children will 'progress slowly' while others will 'remain illiterate all their lives' (Meek, 1982, p. 7). Meek, like Clay, promotes the view here that failure, for a certain proportion of children, is inevitable. What they, as well as the many others influenced by them, fail to realise is that this scenario is only true in the absence of appropriate teaching. Virtually all children, even if they are dyslexic, can learn to read if they are taught properly.

As noted earlier, only 4% of the population is dyslexic or truly predisposed to experiencing reading problems. If there is a greater proportion of children than this who are currently being labelled as dyslexic, the chances are they are not, in actual fact, dyslexic at all. More accurately speaking (and to coin a new word), what they are suffering from is not 'dyslexia' (a problem with reading), but *dysdidaxia* (a problem with the *teaching*). Based on the average 24% rate of reading failure among 7-year-olds, a very conservative estimate, this means that while only 4% of children might be suffering from dyslexia, at least 20% of children are suffering from *dysdidaxia*.

Some classroom teachers may rely on specialist staff to help those children who are dysdidaxic. In one survey of forty schools, for example, it was discovered that most children are fortunate if they read with the teacher for five minutes a week, unlike special needs pupils who may read with a teacher four or five times a week (Tregenza, 1994). Perhaps reflecting parents' awareness of this problem the results of the survey, cited earlier, found that 90% of parents were anxious that more emphasis be given to the teaching of reading in primary schools (Moller, 1994). The vociferous teacher opposition against government cutbacks in the funding of remedial programmes which has been reported in the press recently is illustrative of attitudes. Expectations are that ordinary classroom teaching must inevitably result in a large proportion of children failing to learn how to read, and additional specialist help is therefore regarded as a necessary adjunct to classroom teaching, a service that will always be needed (Parkinson, 1994).

While teachers assume that a certain proportion of children must fail at reading, teacher expectations for *all* pupils are inclined to be low. In the same survey of forty schools, it was found that teachers expect the majority of pupils to reach, on average, a standard of reading that is below national norms (Tregenza, 1994). Teachers may not be aware that their expectations are so low. When asked whether the government's Statements of Attainment were necessary because teachers' expectations of pupils were too low, 94% of teachers denied this to be the case (NUT, 1992). Yet inspectors' reports frequently note the problems of low expectations, superficial teaching and learning, and inadequate monitoring of standards. Evidence of teachers' low expectations is seen, too, when comparing the reading levels awarded by teachers with the results obtained on National Curriculum tests; teacher-awarded levels are consistently higher than those achieved on national tests. In fact, since the abolition of the 11-plus examinations twenty years ago, in most parts of Britain there have been no external measures or adequately defined standards for this age group, a state of affairs which has made it difficult for teachers to know exactly what their objectives should be.

(b) Particular Problems Learning How to Read

In the absence of appropriate instruction, at least 25% of children (those with poor phonological skills) will have difficulty learning how to read. Results available from National Curriculum tests (DFE, 1992, 1994b) indicate that almost exactly this proportion of children are currently experiencing difficulty learning how to read. Understandably, many parents are upset. Parents who have a child, or children who, for whatever reason, lack sensitivity to the individual speech-sound structure of words, often find themselves in a desperate situation in their attempt to get help.

The school system in England is such that children who experience particular learning problems are entitled to free specialist help, provided that they are issued with a 'statement' from their local school authority that the child qualifies for this help. On a television programme, distressed parents reported their dismay at the difficulty of obtaining 'statements' for their children (Kilroy, BBC1, 1994). Parents are told that their child has to be at least three years behind in his or her reading achievement in order to qualify for assessment procedures, the results of which, may or may not lead to the granting of a 'statement'. One can sympathise with teachers who would like to remediate reading problems but who 'don't know what to do to help', or even with local authorities, who would like to help but have limited funds, but most especially with parents, who must witness their children in a state of increasing distress as year after year goes by, still having not learned how to read, having not received the appropriate instruction in school, and having not received a 'statement' from their local school authority entitling them to specialist help. Some parents report that, under these conditions, children become 'suicidal' (Kilroy, as above).

(c)Incidence of Reading Disabilities

In spite of the research demonstrating that virtually all children, including those at risk, can successfully learn to read if they are given the appropriate code-emphasis instruction, many children are now experiencing serious reading problems. Currently there are about 350,000 children in UK schools who need specialist help (Brooks, 1994).

However, while it is estimated that 20% of pupils in English primary schools are in need of specialist help (Doe, 1994; Pyke, 1994a; Warnock, 1994), many are not receiving it. As most authorities only issue statements to between 2 and 4% of pupils (Doe, 1994), there has been a resulting 'exponential rise' in Special Educational Needs court cases (Pyke, 1994b), the major proportion of these involving reading problems or dyslexia. The number of children in Gloucestershire classed as having special educational needs has more than doubled in the two years 1991-93 (*The Citizen*, 1993).

Gender Differences

The declining reading standards and the high incidence of reading failure among boys are increasingly causing concern. In 1992, nearly a third of boys at age 7 were struggling to read, compared to a fifth of girls (DFE, 1992), and in 1994, almost a quarter of boys aged 7 had failed to learn to read compared to about one-seventh of girls (DFE, 1994a). In schools for children with learning difficulties, boys now outnumber girls two to one. A survey in Humberside (Ofsted, 1993b) found that boys begin to suffer from a lack of interest and/or confidence in English before Key Stage 2. It was noted that at age 7, both girls and boys are enthusiastic about all learning, but by age 11 there is a marked change, with boys rapidly losing interest.

Results from the standardised Edinburgh Reading test (standardised in 1971-72) given to Scottish 8-year-olds in 1978, 1981, and 1984 found no significant sex differences in performance (Scottish Education Department, 1988); when English children were included in the restandardisation sample of this test in 1975, however, a significant sex difference of about 5 months of reading age between the sexes was discovered (University of Edinburgh, 1994). In addition, both in the years 1988 and 1992, sex differences in England among 7- to 9-year-old children were apparent: in 1988, in a survey using the London Reading Test, 32% of boys compared to 19% of girls obtained scores indicating severe reading difficulty (Mortimore, Sammons, Stoll, Lewis, & Ecob, 1988a); in 1992, in restandardising the Edinburgh Reading Test, sample populations were drawn from England only, and a significant sex difference was revealed, with girls substantially outperforming boys. (In 1975, when Scottish children were included in the sample the sex difference was 5 months, but in 1992 with English children only in the sample, the sex difference was 12 months (University of Edinburgh, 1994).

Although it has been shown that a particular type of instruction is needed in order for all children to experience early success with reading, there is widespread resistance to this concept. More fashionable whole-word, child-centred methods reign, so that in practice there are still many today who would agree with Margaret Meek, who stated in 1982 that 'we have still not discovered the best means of helping all children to learn' (p. 7), and if a child 'thinks he is a failure...what he needs, above all, is more reading experience, a purpose of his own for reading' (p. 114), (i.e. more individualised, context-oriented instruction).

Summary

Instead of selecting reading instruction that suits the needs of all children during different stages of learning to read, teachers adhere to a individualised, mixture-of-methods philosophy, a stance that effectively deflects attention from teaching methods as a possible cause of poor reading standards. Other factors are blamed, including differences in children's individual styles of learning, in their abilities and interests, and in their socioeconomic backgrounds. The failure of local school authorities to supply adequate specialist help, regarded by many in the profession as a service that will always be needed for a large proportion of children, is also identified as a contributing factor.

6 | The Politics of Reading Assessment

If we are concerned that all children learn to read to the best of their abilities, like any high-risk enterprise, trial-and-error methods of operation are undesirable. In the field of early reading instruction, such methods are also unnecessary. Scientific research has demonstrated precisely what beginning readers need to know and which methods produce the best results. If we are to ensure that reading methods are as closely aligned as possible with this research knowledge, the careful measurement and systematic evaluation of children's reading performance is of key importance. Information gained from such measurement permits the fine-tuning of reading methods, so that maximum success in learning to read is guaranteed for all children.

However, what we find in practice is that reading is assessed in ways which are unreliable and unnecessarily expensive; and that the monitoring of teachers' performance in enabling children to read is entirely subjective and, again, exceedingly expensive. Moreover, it is clear that the the nature of teacher training and the 'research' on which this training is based is suspect. Much of the inadequacy can be traced to the politicisation of reading assessment, the subject of this chapter.

Assessing Children's Reading

How should pupils' reading achievement be measured? It is important that test measures yield the sort of information that will help teachers perfect their teaching methods in order to produce the highest reading standards possible. With this purpose in mind, what kind of test measures are available and what are their specific advantages and disadvantages?

Essentially there are two criteria involved with testing children's early reading achievement: first, the test should actually measure what it sets out to, that is, how well the child is able to read (*validity*); and second, the test should give consistent results, from one use of the test to another and from one child to another of the same reading ability (*reliability*). A reading test, for example, that requires a child to read a story that has been memorised will not be testing how well the child can read, but how well the child has memorised, and hence will lack validity as a test of reading. Similarly, lack of reliability can arise if a test uses a very coarse scale of measurement, dividing readers into, for example, three broad levels, which may result in children of similar reading ability being awarded different level scores, or those very different in ability being awarded identical scores.

For the purposes of our discussion here, we need to contrast the procedures of the National Curriculum Standard Attainment Tests (SATs) with those of norm-referenced or standardised tests of reading. The SATs use criterion-referencing, where what is measured is how well a child meets certain criteria: for example, the child is able to 'read and understand three typical classroom signs or captions' (English Key Stage 1, Level 1), or the child is able to 'retell the content of a passage read including at least two of the main points and makes a sensible prediction about what might happen next' (English Key Stage 1, Level 2, National Curriculum reading tests) (SCAA, 1994e). Children are assessed individually to determine whether or not they meet the criteria demanded of the level description. The teacher then makes a subjective judgement as to whether or not the criteria have been met.

Norm-referenced or standardised reading tests, on the other hand, furnish tables of norms, based on prior sampling of a population; such tables permit teachers to convert a child's score into a reading quotient which takes chronological age into account; this quotient gives some indication of the child's standing relative to that of the population to which he belongs. Standard procedures for conducting such tests are clearly stipulated. Timing of the test, the test materials used, and objective marking procedures are the same for all pupils. These tests usually yield scores on a relatively fine scale of measurement, they require limited administration time since they are usually administered to the class as a whole; and in scoring, each item is either right or wrong. The *Young's Group Reading Test* is an example of this type; it measures a child's ability to read and understand single words, and short sentences of increasing difficulty.

Value of Different Kinds of Tests

Each type of test measure has advantages and disadvantages. Criterion-referenced tests such as the SATs can be designed to match curriculum targets closely, with the result that they may help teachers to define specific teaching goals. They also permit every student to achieve at least some of the specified targets. On the other hand, they may be very time-consuming and expensive to administer and mark. They do not furnish any reliable information about relative standing, and criteria must be worded so specifically that there is no doubt about what constitutes attainment of each criterion. Judgements about whether or not criteria have been met, or whether the test actually measures reading ability, for example, are totally subjective in nature, and therefore, validity and reliability are reduced.

Standardised reading tests can save time both in administration and marking, involve, therefore, less cost, and yield useful information about relative standing between pupils, schools, school districts, and about comparative standing over time. Standardised tests are regarded by statisticians as 'the products of a high degree of professional competence and skill in test-writing and, as such, are usually quite reliable and generally valid' (Kerlinger, 1986, p. 451). These tests are subjected to rigorous item analysis in order to ensure that the test actually measures what it sets out to. For this reason, standardised tests are more likely to provide a valid measure of a child's reading ability; and because marking of the test is objective, the reliability of the scores obtained is high. Standardised scores, represented as they are on a relatively fine scale, may be useful in allowing teachers to evaluate different teaching methods and in encouraging teachers to produce even the smallest improvements.

The one primary advantage standardised tests have over the criterion-referenced SATs is the more reliable comparisons of results that can be made over time, making them more suitable as tools for helping to improve reading standards. Since to a large extent SATs outcomes are based on subjective judgement, the danger is that, with the use of such tests, judgements could gradually become more liberal, and reading standards could decline, perhaps dramatically, without being detected. On the other hand, standardised tests can be used to make more reliable comparisons of results over months or years and they thus permit more careful monitoring of trends in reading attainment. These tests can also be used to draw tentative conclusions: conclusions, for example, about the relative effectiveness of different teaching methods between schools, in different years, or under different circumstances. In short, the knowledge gained, under the more controlled conditions of standardised tests, can be much more valuable in helping to shape effective reading practice over the long term.

Ineffective Tuning Methods?

What is happening in practice with regard to the assessment of readers? Turner's investigations into reading standards in 1990 helped to raise concern in England that reading standards among 7-year-olds were too low and in serious need of improvement (Turner, 1990). Since that time, the government has introduced a national curriculum along with compulsory tests for 7-, 11- and 14-year-olds. Will the National Curriculum tests in reading for 7-year-olds help to raise expectations as to what is possible and help to improve reading standards among this age group? How reliable and valid is this form of assessment? And what other forms of assessment of reading are being used in classrooms?

Some assessment of children's reading abilities is contained in teachers' own reports. These, however, are extremely subjective and descriptive in nature. In a recent Ofsted report (1995), school inspectors complained that the type of reporting contained in children's Records of Achievement (required when children transfer from or leave a school) is often unclear, jargon-filled and overly positive; inspectors were concerned that more than half the reports examined failed to diagnose problems and that the nature of these reports gave the false impression that standards were higher than they actually were. Although some standardised reading assessment does take place in schools, a 1991 report on reading standards revealed that only 59 out of 116 LEAs carried out standardised testing of primary school reading at some point in the previous ten years (Cato & Whetton, 1991).

In general, whether standardised testing is conducted or not, school inspectors report that very few schools have 'effective' systems for monitoring the standards of work achieved by pupils (Ofsted, 1994). In this one report, they concluded that in only 4% of schools did headteachers make an attempt to monitor the standards of work achieved by pupils, and among teachers inspected, only 50% made provision for systematic monitoring and evaluation of pupils' performance.

Shortcomings of the National Curriculum Tests

As the only reading results available for 7-year-olds on a national scale at the present time are those from the National Curriculum Key Stage 1 tests in Reading, these clearly deserve serious attention here. While some form of testing may possibly be better than no testing at all, there are in fact serious shortcomings with these particular tests. The remarkable degree to which progressive attitudes towards reading extend is seen in the government's choice of a measuring device to assess reading standards among 7-year-olds. For we see that the National Curriculum assessments use a whole-word, meaning-emphasis procedure to measure reading ability: this is none other than the 'miscue' inventory, invented by the popular whole language advocate, Kenneth Goodman.

The fact that the (now) Department of Education & Employment has decided to test in this manner is significant. The method used to measure how well children read is symptomatic of how they are being taught, or not being taught, to read: teachers attest that this manner of assessment is suited to the type of instruction being given and to the philosophies adhered to. When teachers were asked if the National Curriculum forms of assessment provided grades which were a valid reflection of children's reading abilities, 74% of teachers agreed that they did (NUT, 1992).

Why has the Department of Education chosen to measure reading ability with techniques approved by progressive, whole-word advocates rather than with a conventional standardised reading test? In explaining how this happened, Seaton (1994a) has pointed out how 'the Government unwittingly appointed educationists to the National Curriculum Council' (to design the curriculum), 'and the School Examinations and Assessment Council' (to devise the tests) 'who were mainly progressive in outlook'. Many of those chosen for these tasks are members of NATE (National Association for the Teaching of English) and/or LATE (London

Association for the Teaching of English), organisations that are vociferous in their opposition to traditional, research-based forms of teaching and testing. There are four main shortcomings of the National Curriculum SATs tests for seven-year olds:

(a) Assessment is Entirely Subjective in Nature

There is opportunity for a wide margin of error since the reading material used, the timing of test administration, the child's age when tested, and the teacher evaluation of performance can all vary widely; none of these aspects has been standardised. Teachers can choose from a list of ordinary story books (which vary widely in difficulty) whatever text they want a particular child to read; teachers may then 'familiarise' the child with the chosen text to whatever degree they like; they can conduct tests at any time they choose over several weeks; they may vary with each child tested the amount of time and assistance allowed during testing; they do not have to consider the age of the child when scoring; and they are required to make subjective judgements about each child's reading fluency, accuracy, and understanding.

(b) Reliability of the Tests is Low

The non-standardised, imprecise nature of these tests make it impossible to determine in a reliable way what 'national standards' are; reliable comparison between children, between schools, or between different school years cannot be made.

The tests invite variation. Subjective evaluation means that teachers may vary from year to year, from to school to school, or from child to child in the manner in which they award a score. The reading passages designated for use in these tests (derived from a long list of story books) vary widely on a number of factors, so that a child's performance may depend entirely on which story passage is selected. In 1994, for example, there were fourteen story books with designated reading passages from which teachers could choose. Since each passage is different, the skills being tested by each passage are likely to vary. One child may score highly because a particular word that the child has memorised well is liberally repeated throughout the selected test passage. Another child may score highly because the test passage, selected subjectively by the teacher, is familiar to the child or almost completely committed to memory. Yet another child may achieve an inflated score because the passage selected is shorter than others, allowing more time to discuss the content with the teacher and guess from the pictures.

Such children may not have the ability to decode unfamiliar words, and may not understand that reading is more than recognising memorised words on the page or guessing from the pictures. This inability is acceptable in the eyes of whole-word advocates: 'children should know what they are going to read before they read it' (Waterland 1985, p. 14). The vast opportunities for teacher variation in judging what good reading ability actually is mean that one can depend very little on the accuracy of the results obtained.

Furthermore, there has been year-to-year variation in test content and procedures. In 1996, for example, the list of twelve story books to be used for Key Stage 1 tests differed to a considerable degree from the nineteen books listed in 1995, and from the fourteen books listed in 1994. In 1995, teachers were to determine an accuracy level based on a child's number of oral reading errors in a particular book passage, whereas in 1996, accuracy scores were no longer included in the assessment procedures. In 1994, teachers were to select the book for testing, while in 1996, children were to select from among three or four books chosen by the teacher.

In every year, teachers were to determine whether a child had reached Level 1, 2 or 3 in his or her reading ability, Level 2 being the standard expected of a 7-year-old. There is, however, a huge leap in performance represented between Levels 1 and 2. Those assessed as Level 1 in ability need only recognise one word and a few letters, while those who are categorised as Level 2 must be able to read a simple piece of text with 'reasonable accuracy' (SCAA, 1994d).

More specifically, requirements for various levels are as follows:

Level 1   shows interest in a book, verbally or non-verbally, talks about the content of a book, shows understanding that print carries meaning, and recognises at least one word and at least three letters.

Level 2   reads aloud from one of a number of designated books with no more than eight words told (words that make sense are permitted).

144

In some cases, depending on the particular book, a child need have only six to eight words marked correct in order to attain Level 2 (based on 1994 material). Some of the words permitted as correct may not be the actual words on the page, but words permitted because meaning is preserved. Words omitted that do not disturb the sense of the passage are not counted as errors either (SCAA, 1994e, p. 8). When accuracy rate was part of the test procedures, the accuracy rate for different story passages required to pass Level 2 could range from six to twenty words correct. But this method of compensation for variance in passage difficulty does not account for factors such as the number of irregularly spelled words, the number of multisyllabic words, the degree of advantage provided by picture cues, or the amount of repetition in words or phrases that may occur in a passage. An in-depth analysis of these passages shows that they are not comparable in difficulty, and an examination of the present system for dealing with the differences in passage difficulty is shown to be inadequate (Morris, 1993).

Thus, among the 76% of children who attained Level 1 on the national curriculum tests in 1992, for example, it is likely that a very wide range of reading abilities was represented. Addressing this issue, an investigation comparing pupils' standardised reading scores with their level of attainment on national curriculum tests is starkly illustrative (Pumfrey et al., 1991). Children who had been assessed as having attained Level 2 (the average expected for their age) on national curriculum tests, were found to have reading ages, determined from standardised testing, ranging from 5·7 to 12·9 years. That is, within the group of pupils all categorised as Level 2, there was an *incredible 7-year range* in the actual reading abilities represented. Similarly, those categorised as Level 1, were found to have reading ages ranging from 5·0 to 9·6 years.

The Secretary for State for Education and Employment, Gillian Shephard, has stated that 'educational reforms' (such as the national curriculum testing and performance tables) 'are helping our children to achieve higher standards' (Shephard, 1995, p. 1). How accurate is this assertion? Are the reading standards among 7-year-olds improving, are teachers becoming more adept at administering the tests, or are the subjective judgements of teachers in deciding whether a child qualifies for Level 1 or 2 perhaps becoming more relaxed?

A recent study sheds a great deal of light on these questions and shows the danger in accepting the results from the National Curriculum assessments without a considerable degree of caution. A comparison of the reading performance of children tested on the National Curriculum assessment tasks in the years 1991 and 1992 with the reading levels attained by the same children on standardised reading tests revealed a discrepancy. Confirming the suspicion that the results from the curriculum tests are inflated, children's performance on the standardised reading test was much poorer than their National Curriculum assessment indicated (Davies, Brember, & Pumfrey, 1995).

Based on the proportions of children found to have a reading age of less than 6 in the samples that were randomly chosen for this study, and comparing these with the children's attainment on the National Curriculum assessments, the evidence would suggest that national reading standards are much worse than they appear. Although National Curriculum assessments indicate 28% (1991) and 24% (1992) of children failing to reach Level 2, evidence extrapolated from this study suggests that the proportion of children failing to learn how to read after two years in school is likely to be closer to 31% in 1991, and 34% in 1992. Most alarming, based on standardised reading comprehension scores obtained in this study, an average drop in reading standard of 2·6 months of reading age occurred over this one-year period. This represents a current annual rate of decline more than three times greater than that reported by past NFER investigations.

Thus, instead of finding that reading standards were improving between the years 1991 and 1992, as the results from the National Curriculum assessments would suggest, these researchers found the opposite trend. Analysis of the raw test scores from a standardised reading test revealed that the means (representing an equivalent standard to that of Level 2 on the national curriculum tests) were lower in 1992 than in 1991, a difference that was highly significant (at the 1% level).

As Professor Peter Pumfrey observes, 'perhaps no one in government wants or needs to know what reading standards are, and whether they are or are not changing? The public *illusion* that this information is important to government could be *all* that is politically required' (Pumfrey 1991, p. 57). If this is so, it is suggested that the national tests are the ideal instruments because, as has been noted by a number of researchers, they do not provide valid or reliable information about national standards (Davies, Brember, & Pumfrey, 1995; Morris, 1993; Pumfrey, 1991; Pumfrey, Elliot, & Tyler, 1991).

(c) Validity of the Tests is Suspect

According to the *Parents Guide to Testing* (DES, 1991b, p. 2.), 'the point of the new tests is to give you and the teachers an exact picture of what your child has learned' so that it will be known 'how your child measures up against *national* standards.' While these may be the stated aims, the truth is that the National Curriculum tests fail to achieve either of these goals. Not only are the test results obtained unreliable for the purpose of making comparisons, they are also of limited use, either for assessing reading performance or as a means to raising reading standards.

The tests for reading are not capable of giving an 'exact picture' of what reading skills have been learned; they may furnish a 'picture' of how the child is *pretending to be a reader*, but this is not reading and the picture furnished is not 'exact'. Because the measuring scale for determining a particular reading level covers such a large range of performance, only a very vague picture of what is regarded as 'reading ability' is obtained.

How 'reading ability' is defined by these tests is not in line with current research-based models of reading; the most important skill which must be acquired during early reading development is not even measured – the ability to decode print alphabetically. Research consistently underlines the fact that fluent reading requires accurate and fluent decoding. Yet instead of using a standardised reading test which measures context-free word-recognition skills, the national curriculum tests focus on assessing the child's ability to make sense of a passage by guessing, by using context or picture cues, or by recognising whole words by their shape. It is more an assessment of the range of a child's learned repertoire of whole-word guessing strategies than an assessment of his or her ability to read.

Indeed, these tests may not be measuring reading ability at all. They may, instead, be measuring the ability to memorise. There is evidence that parents may be increasingly active in helping their children memorise the story books used to test 7-year-olds. Booksellers cannot keep up with the demand.

Schools, having to compete with parents' demand for the books, are having difficulty obtaining the books they require for testing. One book club has been 'actively selling the books from the lists to parents, running a 'buy-two-and-get-one-free' promotion' (Williams, 1996, p. 15).

(d) Financial Costs are High

The national curriculum tests are expensive. Apart from the development and marking costs, the administration costs (in terms of teacher time) are also very high.

The estimated development costs for the years 1991, 1992, and 1993 were approximately £4 million per year. However, in 1991 the eventual costs were £6 million. The cost of hiring outside markers, necessary to secure the co-operation of teachers' unions, is another £30 million per year. Taking into consideration the amount of teacher time required (about forty hours), the National Curriculum assessments are estimated to cost £60 million; the cost per year, then, is roughly $(4 + 30 + 60 =)$ £94 million. If these tests were replaced by standardised, whole-class, paper and pencil tests (taking about two hours in total for administration and marking), the estimated cost is £3 million (Turner, 1991a). Thus, the comparative costs are £94 million (for the present criterion-referenced testing) versus £3 million (for standardised reading testing).

Opposition to Standardised Testing

Teachers' unions have objected strenuously to national testing on both ideological and practical grounds, and consequently, only limited testing was carried out prior to 1994. And, although 90% of schools used the Key Stage 1 tests for testing the reading of 7-year-olds in 1994, only 52% of schools reported the results. Objections to the tests have ranged from the heavy demand made on teachers' time to administer and mark the tests, to the disrespect implied for teachers' own evaluations of student progress. These objections are puzzling, if not illogical; for the teachers' unions themselves demanded criterion-referenced testing, a form of testing which they felt would more closely match their concept of good practice. It should, therefore, come as no surprise that tests which have to be individually administered and which have no right or wrong answers are time-consuming to administer and mark; nor should it be surprising that the information gained is superfluous since teachers' current mode of evaluating pupils' abilities tends to be identical in nature.

However, in spite of the shortcomings of subjective measurement, many teachers are even more opposed to objective forms of testing. A speaker at the 1991 conference of the United Kingdom Reading Association (UKRA) gave three reasons why standardised tests are 'inappropriate': 'Teachers who use a whole language approach to reading instruction in their classrooms have discovered that traditional standardized testing is not an appropriate assessment mode ... since it lacks validity, suitability, and availability' (Leland, p. 238). How justified are these assertions?

(a) Validity

Whether standardised tests are 'valid' or not is dependent on one's concept of what reading is. Traditional standardised reading tests include measures that assess both decoding and reading comprehension ability; they require both the reading of words in lists and the comprehension of short passages read silently. These tests reflect a definition of 'reading' which includes both the ability to decode print and to understand it. However, if 'reading' is now seen purely as the ability to make guesses at words through the use of context, syntax, or pictures, then indeed, such tests would not be valid. The fact that mainstream teachers view standardised reading tests as lacking in validity is a testament to just how widespread this new concept of reading has become. Reading is no longer seen as the dual process of deciphering print *and* comprehending it, as a process where print is decoded in order to achieve the main aim of understanding it. The Nelson-NFER Reading Ability tests are selected for use in NFER surveys because they reflect 'modern conceptions of reading' where the *only* reading-related ability that is seen worthy of measurement is how well children 'make sense of coherent and complete texts' (Gorman & Fernandes, 1992, pp. 3-4); whether children are able to decode print accurately or not is no longer seen as important.

Pertinent to this issue, in 1991, England and Wales accepted an invitation to take part in an international survey of the reading ability of 9-year olds. Ultimately, however, they withdrew from the study, which went ahead in twenty-seven countries, because government officials and researchers at the NFER were 'dissatisfied' with the tests that were to be used.

They protested that the questions measured mainly literal comprehension, were almost entirely objective in nature, and therefore represented an 'outmoded and inadequate model of the reading process' (Brooks, Pugh, Schagen, 1996, p.3).

(b) Suitability

Standardised reading tests are accused of being 'unsuitable' for teachers using a whole-language reading approach. Standardised reading tests measure a child's ability to decode and understand words, short sentences, or short passages. This is accomplished through a variety of tasks: children are required to read words in isolation without the aid of context, and/or to read and understand hitherto unseen short sentences or passages without the aid of accompanying pictures. Under a whole-language régime, the child is not taught how to perform either of these tasks. Thus, in this sense standardised tests do not 'suit' the teaching approach.

On the other hand, standardised tests could be viewed as especially suitable to the whole-language teacher as they may provide information about a pupil that might not otherwise be revealed. One of the most frequent teacher complaints about the National Curriculum tests is that they do not provide any further information about a pupil beyond the teacher's own assessment. Traditional standardised tests, therefore, are particularly 'suitable' in this context. As whole-word methods do not focus directly, or in a systematic fashion on the learning of letter-sound correspondences, for example, standardised reading tests could provide a useful warning of children's lack of progress in this area. Furthermore, standardised reading tests may be particularly 'suitable' in a whole-word classroom, in helping to draw a teacher's attention to some of the shortcomings of such teaching methods.

(c) Availability

As for the 'lack of availability' claim, this assertion is patently untrue. Inexpensive standardised tests are readily available, and have been used by most schools to some degree in the past. It is good quality, criterion-referenced tests that are in short supply. The National Curriculum tests are a case in point, where the results obtained are questionable and the costs in time and money are huge.

Politics and the Reading Debate

Validity, suitability and availability aside, perhaps there is another, overriding reason why such teachers are opposed to testing in any form? It has been frequently noted that the debate on reading methods has become highly politicised (McKenna, Stahl, & Reinking, 1994). Current orthodoxy, and in particular, the whole-language philosophy, is concerned with passing on certain values, engendering certain attitudes and teaching ways of behaving; what it is least concerned with is passing on specific subject knowledge. Reading has been redefined by whole-word advocates to such an extent that reading is no longer viewed in a way that makes testing of reading ability possible. Instead, it has become more 'suitable' to assess various random behaviours, none of which are supported by research as useful strategies for the beginning reader: what kind of guessing strategies children are able to use, whether meaningful word substitutions are made, and whether or not a child has memorised some words by shape.

Whole-word advocates see external tests as a threat to the search for an egalitarian society, a 'more just world' (Goodman, 1992a). External imposition of tests and standards are seen as 'disempowering' children who must be allowed to direct their own learning, to interact with texts individually in their own personal manner and at their own rate. Competition is seen as encouraging élitism; tests are seen as an interfering affront to teacher professionalism. And yet by encouraging reading methods which result in high rates of reading failure especially among boys, are not whole-word supporters causing individuals to be ranked in a way that actually *highlights* individual differences? In their anxiety not to make any child feel inferior, whole-word advocates actually guarantee that certain children will be consigned to a lower status by adhering to methods of instruction which are inadequate, methods which fail to teach *all* children to read. As Gough, a supporter of research-based instruction, states, 'I would "devalorize" no one; I would teach everyone to read' (Gough, 1995, p. 86).

'Progressive' Ideology

Child-centred, discovery, or so-called 'progressive' methods have been practised widely in the UK over the last twenty years, although the idea that children should be engaged in gaining experiences while at school rather than knowledge or facts may have begun as early as 1931 with the Hadow Report. Such methods have been particularly popular during the 1980s, a period when reading standards among 7-year-olds declined (Cato & Whetton, 1991; Turner, 1990). From 1987 to 1991, reading standards revealed evidence of a continued decline (Gorman & Fernandes, 1992).

As Professor Robin Alexander and his colleagues point out, 'over the last few decades the progress of primary pupils has been hampered by the influence of highly questionable dogmas' (Alexander et al. 1994, p. 1). Clarke expressed his concern, as the Secretary of State for Education, that 'present primary practice is not well adapted to effective teaching' (Clarke 1991 p. 9). Long before this, it was the Plowden Report of 1967 that endorsed and helped to enshrine many of the child-centred, progressive tenets: it focused on 'active learning', concentrated on processes rather than the learning of specific subjects or knowledge, and favoured children discovering things for themselves, rather than being directly taught. The advent of this document led to 'an all-embracing, and dogmatic orthodoxy about how children should be taught' (Clarke, 1991, pp. 2-3).

It is perhaps ironic, given the well-known views of Her Majesty's Chief Inspector, Chris Woodhead, that Her Majesty's Inspectorate have, intentionally or otherwise, helped to reinforce the progressive stance, through their establishment of the concept of 'good practice'. Rather than judge teaching practice by the academic results produced, inspectors have judged classroom procedures on how well they fit the mould of 'good practice'.

What is 'good practice' exactly? An HMI report defines classes characterised by 'good practice' as providing opportunities for 'independent work', 'individual initiative', accommodation of the 'needs of individual pupils', and an 'eclectic' approach to the teaching of reading (HMI 1989-90 pp. 13-14).

Throughout the 1970s and 1980s, however, observations made by HMI and others inadvertently reveal some of the undesirable consequences of this 'good practice'. Inspectors note unacceptable noise levels, fragmented reading activities, extreme difficulty managing to cater to the individual needs of all pupils, shortage of time to listen to all children read, assessments that are too generalised (HMI, 1990), decreasing enthusiasm for reading among the less able, lack of systematic attention to poorer readers (HMI, 1990-91), lack of progression, lack of guidance in choosing books, underchallenged readers, and inadequate monitoring of reading progress (DFE, 1989). Researchers note a substantial variance in the use of phonics (Cato et al., 1992), and clear evidence that topic work leads to fragmentary, and superficial teaching and learning (Alexander et al., 1994).

It would be hardly surprising if reading standards are declining, since 'good primary practice' appears to support precisely those practices identified by scientific research as the most detrimental to reading progress. Findings from experimental research have clear and consistent implications for designing instruction that will most enhance reading achievement. In direct contrast to these findings, however, 'good primary practice' encourages the following: incidental learning rather than direct instruction; learning dictated by the child rather than by logical sequence or order of progression; an emphasis on enjoyable reading activities in collaboration with an adult rather than on teaching children how to read so that they are able to derive the real satisfaction that only comes with knowing how to read for themselves; group projects in favour of more productive, whole-class teaching; trying to decode words by context or meaning, instead of decoding words by their sounds; and reading by osmosis, or slow progress whole-word discovery methods (which are usually described as a 'mixture of methods') instead of an early emphasis on systematic, phonological, code-emphasis instruction.

Evidence from researchers based at Bristol University suggests that since the introduction of the new National Curriculum, the majority of teachers still continue to favour progressive, child-centred methods; these are described as methods whereby teacher and pupil are equal partners, tasks are negotiated with pupils, and the teacher offers assistance as the need arises (Osborn & Broadfoot, 1991; Webster, Beveridge, & Reed, 1996).

Assessing Teachers

Just as it is possible to measure children's reading achievement through validity- and- reliability-enhancing objective means, the quality of reading instruction teachers deliver can also be measured this way. If quality of teaching is judged not by subjective evaluation but by the reading results produced, the danger of the wholesale adoption of unproven but fashionable methods can be avoided. Such a policy would allow teachers to direct their attention to producing the highest standards of reading by whatever methods they found to be the most effective. Otherwise, the danger is that attention is directed to satisfying subjective criteria instead, such as how well the teacher is fulfilling the requirements of the National Curriculum, how well the teacher is shaping his or her teaching practice to satisfy the current definition of 'good practice', or how well practice matches what is currently expected by school inspectors, school heads, or governors.

If the most important goal is to ensure that all children learn to read early and well, then the criteria by which teacher performance is judged should be related first and foremost to this issue; teachers should be judged on their ability to perform this task. Children's standardised reading scores are an objective indicator of teacher performance in this regard. Judging the quality of teacher effectiveness by the reading results produced, as well as increasing the validity and reliability of teacher assessment, would have the added advantage of permitting comparisons to be made between different teaching techniques. Under this system, the evaluation of teacher performance would be both more objective and more clearly defined. Effective teachers could be identified and rewarded.

In measuring overall reading achievement over time, it is important to take initial differences into account. As the research demonstrates, being able to hear and identify speech sounds, along with having a knowledge of letter-sound correspondences are the two most important indicators of future reading achievement. An early screening test of these skills could be given as an initial routine to establish children's ability prior to instruction; studies show that such a procedure can accurately identify children at risk, alerting the teacher, right at the outset, to those children who will require more intensive teaching (Hoien et al., 1995; Hurford, Schauf, Bunce, Blaich, & Moore, 1994; Majsterek & Ellenwood, 1995; Torgesen, Wagner, & Rashotte, 1994). Intervening at this stage with intensive phonological and letter-sound instruction has been shown to produce impressive differences in reading achievement, compared to those children at risk who may or may not receive help at a much later stage (Blachman et al., 1994; Felton, 1993). To adopt this procedure as a routine would not only circumvent the need for determining a value-added score for school league tables, but would also considerably reduce the need for reading remediation that may be difficult to arrange, is often expensive and usually limited in its effectiveness.

How does practice in schools measure up to these principles? A teacher appraisal scheme for newly-qualified teachers that was introduced by the government in 1991 fails to monitor teacher progress adequately. Currently such teacher appraisal may consist of one meeting with the training school department head every two years. The National Association of Head Teachers (NAHT) has recently set up a scheme to improve monitoring of teacher effectiveness, through workshops that teach specific target setting and close monitoring of progress. At present, however, teachers do not have a record of their progress, making it difficult for teachers to know what they ought to aim for, or how they might improve.

What many school heads and teachers must aim for is satisfying school inspectors. Inspections reveal that up to 30% of lessons are 'inadequate', 20% of new teachers' performance is 'unsatisfactory', and 10% of teaching is so poor that teachers should not be teaching. What do these descriptions mean? On what basis are lessons and teachers judged? These terms represent inspectors' subjective judgements and lack the precision of, for example, the reading achievement scores produced.

A school's 7+ Average Reading Quotient (ARQ) is the most important indicator of how effectively teachers are carrying out their primary task. The ARQ, a standardised measure, is similar to an Intelligence Quotient in that the average score is 100, a score of 94 indicating that a child is approximately one year retarded in reading, and a score of 106 indicating that he or she is one year advanced.

However, instead of adopting the school's 7+ ARQ as a useful index of teacher performance, confusion reigns. Confusion is created because targets are not specific (what criteria are used to determine if performance is 'satisfactory'?), and the particular biases of the inspector may not be known. In fact, the present system is such that far from being judged on their ability to produce good reading results, teachers are judged on their ability to fit the mould of 'good practice'.

Recently the government (primarily due to the efforts of its Chief Inspector, Chris Woodhead) has attempted to change this concept of 'good practice' where child-centred approaches, and the teacher-as-facilitator view are much applauded, where direct, whole-class teaching are much frowned upon, where results obtained are not important, and where mention of the word 'phonics' is, in the words of one headteacher, 'a capital offence ... certainly it was made clear you wouldn't get promoted using words like that' (Kent, 1996). However, in spite of the government's best efforts to shatter the 'conspiracy of silence' surrounding educational methods (Woodhead, 1996b), to expose the fact that teachers are clinging to reading methods that are 'self-evidently not working' (Ofsted, 1996), and to encourage early systematic phonics instruction, its attempts to bring about change are hampered. Although some teachers may be resistant to change, those who judge teachers' performance must also be considered. Among the inspectorate who once approved of and strongly encouraged this old concept of 'good practice' and whose views one cannot be certain about, are many who now are in positions of power, leading Ofsted teams, in charge of literacy centres, working for government teacher training bodies, or advising important educational officials.

Each school inspection costs £30,000 to £40,000; the Ofsted budget for 1996-7 is £118 million (DfEE, 1996e, p. 165). This huge expenditure on Ofsted inspections perpetuates a system that is, thus far at least, committed to descriptive measurement, and subjective evaluation. If objective, reliable measurement of teacher performance is the desired outcome, then subjective methods of assessment, open to bias, are better avoided. A staggering amount of money could be saved if the standardised testing of reading were to replace national curriculum testing, but even more money could be saved if the results from such tests were used as indicators of the quality of teaching, thus eliminating the need for subjective inspections from government officials. Schools' reading results could be monitored instead; poor reading attainment in a school would then be a situation which would alert government officials to the school's need for inspection, advice, and/or assistance.

Teacher Trainers

The roots of the politicisation of reading are likely to lie with the teacher trainers and educational researchers. To ensure that teacher trainees are equipped with the ability to deliver high- quality reading instruction in the schools, it should be vital that teacher trainers give students a comprehensive theoretical and practical grounding in reading methods, with a focus on what works and what does not. Reading is a field that is heavily researched, so that knowing how children learn to read and how best to teach them are areas of inquiry that now have a very solid research base. Teacher trainers need to ensure not only that their students are well acquainted with this research but also that they are taught the practical details of the particular sequence of instruction that one needs to follow in order to teach all children to read as efficiently as possible. Teachers in training should also be given the opportunity to observe and work in schools with the most effective teachers of reading, those teachers who have a proven record of producing outstanding reading achievement among their pupils.

How do the teacher trainers measure up? After up to four years of teacher training, nearly half of newly trained primary-school teachers feel inadequately prepared to teach reading, with almost two-thirds taught little or nothing about phonics (Brooks et al., 1992). Many frequently express their general dissatisfaction with the quality of training received (Blatchford et al., 1994). They report insecurity at the prospect of facing a child who cannot read. Some students have accused college teachers of putting forward their own individual perspectives, prejudices and progressive theories, at the expense of providing students with the practical, step-by-step details of how best to teach a child to read (Hadfield, 1992).

Indeed, many universities and colleges currently stress the social and political issues related to education, rather than providing students with an objective analysis of current reading research and teaching them the concrete procedures that comprise a well-structured, effectively sequenced

157

programme of reading instruction. In an Institute of Education, University of London course guide, for example, it states that 'literacy should thus be regarded as socio-cultural practice and not a neutral technical skill'; 'learning to read and write thus means being socialised into particular views of the meaning of literacy events' (University of London, 1992, p. 29).

Such views are not isolated; evidence suggests that they represent the majority view adopted by teacher training institutions today. Recently, leaflets were handed out at a King's College, London, conference in which Brian Cox comments on the National Curriculum, a document that he sees as 'muddled on vital issues' owing to continual 'political interference'; he goes on to state, 'The new curriculum will do much harm ... sensible teachers will adapt the proposals according to their knowledge of good practice' (Cox, 1994). Students at this conference, who were offered the chance to discuss teaching methods, refused on the grounds that they were 'too stressed and too frightened to accept'; although aware of the bias in the education they were receiving, they were reluctant to speak against it for fear of jeopardising their prospects of qualifying.

Experimental research is strongly at variance with the child-centred, progressive views upheld by most of today's universities, but if attacked for ignoring research findings, these colleges are enormously defensive. The progressive bias present in the teaching of reading in three teacher-training centres, Exeter University, London University and the University College of Ripon and York St John, was exposed through an analysis of their publications, reading lists, pamphlets and brochures (Seaton, 1993). The reaction of academics at London and Exeter universities was to threaten legal action (Salmon, 1993).

It is suggested that there is 'deep insecurity and confusion among teacher trainers that induces ... close-minded antagonism to any reforms that challenge ... existing assumptions' (Hargreaves, 1994). As one recent example of the general stance taken, a student Diploma in Education booklet, *Curriculum Studies and the Primary School* (from the London Institute of Education), asks students what they think about the strongly progressive Plowden Report and various attempts on the part of the present government to sabotage the Plowden ideal. This booklet, transparently manipulative, then proceeds to enquire of students, 'Are you offended by the suggestion that teachers lack the intelligence to become the Plowden ideal?' (Institute of Education, 1992, p. 14).

Furthermore, there is no doubt that a large industry has grown up in connection with education, not least in the field of publishing. There are powerful vested interests at stake. A brief description of the birth of the International Reading Association, one of the most influential bodies today in the field of reading education, serves as just one case in point. In 1956, William Scott Gray and his American colleagues formed the International Reading Association (IRA). This event came one year after Rudolph Flesch's best-selling book, *Why Johnny Can't Read*, was published. Flesch's book identified and publicised widely for the first time why so many children were failing to learn how to read: they were being taught by the look-and-say reading programmes of Gray and others. The Scott Foresman 'Dick and Jane' readers, first published in 1930, were the dominant texts used throughout American primary schools. Their use represented a multi-million dollar industry; teaching children to read with the new look-and-say basal readers, with their controlled vocabularies, was far more expensive than teaching children phonics, three to eight times more expensive according to some estimates (Armstrong, 1989).

However, parents were beginning to be unhappy with the results; in schools, 'remedial reading' and 'reading disability' were suddenly new phenomena. With the advent of Flesch's book, parents became more vociferous in their disapproval of look-and-say methods. It was necessary for those such as Gray, who had established an extremely lucrative industry by this time, to fight back; amalgamating two previously formed reading organisations (formed in response to growing reading problems), the International Reading Association was created. It was to become 'the impregnable citadel' of the look-and-say method (Blumenfeld, 1990, p. 121). Gray was elected as its first president. Subsequent presidents have been strong proponents of look-and-say methods, more recently termed *whole language*. In 1956, in its first year, the IRA had 7,000 members; in 1995, it had more than 92,000 members in ninety-nine countries and recent conferences have been attended by more than 16,000 people (IRA, 1995).

An organisation of such size wields a powerful influence in shaping the attitudes of educational professionals. A total of

1,609 reading professors on an IRA list of American and Canadian university and college professors were asked to list which reading authorities of all time, in their opinion, had written the most significant, worthy, 'classic' studies in reading; the top three individuals listed were: Frank Smith, Kenneth Goodman, and Edmund Huey (Froese, 1982). Needless to say, these three represent some of the most dedicated advocates of whole-word, look-and-say methods. Kenneth Goodman, who succeeded Gray as a senior author of the Scott Foresman basal reading series (Flesch, 1983), became president of the IRA in 1981.

In England, the United Kingdom Reading Association (UKRA) contributed their support and encouragement of look-and-say methods in 1962 by becoming a branch affiliation of the IRA. By the early 1970s, teacher trainers began to develop closer links with publishers. Up until this time, publishers in England had been cautious and had resisted the progressive, child-centred movement. Organisations such as NATE, the National Association for the Teaching of English, played an influential rôle, in collaboration with universities, colleges, and publishers, in establishing the progressive movement over a number of decades (NATE, 1986). Currently, whether because vested interests are at stake or not, academics continue in their steadfast refusal to acknowledge the leading empirical research in the field, research which is conducted, and consistently confirmed, not only in the United States and England, but in many other countries of the world.

In their concern to preserve the status quo it is now quite likely that many teacher trainers have neither the knowledge nor the skills needed to ensure that their students are taught how to teach reading effectively. Prominent professionals express the popular view that phonics is too complicated, abstract or 'overrated' (Clay, 1991). Some others express their pride at being totally ignorant about the subject (Hynds, 1994).

As for giving trainee teachers the opportunity to observe effective teachers in action and to practise the skills of such teachers, financial concerns may play a rôle here too. Since September 1994, teacher trainees are required to spend most of their time in schools. In the past, schools were happy to have students because they came for a limited period and were supervised by college tutors. Much of this supervisory work now falls to already overburdened teachers, with the result that many are reluctant to take students. Colleges pay schools that are willing to take students at £600 to £1600 per place. As a result, instead of placing students in classrooms where high standards of reading are achieved, the criterion determining placement are how much colleges are willing or able to pay, and which schools are prepared to accept the offers.

The concept of offering trainee teachers a more practically based training is a positive step, but only so long as quality is assured. At present, the quality of placements students receive is based purely on chance. There is a high probability that the shortcomings of the teacher training to which students are subjected in college are simply compounded by school-based training that may be similarly biased, inadequate, or of poor quality.

Evaluating Reading Research

Any research on which teachers are to base their teaching practice should be dependable. A scientific approach to research has one characteristic that no other method of gaining knowledge has: self-correction. Checks are designed and used to control and verify scientific procedures and conclusions, to satisfy the one ultimate aim of obtaining dependable knowledge. Even where an hypothesis is apparently supported by experiment, a scientist will not accept statements as true, even though first evidence appears promising. Hypotheses are tested and retested and open to public scrutiny. The checks are designed to prevent the possibility of the scientist's personal beliefs, opinions, attitudes, and biases from influencing results. They are designed to ensure objectivity. The level of objectivity brought about by using such checks helps to ensure that the findings of an experiment can be replicated and that any predictions made from these are as dependable as possible.

In the field of education, there are two kinds of reading research conducted: experimental and non-experimental. Experimental research is also known as *controlled, scientific,* or *quantitative* research; non-experimental research may be termed *descriptive, naturalistic, ethnographic,* or *qualitative* research. These terms hint at the differences between them.

Experimental research is characterised by the checks described above; investigations are controlled and objective test measures (including standardised tests) are used. Non-experimental research, on the other hand, is characterised by a lack of control, and the use of descriptive, subjective measures.

In experimental research it is not assumed that because there is a correlation between two variables, that A causes B; checks are made to rule out other influences that could possibly have contributed to the correlation. If, for example, one wanted to investigate if the amount of letter-sound instruction a child received was correlated with later reading achievement, it would be necessary to consider what other factors might have influenced the measured reading achievement. Some examples of the sort of checks or controls imposed to help rule out the effects of outside factors or extraneous variables are: the random assignment of subjects to experimental groups, the selection of large sample sizes or the use of statistical procedures that remove or partial out the effects of extraneous factors.

In non-experimental research, however, it often seems to be assumed, on the basis of descriptive data analysis (and in the absence of controls or checks), that A is correlated with B or even that A causes B. However, such assertions cannot be made with the same degree of confidence as under experimental conditions, and reliable conclusions cannot be drawn. For example, the observation might be made that children appear to read words better in the context of a story than they do in lists, and it is therefore concluded that context assists decoding. However, if during such observations, the children are always required to read the words in lists first, and words in context, second, this unvarying presentation order could be a factor influencing results. Children may find the words appearing in context easier to read simply because of the practice afforded them during the prior viewing of these same words in lists. By failing to take this factor into account, counterbalancing practice effects by varying the presentation order, the experimenter could easily draw the wrong conclusion.

This is exactly what happened in the case of Kenneth Goodman's non-experimental research on context effects (Goodman, 1965), which constitutes the only evidence ever offered by whole-word advocates in support of the rôle of context in reading (Vellutino, 1991). Goodman not only failed to take practice effects into account, he also failed to account for differences between good and poor readers. Others have tried to verify Goodman's findings, but under experimental research conditions where such factors have been controlled, the effects reported by him have not been replicated (Nicholson, 1991). In fact, the contradictory evidence is definitive and highly reliable (Gough et al., 1981; Perfetti, 1985; Stanovich, 1980); unfortunately, compared to Goodman's flawed study, it appears to be little known. The detrimental effects of Goodman's erroneous conclusion are seen in today's classrooms where children are encouraged to follow the fruitless practice of guessing at words from context, a practice which not only has been proven unproductive but which also contradicts the scientific research demonstrating what skilful readers do.

This example helps to highlight one of the inherent weaknesses of non-experimental research: the risk of drawing erroneous conclusions. The danger of improper interpretation is high in non-experimental research where data is simply collected, and then interpreted. There is no attempt to control for the difference factors between groups being compared, no attempt to control or equalise experimental treatment conditions of groups under comparison, no attempt to ensure that sample sizes are large, and no random assignment of subjects to groups, which would help reduce the bias likely to occur when none of the foregoing procedures are used. Under these uncontrolled conditions, plausible explanations may be compelling, but often quite wrong. A further difficulty is that once plausible explanations are found and believed, they are often difficult to test, and at the same time, new interpretations can invariably be found to fit the facts (Kerlinger, 1986).

As far as determining teaching practice is concerned, if results from experimental research were not available, we would have to make do with the less objective findings from non-experimental research; but they are. Most of the references in this book are to sophisticated, large-sample studies, conducted under controlled conditions, where the data has been subjected to proper statistical analyses and the results obtained can be replicated.

Again, we can ask: what sort of research do teacher training institutions seem to favour?

As mentioned earlier, the top thirty most recommended teacher training texts (Brooks et al., 1992) do not include one text that provides an objective review of experimental research findings, and the majority of these texts do not even mention this type of research. It is absolutely extraordinary, for example, that a text such as *Beginning to Read: Thinking and Learning about Print* by Marilyn Jager Adams (1990), which provides one of the most contemporary, comprehensive and objective reviews of research findings in the field of reading education, does not appear anywhere on the list of the thirty most recommended teacher training texts.

The texts that *are* on this list repeatedly cite the 'research' of such authors as Frank Smith, Kenneth Goodman, Margaret Meek, and Liz Waterland. None of these people has conducted experimental research; a careful examination of their writing reveals that their research consists of 'assumptions', personal 'beliefs', 'theories', or 'observations'. In an endless cycle, these four authors cite the 'research' of others, or even each other, which upon investigation is found to consist once again of anecdote or speculation. Students reading their books are exposed, perhaps very often without realising it, to an extraordinary bias against experimental studies. As a result, students in teacher training programmes today, tutored as they are in popular theories, opinions, or personal beliefs, are most unfortunately deprived of a wealth of valuable and practical information.

The following statements show each author's bias against empirical research (Words antithetical to experimental research have been italicised):

Margaret Meek

'Any significant research I have done rests on my having treated *anecdote*s as evidence' (1979, p.8).

'Where the partnership of home and school takes into account the *views* of parents, teachers and children and records these as words, *not numbers*, we can already see what modern literacy looks like.' (1982, p. xiii).

Kenneth Goodman

'For me research is never neutral. It is always for or against something or somebody. I could never do *amoral and atheoretical* research. Nor could I do contrived studies on bits and pieces ...' (1992a, p. 192).

Goodman dismisses people who favour experimental research as 'academic elitists (sic) who view many learners as incapable'. The experimental researchers themselves are condemned as being 'amoral' people who depend on *'one-legged models of inquiry'* (1992a, p. 198).

'I am weary, oh so weary, of attacks on whole language ... their disagreement does not make my view wrong ... whole language is *...beliefs expressed in texts'* (1994, pp. 340, 345).

Frank Smith

'The main instructional implication of *the analysis of this book* is that children learn to read by reading' (1978, p. 3).

'My present *assertion* is that any written language is read as Chinese is read, directly for meaning' (1988, p.153).

There have been other indications of a desire to replace experimental research with subjective observations, anecdotes, or 'naturalistic research'. The changes seen in the content of a number of reading research journals and the content of government curriculum or policy documents reveal an acceptance of concepts which are based on theories and assumptions shown by empirical research to be false.

Journals such as *Reading* (published by the United Kingdom Reading Association), *The Reading Teacher*, and *The Reading Research Quarterly* (both published by the International Reading Association, whose past presidents include Marie Clay, and Kenneth Goodman) show a definite bias towards non-experimental research.

The April 1994 issue of *Reading* was devoted entirely to 'teacher research', teachers' personal observations, or 'reflections' (Manning & Harste, 1992, p. 2). During the period from 1986 to 1991, *The Reading Teacher*, hitherto providing a relatively open forum on different points of view as to the best method of teaching reading, published 115 articles in favour of 'whole-language' teaching (an approach based on popular beliefs and anecdote), and 24 articles that described teaching methods opposed by whole-language advocates (methods based on experimental research) (Groff, 1992). The April 1990 issue of *The Reading Teacher* was entirely devoted to 'whole-language'. The winter 1994 issue of *The Reading Research Quarterly*, no longer able to ignore the popularity of whole-language methods of teaching, and descriptive research, devoted almost the entire journal to a debate over the 'rhetoric of whole language' (Moorman, Blanton, & McLaughlin, 1994, p. 309).

For many professionals, publication means promotion. The fact that such articles are being published does not merely show the current popularity with anecdotal, 'classroom research' (and also, the current tendency to ignore scientific research), but it also helps to demonstrate how vitally dependent many professionals are on journal bodies for furthering their careers. The kind of articles that are published certainly play a part in determining the fashionable attitudes which evolve and become powerfully entrenched.

Government documents also influence attitudes. The Hadow Report (1931), the Plowden Report (1967), the Bullock Report (1975), the Cox Report (1989) and the final draft orders for the National Curriculum (1994) are government policy directives, all of which endorse progressive, child-centred methods to some degree. As each of these documents demonstrates support for theories that have been shown to be false when subjected to strict empirical investigation, they all represent at least indirectly a denigration of experimental research.

As an example, the new National Curriculum final draft orders for English Key Stage 1, Reading, contain the wholesale endorsement of 'real books'. The first statement that appears is: 'Pupils should be given extensive experience of children's literature' (p. 6). Instead of stating that the main goal is to teach children how to read, the primary aim is to have children 'experience' literature. In support of using guessing and context to decode words, the orders state that pupils are to be 'taught to recognise the value of surrounding text in identifying unknown words' (p. 7). In support of whole-word, meaning-emphasis approaches such as shared reading, apprenticeship reading or paired reading, where the child is to 'read' texts over and over with an adult until he or she has memorised the story and is able to join in, the orders state that pupils should be 'focusing on meaning' (p. 7) and given opportunities to 'reread favourite stories and poems, learning some by heart' (p. 8).

Although the curriculum orders do contain a number of concepts that are supported by empirical research, all of the dictated procedures outlined above are not. On the contrary, there is a substantial amount of research which shows that directing a child to behave like a reader or 'experience' literature, to decode words by using guessing and context, and to treat reading as if it were a memorisation task, are all procedures which have been shown to be ineffective in, and even detrimental to, teaching a child how to read.

In addition, the government's national curriculum tests (SATs) are measures which are derived from subjective research. The government's decision not to use objective tests and to use this sort of measure instead, is seen as 'another vote of confidence in teacher professionalism' (Rowan, 1994); in other words, another concession to the progressive establishment, further support of their rejection of scientific research findings.

Thus both the curriculum orders and the national tests represent, to some degree, government support of fashionable theory; indirectly, these also represent the rejection of experimental research findings and scientific investigation itself as a valuable method of enquiry.

Summary

Although research indicates that the most valid and reliable assessment is through the use of objective, standardised measures, in practice children's reading ability, teachers' ability to teach reading effectively, and teacher-trainers' ability to produce effective teachers of reading are all evaluated through the use of subjective, error-prone assessment measures. Reading standards will not improve so long as there is no year-to-year system of assessment in place that is capable of giving an accurate and reliable picture of what reading standards really are, there is no monitoring of classroom teachers' reading methods linking these with pupil reading attainment produced, and there is no routine, objective assessment of the quality of teacher-training courses.

In addition, the type of research on which teachers and others in the field of education most often judge acceptable enough to base practice consists of descriptive, non-experimental research. As long as practice is to be based on fashionable anecdotal or 'naturalistic research', the reading standards among 7-year-olds will continue to be under threat.

7 | Conclusion
Why Schoolchildren Can't Read: Problem and Solution

The Problem: The Research/Practice Gap

In England, the chances are that more than one child in three will not have learned how to read after spending two years in primary school. At least half the student population in older grades are still struggling to read. For those acquainted with the nature of current teaching practice, this state of affairs will come as no surprise at all. Although research demonstrates unequivocally that certain skills need to be taught to beginning pupils, typically this is not happening in Key Stage 1 classrooms in this country. The failure to provide children with the structured, sequential, explicit phonological and code-oriented instruction that they need is depriving them of the best opportunity to learn to read, write, and spell at an early age, as well as reducing their capabilities at every stage in the future.

Over the past thirty years, reading itself has been redefined. Learning to read is currently seen as little more than a memorisation and guessing exercise. Many children cannot make the transition from this behaviour to proper reading. It is not the teachers, who as a group have come under heavy criticism over declining standards, who are to blame. They are merely doing what they have been taught to do. No – one must look higher up the chain of command. Responsibility for poor reading standards lies with the many primary school heads, local education authority officials, school inspectors, teacher trainers, and national teacher organisations and unions who advocate methods of reading instruction radically at variance with the findings from empirical research. It is they who most influence practice, dictating methods of instruction that do not work. In effect, it is as if they are happy to send their educational troops into battle each day armed with blanks.

England is not the only country where a discrepancy between research and practice has developed. There is the same dis-ease between teaching practice and reading research evident in such countries as the USA, Canada, Australia, and New Zealand. In Europe also, in countries where traditional, more research-compatible methods have been the norm (Switzerland, for example) the continuation of these practices is coming under threat.

In this country, there has to be change and it will need to come quickly to avoid failing further generations of children.

The Solution

While it might be relatively clear how to solve the problem, it is less easy to see how the problem might be solved quickly. The more accurately teaching practice encapsulates the findings from reading research, the higher the reading attainment produced. Altering teaching practice so that it becomes as closely aligned as possible with the findings from research is the way to solve the problem, but how might the changes required be expedited?

First, that which is dogma needs to be recognised and discarded. Within today's educational establishment, entrenched beliefs, certain assumptions that are based on false premises, are stubbornly adhered to. These need to be challenged. As a first principle, before any new practice is implemented, its effectiveness should be scientifically demonstrated. The first question one must ask before implementing practice is: where is the evidence that this practice works? Practices which are not based on solid evidence that they are effective need to be eradicated.

The public would be outraged if a drug with damaging side-effects were released onto the market and used widely to treat patients without its having been rigorously tested and proven safe; in the field of medicine, a reliance on belief rather than evidence is not permitted. Yet, instruction in English classrooms operates on this basis regularly. New ideas or old ideas dressed up in new terminology are held up as the latest theories to be put into practice, when in fact, they are simply examples of ideology being incorporated into practice. In this case, it is our schoolchildren who are the principal casualties of this carelessness; it is they who are the victims of the instructional shortcomings and who must suffer the many far-reaching and detrimental side-effects of not being able to read.

Second, it is essential that those with the power to influence practice recognise that there is indeed a problem. Assessment procedures and the results produced must be questioned. How many times have we heard a senior politician or educationalist assert that standards are actually improving, that reports of widespread reading failure are alarmist, or exaggerated, or even, politically motivated, that, in short, there is no problem? Usually quoted are the rising numbers of A level and GCSE passes, the improving National Curriculum test results. But, is this evidence to be trusted? Many parents in the country worry that reading standards have fallen, and that illiteracy amongst the young is on the increase. The constant shifting of goalposts to create a positive impression does not fool the parents of children who cannot read – nor does the replacing of letter grades with anecdotal, non-graded, no-fail report cards.

The same question that must be asked about teaching practice must be asked of the present system for monitoring reading standards: does it work? The national curriculum tests in reading describe (through a teacher's particular interpretation of events via a running record) how a child behaves when faced with a reading passage he or she is likely to have seen before. This system of assessment is entirely consistent with the child-centred philosophy that no child can be seen to fail; a child's self-esteem must be preserved at all cost, and if one looks very hard and sufficiently lowers the benchmarks, there will always be some behaviour that one can find to praise. What must be asked, however, is: what evidence is there to support this way of thinking? In the first place, if a child fails to read, what evidence is there that it is the child's fault and not the fault of the instructional setting? Whose self-esteem is really at stake – the child's, or the teacher's? In the second place, what evidence is there that the present system for assessing reading ability is the most accurate means of doing so? The present nature of testing reading, which ensures that accurate comparisons between children, between schools, or over time cannot be made, looks suspiciously designed to obscure evidence rather than make it available as a tool for creating change.

Third, when challenging those who are in a position to dictate or influence practice to choose only instructional and assessment methods that work, that have evidence to support them, the nature of 'evidence' needs to be examined. From a scientific perspective, the only source of information that has implications for effective practice is comparative intervention research where one procedure is compared to another under repeated, controlled experimental conditions. Descriptive studies explore and describe existing problems but they do not provide the sort of data from which effective solutions can be inferred.

The whole-word method of instruction and its variants are derived from the descriptive studies of child development and learning. But these have not been subjected to empirical investigation and therefore represent nothing more than untested hypotheses. They are 1960s ideology which has become fixed as 1990s dogma. There was no reason to suppose that these methods would ever have worked but they suited the ideology of the times. Their introduction was an experiment, a kind of educational vivisection carried out on the school population.

Instead of experimenting on children by implementing these untested ideas, the results from controlled experiments and their implications for instruction need to be recognised as the more reliable evidence available, the evidence upon which teaching practice should be based. The neglect of empirical data, and resistance to objectivity, seen in both present intructional practice and assessment procedures does not make sense if one is truly interested in ensuring that all children learn how to read.

Fourth, there is a need to recognise, too, the impossibility of implementing current theories. Whole-word, child-centred, individualised methods, adopted in the sixties, were perhaps an understandable reaction to such traditional and élitist practices as the eleven-plus examinations, to a long tradition of authoritarianism and control. However well-meaning the intent of whole-language methods, which have been widely promoted as the route to greater teacher 'empowerment', the cruel truth is that such methods are next to impossible for any teacher, no matter how talented, to implement in practice. However well-meaning the progressive ideas of shared reading, 'real books', 'emergent literacy', 'invented spelling', 'teacher-as-facilitator', it is impossible for one teacher to 'facilitate' and supervise these practices to any real degree in a class of twenty-five to thirty children; the amount of 'facilitation' a teacher will be able to provide in such circumstances will be marginal at best. Perhaps these ideas, if tested empirically, would prove effective compared to other methods if each teacher were given only one child to teach? This, however, is not, nor has it ever been, the reality that teachers must deal with. At best, any teacher faced with a classroom of twenty to thirty non-reading five-year-olds will feel severely challenged in attempting to adopt individualised, whole-word methods in such circumstances. Rather than feeling 'empowered', it is far more likely that he or she will feel defeated.

Thus, however attractive progressive ideas might be, there needs to be greater honesty in questioning the practicality of implementing such ideas within a normal classroom setting. And the same questions need to be asked of current individualised methods of assessment: how practical are these for the purpose and might not a teacher spend his or her time in more productive ways? In teaching or testing reading, a pragmatic rather than an ideological view must be taken.

Finally, those in positions of power must question whether it is largely fear that determines present teaching practice and if so, attempt to overcome it. Those who have advocated practices that do not work must not be afraid to admit that perhaps they were wrong. Others have had the courage to do so. Since whole language methods were introduced to the state of California in 1982, reading standards, once among the best in the country, began to decline and eventually, in 1995, plummeted to the very worst in the country. Yet, Bill Honig, who had encouraged and presided over these methods from 1982 to 1992 as California's superintendent of schools, was brave enough to admit his mistake. Speaking before the state assembly's education committee in 1995, he explained that he had changed his mind since researchers in the past 10 years had discovered the importance of phonological processes in reading. Phonics methods are now being reintroduced to the state of California.

In England, there may be the fear that phonological and code-emphasis methods of instruction represent a return to all that is old-fashioned, to didacticism, competition, élitism, and selection. This need not be the case. Instead, the simple policy one must adhere to is that no practice should be embraced without evidence to support its effectiveness. Rather than increase differences among children, differences will diminish if all children receive the sort of instruction that teaches them to read.

BIBLIOGRAPHY:

Ackerman, P.T., Anhalt, J.M., & Dykman, R.A. (1986). 'Inferential word decoding weakness in RD children', *Learning Disability Quarterly*, 9, 315-324.

Ackerman, P.T., & Dykman, R.A. (1993). 'Phonological processes, confrontational naming, and immediate memory in dyslexia', *Journal of Learning Disabilities*, 26(9), 597-619.

Ackerman, D., & Mont, H. (1991). *Literacy for All: a Whole Language Approach to the English National Curriculum for Pupils with Severe and Complex Learning Difficulties*. Manchester University School of Education.

Adams, M.J. (1990). *Beginning to Read: Thinking and Learning about Print.* Cambridge, MA: MIT Press.

Adams, M.J., & Bruck, M. (1993). 'Word recognition: The interface of educational policies and scientific research', *Reading and Writing: An Interdisciplinary Journal*, 5, 113-139.

Aguiar, L., & Brady, S. (1991). 'Vocabulary acquisition and reading ability', *Reading and Writing: An Interdisciplinary Journal*, 3(3/4), 413-425.

ALBSU (Adult Literacy and Basic Skills Unit). (1991). *Extending Reading Skills*. London: ALBSU.

ALBSU (Adult Literacy and Basic Skills Unit). (1992). *The Basic Skills of Young Adults*. The Social Statistics Research Unit, London: ALBSU.

ALBSU (Adult Literacy and Basic Skills Unit). (1994). *Making Reading Easier*. London: ALBSU.

ALBSU (Adult Literacy and Basic Skills Unit). (1995). *Read and Write Together: BBC Education.*

Alegria, J., & Morais, J. (1991). Segmental analysis and reading acquisition. In L. Rieben, & C.A. Perfetti (Eds), *Learning to Read: Basic Research and its Implications* Hillsdale, New Jersey: Lawrence Erlbaum Associates pp.135-148.

Alegria, J., Pinot, E., & Morais, J. (1982). 'Phonetic analysis and memory codes in beginning readers', *Memory & Cognition*, 104, 451-456.

Alexander, R. (1992). *Policy and Practice in Primary Education*. London: Routledge.

Alexander, A., Anderson, H. Heilman, P., Voeller, K, & Torgesen, T. (1991). 'Phonological awareness training and remediation of analytic decoding deficits in a group of severe dyslexics', *Annals of Dyslexia*, 41, 193-206.

Alexander, R., Rose, J., & Woodhead, C. (1994). *Curriculum Organisation and Classroom Practice in Primary Schools: A Discussion Paper*. Department of Education and Science.

Allington, R.I. (1983). 'The reading instruction provided readers of differing reading abilities', *The Elementary School Journal*, 83, 548-559.

Anderson, M. (1992). *Intelligence and Development: A Cognitive Theory*. Oxford: Blackwell Publishers.

Anderson, R.C., Hiebert, E.H., Scott, J., and Wilkinson, I. (1985). *Becoming a Nation of Readers*. Washington, DC: National Institute of Education.

Arter, J.A., & Jenkins, J.R. (1977). 'Examining the benefits and prevalence of modality considerations in special education'. *Journal of Special Education*, 11, 281-298.

Backman, J. Bruck, M. Hebert, M, & Seidenberg, M. (1984). 'Acquisition and use of spelling-sound correspondences in reading'. *Journal of Experimental Child Psychology*, 38, 114-133.

Badian, N.A. (1993). 'Phonemic awareness, naming, visual symbol processing, and reading', *Reading and Writing: An Interdisciplinary Journal*, 5(19), 87-100.

Badian, N. A. (1994). 'Do dyslexic and other poor readers differ in reading-related cognitive skills?', *Reading and Writing: An Interdisciplinary Journal*, 6, 45-63.

Bakker, D.J. (1992). 'Neuropsychological classification and treatment of dyslexia', *Journal of Learning Disabilities*, 25(2), 102-109.

Bakker, D.J., Bouma, A., & Gardien, C. (1990). 'Hemisphere-specific treatment of dyslexia subtypes: a field experiment', *Journal of Learning Disabilities*, 23(7), 433-438.

Bakker, D.J., & Moerland, R, (1981). 'Are there brain-tied sex differences in reading?' In A. Ansara, N. Geschwind, A. Galaburda, M. Albert, & N. Gartrell (Eds), *Sex Differences in Dyslexia* . Towson, Maryland: The Orton Dyslexia Society, pp.109-118.

Ball, E. W. (1993). 'Phonological awareness: what's important and to whom?', *Reading and Writing: An Interdisciplinary Journal*, 5(2)142-160.

Ball, E.W., & Blachman, B.A. (1988). 'Phoneme segmentation training: Effect on reading readiness', *Annals of Dyslexia*, 38, 203-225.

Ball, E.W., & Blachman, B.A. (1991). 'Does phoneme segmentation training in kindergarten make a difference in early word recognition and developmental spelling?', *Reading Research Quarterly*, 26, 49-66.

Bald, J. (1994, 8 July). Phonics arising. *Times Educational Supplement*, p. 17.

Barber, M. (1996). *Young People and their Attitudes to School: An Interim Report of a Research Project in the Centre for Successful Schools*. Keele: Keele University.

BBC1, (1994, October 24). Panorama programme on why boys are failing. London

Beard, R. (1994) Coming to terms with the written word. *Times Educational Supplement*, , 30 September, p. 8.

Beck, I.L. (1981). Reading problems and instructional practices. In G.E. Mackinnon & T. G. Waller (Eds), *Reading research: Advances in Theory and Practice* New York: Academic Press, vol 2, pp.53-95.

Becker, W.C. & Gersten, R. (1982). 'A follow-up of Follow Through: The later effects of the direct instruction model on children in fifth and sixth grades', *American Educational Research Journal*, 19, 75-92.

Bialystok, E. & Niccols, A. (1989). 'Children's control over attention to phonological and semantic properties or words', *Journal of Psycholinguistic Research*, 18(4), 36-386.

Biemiller, A. (1977-8). 'Relationships between oral reading rates for letters, words, and simple text in the development of reading achievement', *Reading Research Quarterly*, 13, 223-253.

Biemiller, A. (1979). 'Changes in the use of graphic and contextual information as functions of passage difficulty and reading achievement level', *Journal of Reading Behaviour*, 11, 307-319.

Bishop, J.E. (1993). 'Word processing: Stroke patients yield clues to brain's ability to create language', *The Wall Street Journal*, , 12 October, p. A14.

Blachman, B.A. (1984). 'Relationship of rapid naming ability and language analysis skills to kindergarten and first-grade reading achievement', *Journal of Educational Psychology*, 76, 610-622.

Blachman, B.A. (1987). The alternative classroom reading program for learning disabled and other low-achieving children. In R. Bowler (Ed.), *Intimacy with Language: A Forgotten Basic in Teacher Education* . Baltimore: The Orton Dyslexic Society, pp.49-55

Blachman, B.A. (1994). 'What we have learned from longitudinal studies of phonological processing and reading, and some unanswered questions: A response to Torgesen, Wagner, and Rashotte', *Journal of Learning Disabilities*, 27(5), 287-291.

Blachman, B.A., Ball, E. W., Black, R. S., Tangel, D. M. (1994). 'Kindergarten teachers develop phoneme awareness in low-income, inner-city classrooms', *Reading and Writing:An Interdisciplinary Journal*, 6(1), 1-18.

Blatchford, P., Ireson, J., & Joscelyne, T. (1994). 'The initial teaching of reading: what do teachers think?', *Educational Psychology*, 14(3), 331-344.

Bleismer, E.P., & Yarborough, B.H. (1965). 'A comparison of ten different beginning reading programs in first grade. *Phi Delta Kappan, June 46* (10), 500-504.

Blumenfeld, S.L. (1990). *N.E.A. Trojan horse in American Education*. Boise, Idaho: The Paradigm Company.

Boder, E. (1973). 'Developmental dyslexia: A diagnostic approach based on three atypical reading-spelling patterns', *Developmental Medicine and Child Neurology*, 15, 663-687.

Body, W. (1990). *Help Your Child with Reading*. BBC Education.

Bowers, P.G., & Swanson, L.B. (1991). 'Naming speed deficits in reading disability: multiple measures of a single process', *Journal of Experimental Child Psychology*, 51, 195-219.

Bowey, J.A., & Francis, J. (1991). 'Phonological analysis as a function of age and exposure to reading instruction', *Applied Psycholinguistics*, 12, 91-121.

Bradley, L. (1987). *Categorising Sounds, Early Intervention and Learning to Read: A Follow-Up Study*. Paper presented at the BPS London Conference.

Bradley, L., & Bryant, P. (1983). 'Categorising sounds and learning to read – A causal connection', *Nature*, 303, 419-421.

Bradley, L., & Bryant, P. (1985). *Rhyme and Reason in Reading and Spelling*. MI: University of Michigan Press.

Brigham, F.J. (1992). Spatial learning and instruction of children with learning disabilities. In T. E. Scruggs & M. A. Mastropieri (Eds). *Advances in Learning and Behavioural Disabilities*. Connecticut: Jai Press.

Bristow,. P.S. (1985). 'Are Poor Readers Passive Readers?: Some evidence, possible explanations, and potential solutions',. *The Reading Teacher*, 39, 318-325.

Brooks, E. (1994). Dyslexia: Letter to the Editor (from the Director of the Dyslexia Institute, Staines). *The Sunday Times*, 1 May.

Brooks, G., Gorman, T., Kendall, L. & Tate, A. (1992). *What Teachers in Training are Taught about Reading: The working papers*. National Foundation for Educational Research.

Brooks, G., Pugh, A.K.,& Schagen, I. (1996). *Reading Performance at Nine*. Slough: NFER.

Brouininks, R. (1969). 'Auditory and visual perceptual skills related to the reading performance of disadvantaged boys', *Perceptual and Motor Skills*, 29, 179-186.

Brown, I.S., & Felton, R.H. (1990). 'Effects of instruction on beginning reading skills in children at risk for reading disability', *Reading and Writing: An Interdisciplinary Journal*, 12(3), 223-241.

Bruck, M. (1990). 'Word recognition skills of adults with childhood diagnoses of dyslexia', *Developmental Psychology*, 26, 439-454.

Bruck, M., & Treiman, R. (1992). 'Learning to pronounce words: The limitations of analogies', *Reading Research Quarterly*, 27(4), 375-387.

Brunner, M.S. (1993). *Retarding America*. Portland, Oregon: Halcyon House.

BSA (The Basic Skills Agency) (1994). *Basic Skills in Prisons: Assessing the Need*. London: BSA.

Buffery, A.W.H. (1976). Sex differences in the neuropsychological development of verbal and spatial skills. In R.M. Knights and D.J. Bakker (Eds), *The Neuropsychology of Llearning Disorders: Theoretical Applications*. Baltimore: University Park Press.

Buffery, A. W. H., & Gray, J. A. (1972). Sex differences in the development of spatial and linguistic skills. In C. Ounsted & D. C. Taylor (Eds), *Gender Differences: Their Ontogeny and significance*. Edinburgh: Churchill Livingstone.

Bullock Report (1975). *A Language for Life: Report of the Commission of Inquiry Appointed by the Secretary of State for Education and Science under the Chairmanship of Sir Alan Bullock.* London: Department of Education and Science.

Burkard, T. (1996). 'Phonological training in reception year', *British Journal of Curriculum and Assessment*, 6(3), 7-10.

Byrne, B. (1991). Experimental analysis of the child's discovery of the alphabetic principle. In L. Rieben, & C.A. Perfetti (Eds), *Learning to Read: Basic Research and its Implications.* Hillsdale, New Jersey: Lawrence Erlbaum Associates, pp.75-84.

Byrne, B. (1992). Studies in the acquisition procedure for reading: Rationale, hypothesis, and data. In P. B. Gough, L. Ehri, & R. Treiman (Eds), *Reading Acquisition.* Hillsdale, NJ: Erlbaum, pp.1-34.

Byrne, B., & Fielding-Barnsley, R. (1989). 'Phonemic awareness and letter knowledge in the child's acquisition of the alphabetic principle', *Journal of Educational Psychology*, 81, 313- 321.

Byrne, B., & Fielding-Barnsley, R. (1990). 'Acquiring the alphabetic principle: a case for teaching recognition of phoneme identity', *Journal of Educational Psychology*, 81, 313-321.

Byrne, B. & Fielding-Barnsley, R. (1991). 'Evaluation of a program to teach phonemic awareness to young children', *Journal of Educational Psychology*, 85(1), *104-11.*

Byrne, B. & Fielding-Barnsley, R. (1993). 'Evaluation of a program to teach phonemic awareness to young children: a 1-Year follow-up', *Journal of Educational Psychology*, 85(10). 104-111.

Byrne, B, & Fielding-Barnsley, R. (1995). 'Evaluation of a programme to teach phonemic awareness to young children: A 2- and 3- year follow-up and a new preschool trial', *Journal of Educational Psychology*, 87 (3), 488-503.

Byrne, B., Freebody, P., & Gates, A. (1992). 'Longitudinal data on the relations of word-reading strategies to comprehension, reading time, and phonemic awareness', *Reading Research Quarterly*, 27, 140-151.

Byrne, B., & Ledez, J. (1983). 'Phonological awareness in reading disabled adults', *Australian Journal of Psychology*, 35, 345-367.

Calfee, R. (1983). 'The mind of the dyslexic', *Annals of Dyslexia*, 33, 9-28.

Calfee, R. (1995). 'A behind-the-scenes look at reading acquisition', *Issues in Education*, 1(1), 77-82.

Calfee, R., Lindamood, P. & Lindmood, C. (1973). 'Acoustic-phonetic skills and reading: kindergarten through twelfth grade', *Journal of Educational Psychology*, 64(3), 293-298.

Camp, L.W., Winbury, N.E., & Zinna, D.R. (1981). 'Strategies for initial reading instruction', *Bulletin of the Orton Society*, 31, 175-189.

Cary, L., & Verhaeghe, A. (1994). 'Promoting phonemic analysis ability among kindergartners: effects of different training programs', *Reading and Writing: An Interdisciplinary Journal*, 6(3), 251-278.

Cato, V. & Whetton, C. (1991). *An Enquiry into LEA Evidence on Standards of Reading of 7 Year Old Children – A Report by the National Foundation for Educational Research*, DES.

Cato, V., Fernandes, C., Gorman, T. Kispal, A., & White, J. (1992). *The Teaching of Initial Literacy: How Do teachers Do It?* National Foundation for Educational Research.

Center, Y., Wheldall, K, & Freeman, L. (1992). 'Evaluating the effectiveness of reading recovery: A critique', *Educational Psychology*, 12(3 & 4), 263-274.

Chall, J. S. (1967). *Learning to Read: The Great Debate*. New York: McGraw-Hill.

Chall, J. S. (1979). The great debate: Ten years later with a modest proposal for reading stages. In L.G. Resnick, & P.A. Weaver (Eds), *Theory and Practice of Early Reading*. Hillsdale, NJ: Erlbaum Associates, vol 1, pp.29-56.

Chall, J. S. (1983). *Learning to Read: The Great Debate (2nd ed)*. New York: McGraw-Hill.

Chall, J. S. (1989). "Learning to read: The great debate 20 years later – A response to 'debunking the great phonics myth'", *Phi Delta Kappan*, March, 521-537.

Chall, J. S. (1995). Ahead to the Greeks. *Issues in Education*, 1(1), 83-85.

Chapman, J.W., Lambourne, R.,& Silva, P. A. (1990). 'Some antecedents of academic self-concept: a longitudinal study', *British Journal of Educational Psychology*, 60, 142-152.

Chapman, J., & Tunmer, W. (1991). 'Recovering reading recovery', *Australia and NewZealand Journal of Developmental Disabilities*, 17, 59-71.

Chazan, M. (1972). A critical appraisal of standards and progress in reading. In J. Morris (Ed.). *The first R*. London: NFER.

Clarke, K. (1991). *Primary Education: A Statement by the Secretary of State for Education and Science*. Stanmore: DES.

Clay, M. (1985). *The Early Detection of Reading Difficulties*. Auckland, New Zealand: Heinemann.

Clay, M. (1991). *Becoming Literate: The Construction of Inner Control*. Auckland, New Zealand: Heinemann.

Clay, M. (1992). A second chance to learn literacy: by different routes to common outcomes (the reading recovery programme). In T. Cline (Ed.), *The Assessment of Special Educational Needs: International Perspectives*. NY: Routledge, Chapman, & Hall Inc.

Clay, M. (1993). *Reading Recovery: A Handbook for Teachers in Training*. Auckland: Heinemann Educational.

Content, A., Kolinsky, R., Morais, J., & Bertelson, P. (1986). 'Phonetic segmentation in prereaders: Effect of corrective information', *Journal of Experimental Child Psychology, 42*, 49-72.

Coventry LEA (1981). *Towards a Language Policy; A Discussion Paper on Reading for Heads and Staff*. Coventry: Elm Banks Teacher's Centre.

Cowling, K. (1994). *Toe by Toe*. 8 Green Rd., Baildon, West Yorkshire, BD17 5LH.

Cox, B. (1989, June). *English for Ages 5 to 16*. London: Department for Education and Science and the Welsh Office. HMSO.

Cox, B. (1994, 4 July). Comment in a leaflet distributed at a conference entitled, *Will the New National Curriculum proposals raise standards?* King's College, London University, Kensington Campus.

Cunningham, A.E. (1990). 'Explicit versus implicit instruction in phonemic awareness', *Journal of Experimental Child Psychology, 50*, 429-444.

Cunningham, A.E., & Stanovich, K. (1993). Children's literacy environments and early word recognition skills. *Reading and Writing: An Interdisciplinary Journal, 5*, 193-204.

Davidson, M. & Jenkins, J. R. (1994). 'Effects of phonemic processes on word reading and spelling', *Journal of Educational Research, 87*(3), 148-157.

Davies, A. & Ritchie, D.(1996). *THRASS Teaching Handwriting, Reading, and Spelling Skills*. London: Collins Educational.

181

Davies, J. & Brember, I. (1994). The first mathematics assessment tasks at Key Stage 1: issues raised by a five-school study. *British Educational Research Journal*, 20, 35-40.

Davies, J, Brember, I., & Pumfrey, P. (1995). 'The first and second reading Standard Assessment Tasks at Key Stage 1: a comparison based on a five-school study', *Journal of Research in Reading*, 18, 1-9.

Defior, S. & Tudela, P. (1994). 'Effect of phonological training on reading and writing acquisition', *Reading and Writing: An Interdisciplinary Journal*, 6(3). 279-320.

DES (Department of Education and Science) (1978). *Primary Education in England*. A Survey by HMI Inspectors of Schools.

DES (Department of Education and Science) (1991a). *Testing 7 Year Olds in 1991: Results of the National Curriculum Assessments in England*. London: HMSO.

DES (Department of Education and Science) (1991b). *How Is Your Child Doing at School? A Parent's Guide to Testing*. London: DES.

DES (Department for Education and Science) (1992a, February). *The Government's Expenditure Plans 1992-93 to 1994-95*. London: HMSO, p. 18.

DES (Department of Education and Science) (1992b). *English Key Stages 1, 2, and 3: A Report by H M Inspectorate on the Second Year, 1990-91*. London: HMSO.

DfE (1989). *HMI Report: Reading Policy and Practice at Age 5-14*. London: HMSO.

DfE (Department for Education) (1992). *Testing of 7 Year Olds in 1992: Results of the National Curriculum Assessments in England*. London: HMSO.

DfE (Department for Education) (1994a). *Testing of Seven and Eleven Year Olds in 1994: Results of the National Curriculum Assessments in England*. London: HMSO.

DfE (Department for Education) (1994b, June 15). *House of Commons session 1993-1994: Department of Education Expenditure Plans 1994-1995 – Minutes of Evidence*. London: DFE

DfE (Department for Education) (1995). *Testing of 7 Year Olds in 1994: Results of the National Curriculum Assessments in England*. London: HMSO.

DfEE (Department for Education and Employment) (1996a). *Results of the 1995 National Curriculum Assessment of 11 Year Olds in England.* London: DfEE.

DfEE (Department for Education and Employment) (1996b). *Results of the 1995 National Curriculum Assessment of 7 Year Olds in England.* London: DfEE.

DfEE (Department for Education and Employment) (1996c). *Key Stage 1 English Tasks 1996: Reading and Writing Teacher's Handbook.* London: DfEE.

DfEE (Department for Education and Employment) (1996d). *The Government Expenditure Plans 1996-97 to 1998-99. Department for Education and Employment and Office for Standards in Education Departmental Report. London: HMSO.*

Doe, B. (1994, 11 March). Silent role in disputes over special needs. *Times Educational Supplement.*

Dombey, H. (1990-91). Memorandum by the Faculty of Education, Brighton Polytechnic. In A. Markham, *Letter to the Clerk of the Committee from the Dean of the Faculty of Education, Brighton Polytechnic.* DFE, House of Commons Session Third Report, Volume II, Minutes of evidence and appendices, Appendix 13, 80-91.

Dombey, H. (1992). *Words and Worlds: Reading in the Early Years of School.* National Association of Teachers of English.

Dombey, H. (1994a, 23 November). Letter to the editor. *Times Educational Supplement.*

Dombey, H. (1994b, 29 November). Reading teaching. Letter to the editor, in the Education section, *Guardian*, p.6.

Doncaster Local Education Authority (1983). *Reading.* Produced by the teaching support service Doncaster Metropolitan Borough Council.

Douglas, J. (1969). *The Home and the School.* London: Macgibbons & Kee.

Dyslexia Institute. (1996). *Units of Sound: An Audiovisual Reading Development Programme.* Staines: The Dyslexia Institute.

Ehri, L.C. (1983). A critique of five studies related to letter-name knowledge and learning to read. In L.M. Gentile, M.L. Kamil, and J. S. Blanchard (Eds), *Reading Research Revisited, (143-153).* Columbus, Ohio: Charles E. Merrill.

183

Ehri, L.C. (1985). Effects of printed language acquisition on speech. In D. Olson, N. Torrance, & A. Hidyard (Eds), *Literacy, Language, and Learning* . New York: Cambridge University Press, pp.333-367.

Ehri, L.C. (1989). 'The development of spelling knowledge and its role in reading acquisition and reading disability', *Journal of Learning Disabilities*, 22, 336-365.

Ehri, L.C. (1991). Learning to read and spell words. In L. Rieben, & C.A. Perfetti (Eds), *Learning to Read: Basis Research and its Implications* . Hillsdale, New Jersey: Lawrence Erlbaum Associates, pp.57-74.

Ehri, L.C. (1992). Reconceptualizing the development of sight word reading and its relationship to recoding. In P. B. Gough, L. C. Ehri, & R. Treiman, (Eds), *Reading Acquisition*. Hillsdale, NJ: Erlbaum Associates, pp.107-143

Ehri, L.C. (1995). 'Phases of development in learning to read words by sight', *Research in Reading*, 18(2), 116-125.

Ehri, L.C., & Robbins, (1992). 'Beginners need some decoding skill to read words by analogy', *Reading Research Quarterly*, 27, 12-26.

Ehri, L.C., & Wilce, L.S. (1983). 'Development of word identification speed in skilled and less skilled beginning readers', *Journal of Educational Psychology*, 75, 3-18.

Ehri, L.C., Wilce, L. & Taylor, B. (1987). 'Children's categorization of short vowels in words and the influence of spellings', *Merrill-Palmer Quarterly*, 33, 393-21.

Ellis, N. (1990a). 'Reading, phonological skills and short-term memory: Interactive tributaries of development', *Journal of Research in Reading*, 13(2), 107-122.

Ellis, A. W. (1993). *Reading, Writing, and Dyslexia: a Cognitive Analysis* . Hove, UK: Lawrence Erlbaum, ch.7

Enfield, M. L. (1987). A cost-effective classroom alternative to 'pull-out programs'. In R.F. Bowler (Ed.), *Intimacy with Language: A Forgotten Basic in Teacher Education*. Baltimore: Orton Dyslexic Society, pp.45-55.

Englemann, Z. (1993). Zig Englemann's closing address on standards. *Twenty Years of Effective Teaching*. Paper presented at the 20th Annual Eugene Conference and Celebration of the Association for Direct Instruction. Eugene, Oregon, USA.

Engelmann, Z., & Bruner, E. (1983). *Reading Mastery I and II: DISTAR Reading*, Chicago, ILL: Science Research Associates.

Etting, O. (1993, 21 November). Shut state schools. *Sunday Telegraph*, p. 33.

Evans, M., & Carr, T. (1985). 'Cognitive abilities, conditions of learning and the early development of reading skill', *Reading Research Quarterly*, 20, 327-350.

Feitelson, D. (1973). Adaptive teaching practices. In M.A. Just & P.A. Carpenter (1987), *The Psychology of Reading and Language Comprehension*. Boston: Allyn & Bacon.

Feldman, E., Levin, B., Fleischmann, J., Jallad, B., Kushch, A., Gross-Glenn, K, Rabin, M, & Lubs, H. (1995). 'Gender differences in the severity of adult familial dyslexia', *Reading and Writing: An Interdisciplinary Journal*, 7. 155-161.

Felton, R.H. (1993). 'Effects of instruction on the decoding skills of children with phonological-processing problems', *Journal of Learning Disabilities*, 26(9), 583-589.

Felton, R.H., & Brown, I.S. (1990). 'Phonological processes as predictors of specific reading skills in children at risk for reading failure', *Reading and Writing: An Interdisciplinary Journal*, 2, 39-59.

Finucci, J.M., & Childs, B. (1981). In A. Ansara, N. Geschwind, A. Galaburda, M. Albert, & N. Gartrell. *Sex Differences in Dyslexia*, . Maryland: The Orton Dyslexia Society, pp.1-10.

Fisher, C. W., & Berliner, D. C. (1985). (Eds), *Perspectives on Instructional Time*. London: Longman.

Fleischer, L.S., Jenkins, J.R., & Pany, D. (1979). 'Effects on poor readers' comprehension of training in rapid decoding', *Reading Research Quarterly*, 15, 30-48.

Flesch, R. (1983). *Why Johnny Still Can't Read: A New Look at the Scandal of our Schools*. New York: Harper Colophon.

Flowers, L. (1993). 'Brain basis for dyslexia: A summary of work in progress', *Journal of Learning Disabilities*, 26(9), 575-582.

Flynn, J., Deering, W., Goldstein, M, & Rahbar, M. H. (1992). 'Electrophysiological correlates of dyslexic subtypes', *Journal of Learning Disabilities*. 25(2), 130-141.

Foorman, B.R., & Francis, D.J. (1994). 'Exploring connections among reading, spelling, and phonemic segmentation during first grade',. *Reading and Writing: An Interdisciplinary Journal*, 6(1), 65-92.

Foorman, B.R., Francis, D.J., Novy, D.M., & Liberman, D. (1991). 'How letter-sound instruction mediates progress in first-grade reading and spelling', *Journal of Educational Psychology*, 83, 456-469.

Forell, E. R. (1985). 'The case for conservative reader placement', *The Reading Teacher*, 35, 857-862.

Fox, R (1991). Meaning well. In *Standards in Reading: Perspectives 44*. Outdoor Education Media.

Fox, B., & Routh, D.K. (1980). 'Phonemic analysis and severe reading disability in children', *Journal of Psycholinguistic Research*, 9, 115-119.

Fox, B., & Routh, D.K. (1984). 'Phonemic analysis and synthesis as word attack skills: Revisited', *Journal of Educational Psychology*, 76, 1059-1064.

Foxman, D, Gorman, T., & Brooks, G. (1992-1993, December). *Standards in Literacy and Numeracy*. National Commission on Education Briefing, No. 10. London: Heineman.

Frith, U. (1985). Beneath the surface of developmental dyslexia. In K.E. Patterson, J.C. Marshall, & M. Coltheart (Eds), *Surface Dyslexia*. Hillsdale, New Jersey: Erlbaum Associates, pp.301-330

Froese, V. (1982). 'Classics in reading: A survey', *The Reading Teacher*, 36(Dec), 303-307.

Gallaburda, A. M. (1994). 'Developmental dyslexia and animal studies: at the interface between cognition and neurology', *Cognition*, 50, 133-149.

Gallagher, A. & Frederickson, N. (1995). 'The phonological assessment battery (PhAB): an initial assessment of its theoretical and practical utility', *Education and Child Psychology*, 12(1), 53-67.

Garrod, S. (1995). *Reading for Meaning: Decoding versus Matching Expectations*. Reading 2000: Recent advances in the science of reading, Human Communication Research Centre Seminar, University of Glasgow, 7 April, 1995.

Gersten,R., & Keating, T. (1987). 'Long-term benefits from direct instruction', *Educational Leadership*, 45, 28-31.

Glasgow University, (1994). Human Communications Research Centre project on eye movements and reading. Glasgow University.

Gleitman, L. R., & Rozin, P. (1977). The structure and acquisition of reading. Relation between orthography and structural language. In A. S. Reber & D. L. Scarborough (Eds), *Toward a Psychology of Reading*. Hillsdale, NJ: Erlbaum, pp.1-53.

Glynn, T., Bethune, N., Crooks,J., Ballard, K., & Smith, J. (1989). 'Reading recovery in context: Implementation and outcome', *Educational Psychology*, 12(3/4), 249-261.

Gold, K. (1994, June 17). Whatever happened to Liz Waterland? *Times Educational Supplement*, section 2, p. 1-2.

Goldstein, D.M. (1976). 'Cognitive-linguistic functioning and learning to read in preschoolers', *Journal of Educational Psychology*, 68, 680-688.

Goodman, K. (1965). 'Cues and miscues in reading: a linguistic study', *Elementary English*, 42, 640.

Goodman, K. (1988). List of dos and don'ts when a reader encounters an unfamiliar word. *Whole Language Teachers Newsletter*.

Goodman, K. (1992a). 'I didn't found whole language', *The Reading Teacher*, 46(3), 188-199.

Goodman, K. (1992b). 'Why whole language is today's agenda in education', *Language Arts*, 69, 354-363.

Goodman, K. (1994). 'Deconstruction the rhetoric of Moorman, Blanton, and McLaughlin: a response', *The Reading Research Quarterly*, 29(4), 340-346.

Gorman, T. & Fernandes, C. (1992). *Reading in Recession*. National Foundation for Educational Research.

Gorman, G., White, J., Brooks, G., & English, T. (1989). *Language for Learning: A Summary Report on the 1988 APU Surveys of Language Performance. Assessment Matters, No. 4*. London: SEAC

Goswami, U. (1988). 'Orthographic analogies and reading development', *Quarterly Journal of Experimental Psychology*, 40, 239-268.

Goswami, U. (1994a). 'Phonological skills, analogies, and reading development', *Reading*, 28(2), 32-37.

Goswami, U. (1994b). 'How do children learn to read', *SPA, summer*, 26-28.

Goswami, U. (1995). 'Phonological development and reading by analogy: what is analogy, and what is it not?', *Journal of Research in Reading*, 18(2), 139-145.

Goswami, U., & Bryant, P. (1990). *Phonological Skills and Learning to Read*. Hove, East Sussex: Lawrence Erlbaum Associates Ltd.

Gough, P.B. (1983). Context, form, and interaction. In K. Rayner (Ed.), *Eye Movements in Reading: Perceptual and Language Processes*. Orlando Florida: Academic Press, pp.203-211.

Gough, P.B. (1993). 'The beginning of decoding', *Reading and Writing: An Interdisciplinary Journal*, 5, 181-192.

Gough, P.B. (1995). 'The new literacy: caveat emptor', *Journal of Research in Reading*, 18(2), 79-86.

Gough, P.B., Alford, J.A., & Holley-Wilcox, P. (1981). Words and contexts. In O.J.L. Tzeng, & H. Singer (Eds), *Perception of Print: Reading Research in Experimental Psychology*. Hillsdale, NJ: Erlbaum, pp.85-102

Gough, P.B., Ehri, L., & Treiman, R. (1992). (Eds), *Reading Acquisition*. Hillsdale, NJ: Erlbaum.

Gough, P.B., & Hillinger, M.L. (1980). 'Learning to read: An unnatural act', *Bulletin of the Samuel Orton Society*, 30, 179-196.

Gough, P.B. & Juel, C. (1987). Is there reading without phonological awareness? paper presented at the annual meeting of the American Educational Research Association, Washington, D.C.

Gough, P.B., & Juel, C. (1991). The first stages of word recognition. In L. Rieben & C. Perfetti (Eds), *Learning to Read: Basic Research and its Implications*. Hillsdale, NJ: Erlbaum, pp.47-56

Gough, P.B., Juel, C., Griffith, P.L. (1992). Reading, spelling, and the orthographic cipher. In P. B. Gough, L. C. Ehri, & R. Treiman (Eds), *Reading Acquisition*. Hillsdale, New Jersey: Lawrence Erlbaum Associates, ch.2.

Gough, P.B., & Tunmer, W.E. (1986). 'Decoding, reading, and reading disability', *Remedial and Special Education*, 7, 6-10.

Gough, P.B., & Walsh, M. (1991). Chinese, Phoenicians, and the orthographic cipher of English. In S. Brady & D. Shankweiler (Eds), *Phonological Processes in Literacy*. Hillsdale, NJ: Erlbaum Associates, pp.199-209.

Government Statistical Service. (1994a, March). *Statistical Bulletin: Pupil-Teacher Ratios and Information on the Length of the Taught Week – for Each Local Education Authority in England*. London: DFE.

Graham, K. (1993, 3 October). Is teaching too hard for teachers? Letter to the editor. *Sunday Times*, p. 4.

Graham, S. (1984). 'Teacher feelings and student thought: an attributional approach to affect in the classroom', *Elementary School Journal*, 85, 91-104.

Green, A. & Steedman, H. (1993). *Educational Provision, Educational Attainment and the Needs of Industry: A Review of Research for Germany, France, Japan, the USA and Britain*. Report Series Number 5, Institute of Education, University of London and National Institute of Economic and Social Research.

Groff, P. (1979). 'Reading ability and auditory discrimination: A further consideration', *Academic Therapy*, 14, 313-319.

Groff, P. (1992). 'Is RT a whole language journal?', Letters to the editors. *The Reading Teacher*, 46(1), 7.

Grogan, S. C. (1995). 'Which cognitive abilities at age four are the best predictors of reading ability at age seven?', *Journal of Research in Reading*, 18(1), 24-31.

Gutierrez, & Slavin, (1992). 'Achievement effects of the nongraded elementary school: A best evidence synthesis', *Review of Educational Research*, 62(4), 333-376.

Hadfield, G. (1992, 19 July). Teacher reveals how her training squeezed out 3Rs. *Sunday Times*.

Hall, K. (1994). 'Conceptual and methodological flaws in the evaluation of the "first" British reading recovery programme', *British Educational Research Journal*, 20(1), 121-128.

Halpern, D. (1992). *Sex Differences in Cognitive Abilities*. Hillsdale, NJ: Lawrence Erlbaum Associates.

Hargreaves, D. (1994, 19 June). Blueprint for a better way of teaching. *Sunday Times*, p. 16.

Harris, A.J., & Sipay, E.R. (1990). *How to Increase Reading Ability*. New York: Longman.

Harris, A.J., Serwer, B.L., Gold, L., & Morrison, C. (1967). *A Third Progress Report on the CRAFT Project: Teaching Reading to Disadvantaged Primary Grade Urban Negro Children* (ERIC Document Reproduction Service No. ED015841).

Harrison, B., Zollner, J., & Magill, W. (1996). 'The hole in whole language: An analysis of the basic skills of 615 students', *Australian Journal of Remedial Education*, 27(5), 6-17.

Harter, R.M. (1991). Event-related potential indices: Learning disabilities and visual processing. In J. E. Obrzut & G. W. Hynd, G. W. (Eds), *Neuropsychological Foundations of Learning Disabilities: A Handbook of Issues, Methods, and Practice*. London: Academic Press, ch.17.

Hastings, N. & Schwieso, J. (1995). 'Tasks and tables: the effect of seating arrangemens on task engagement in primary classrooms', *Educational Research*, 37(3), 279-292.

Hatcher, P., Hulme, C., & Ellis, A. (1994). 'Ameliorating early reading failure by integrating the teaching of reading and phonological skills: The phonological linkage hypothesis', *Child Development*, 65, 41-57.

Hayes, D. P. (1988). 'Speaking and writing: Distinct patterns of word choice', *Journal of Memory and Language*, 27, 572-585.

Hayman, E., & Simpson, A. (Eds). (1996). *Public finance trends 96: A statistical background to public spending and revenues*. London: HMSO.

Henderson, M. (1959). A six year experimental study of two methods of teaching reading in elementary school. Paper presented at the American Education Research Association Convention, Chicago.

Henry, M. K. (1991). 'Introduction: The role of decoding in reading research and instruction', *Reading and Writing: An Interdisciplinary Journal*, 5(2), 105-112.

Hetherington, P. (1994, April 12). Success chalked up by making reading the golden rule. *Guardian*, p. 7.

HMI (1989, February). *Aspects of Reading in English in the Junior School*. HMI (Wales), Occasional paper.

HMI (1989-1990). *English Key Stage 1: A Report by HMI on the First Year*. DFE.

HMI (Autumn, 1990). *The Teaching and Learning of Reading in Primary Schools*. DFE.

HMI (Suffolk) (1991). *The Teaching and Learning of Reading*. DFE.

HMI (1992). *The Teaching and Learning of Reading in Primary Schools 1991*. London: DES.

Hogenson, D. L. (1974). 'Reading failure and juvenile delinquency', *Orton Society Annual Bulletin*, 24, p. 165.

Hohn, W.E., & Ehri, L.C. (1983). 'Do alphabet letters help pre-readers acquire phonemic segmentation skill?', *Journal of Educational Psychology*, 75, 752-762.

Hoien, T., Lundberg, I., Stanovich, K., & Bjaalid, I., (1995). 'Components of phonological awareness', *Reading and Writing: An Interdisciplinary Journal*, 7(2), 171-188.

Holmes, J. (1994, August 27). 'Fast words speed past dyslexics', *New Scientist*, no. *1940*, p.9.

Hornsby, B., & Shear, F. (1976, 1980, 1st & 3rd editions). *Alpha to Omega: The A-Z of Teaching Reading, Writing, and Spelling.* Oxford: Heinemann.

House of Commons, Education, Science, & Arts Committee. (1990-91a). *House of Commons Report: Standards of Reading in Primary Schools.* Volume I. London: HMSO.

House of Commons, Education, Science, & Arts Committee.(1990-91b). *House of Commons Report: Standards of Reading in Primary Schools.* Volume II. London: HMSO.

Hu, C.F., & Catts, H.W. (1993). 'Phonological recoding as a universal process?', *Reading and Writing: An Interdisciplinary Journal*, 5(3), 325-337.

Hurford, D., Darrow, L., Edwards, T., Howerton, C., Mote, C., Schauf, J., & Coffey, P. (1993). 'An examination of phonemic processing abilities in children during their first-grade year', *Journal of Learning Disabilities*, 28(3), 167-177.

Hurford, D., Schauf, J., Bunce, L., Blaich, T., & Moore, K. (1994). 'Early identification of children at-risk for reading disabilities', *Journal of Reading Disabilities*, 27(6), 371-382.

Hymas, C. (1993, 26 September). Knowing alphabet at age of 7 is too demanding, say teachers. *Sunday Times.*

Hynd, G.W. (1992). 'Neurological aspects of dyslexia: Comment on the balance model', *Journal of Learning Disabilities*, 25(2), 110-112.

Hynds, J. (1994, October 18-19). *Reading Roadshow.* The National Association for Special Needs Conference, The Business and Design Centre, Islington, London.

Iacoboni, M. & Zaidel, E. (1996). 'Hemispheric independence in word recognition: Evidence from unilateral and bilateral presentations', *Brain and Language*, 53, 121-140.

ILEA (Inner London Educational Authority). (1985). *Improving Primary Schools: A Report of the Committee on Primary Education.* Chaired by Mr. Norman Thomas.

Institute of Education, (1992). *The External Programme, Diploma in Education, Curriculum Studies and the Primary School.* London: University of London.

IRA (The International Reading Association) (27 October, 1995). Personal communication with Scott Walters, at the IRA head office, Newark, Delaware, USA.

Ireson, J., Blatchford, P, & Joscelyne, T. (1995). 'What do teachers do? Classroom activities in the initial teaching of reading', *Educational Psychology*, 15(3), 245-257.

Iverson, S., & Tunmer, W.E. (1993). 'Phonological processing skills and the reading recovery program', *Journal of Educational Psychology*, 85, 112-126.

Johnson, D., & Baumann, J. (1984). Word identification. In P.D. Pearson, R. Barr, M. Kamil, & P. Mosenthal (Eds), Handbook of Reading Research. New York: Longman.

Johnston, P.H. (1985). 'Understanding reading disability', *Harvard Educational Review*, 55, 153-157.

Johnston, R.S. & Thompson, G.B. (1989). 'Is dependence on phonological information in children's reading a product of instructional approach?', *Journal of Experimental Child Psychology*, 48, 131-145.

Johnston, R. (1995, January). Personal communication about methods of teaching reading in Scotland. University of St. Andrew's, Fife, Scotland.

Johnston, R., & Holligan, C. (1991). 'Reading difficulties and learning to read: insights from academic research', *Reading*, April, 2-4.

Jorm, A.F., & Share, D.L. (1983). 'Phonological recoding and reading acquisition', *Applied Psycholinguistics*, 4(2), 103-147.

Jorm, A.F., Share, D.L., Maclean, R., & Matthews, R. (1984). 'Phonological recoding skills and learning to read: A longitudinal study', *Applied Psycholinguistics*, 5, *201-207*.

Juel, C. (1988). 'Learning to read and write: A longitudinal study of 54 children from first through fourth grades', *Journal of Educational Psychology*, 80, 437-447.

Juel, C. (1994). *Learning to Read and Write in One Elementary School*. New York: Springer-Verlag.

Juel, C. (1995). 'The messenger may be wrong, but the message may be right', *Journal of Research in Reading*, 18(2), 146-153.

Juel, C., Griffith, P., & Gough, P. (1986). Acquisition of literacy: a longitudinal study of children in first and second grade. *Journal of Educational Psychology*, 78, 243-255.

Juel, C., & Roper-Schneider, D. (1985). 'The influence of basal readers on first grade reading', *Reading Research Quarterly*, 20, 134-152.

Just, M. A., & Carpenter, P. A. (1987). *The Psychology of Reading and Language Comprehension*. Newton, MA: Allyn & Bacon.

Kail, M. (1992). Are sex or gender relevant categories to language performance? in M. Haug, R. E. Whalen, C. Aron, & K.L, Olsen. (Eds), *The Development of Sex Differences and Similarities in Behaviour*. Boston: Kluwer Academic Publishers.

Kane, I. (Chairman of the Universities Council for Education of Teachers) (1996, 7 June). Quoted by J. Gardiner, Rearranging tables will not be enough. *Times Educational Supplement*, p. 7.

Kent, M. (1996, 31 May). Reading report reveals U-turn by inspectors. *Times Educational Supplement*, p. 20.

Kerlinger, F. N. (1986). *Foundations of Behavioural Research*. New York: Holt, Rinehart, & Winston.

Kershner, J. & Micallef, J. (1991). 'Cerebral laterality in dyslexic children: Implications for phonological word decoding deficits', *Reading and Writing: An Interdisciplinary Journal*, 3(3/4), 395-412.

Kilroy (1994). Television programme on dyslexia. Produced by BBC1 television. London.

Kirkham, S. (1993, 19 March). Outlook variable. *Times Educational Supplement*.

Kline, C.I. (1994). 'Reading, writing and 'rithmetic taught without a measuring stick', *Effective School Practices*, summer, 13-14.

Knights, R. M., & Bakker, D. J. (Eds). (1979). *The Neuropsychology of Learning Disorders: Theoretical Approaches*. Baltimore: University Park Press.

Ladybird series, (1992). *Say the Sounds Phonic Reading Scheme* (Books 1-8). Loughborough, LEIC: Ladybird Books.

Lamb, B. (1994). *A National Survey of UK Undergraduates' Standards of English*. London: The Queen's English Society.

Landwehrmeyer, B., Gerling, J., & Wallesch, C.W. (1990). 'Pattern of task-related slow brain potentials in dyslexia', *Archives of Neurology*, 47, 791-797.

Layard, R. (1996, June). Presentation at the Institute of Directors meeting, London, England.

Leather, C.V. & Henry, L.A. (1994). 'Working memory span and phonological awareness tasks as predictors of early reading ability', *Journal of Experimental Child Psychology*, 58, 88-111.

Leland, C.H. (1991). An assessment model for whole language classrooms. In F. Satow, & Gatherer, B. (Eds), *Literacy without Frontiers*. Proceedings of the 7th European and 28th UKRA Annual Conference, Herriot-Watt University, Edinburgh, July 1991.

Lennox, C. & Siegel, L. (1996). 'The development of phonological rules and visual strategies in average and poor spellers', *Journal of Experimental Child Psychology*, 62, 60-83.

Levy, B.A. (1981). Interactive processes during reading. In A. Lesgold, & C. Perfetti (Eds), *Interactive Processes in Reading*. Hillsdale, NJ: Erlbaum, pp.1-35.

Liberman, I. (1982). A language-oriented view of reading and its disabilities. In H. Myklebust (Ed.). *Progress in Learning Disabilities*. New York: Grune & Stratton, vol.5, pp.81-101.

Liberman, I.Y., & Liberman, A.M. (1990). 'Whole language vs. code emphasis: Underlying assumptions and their implications for reading instruction', *Annals of Dyslexia:* 40, 51-78.

Liberman, I.Y., & Liberman, A.M. (1992). Whole language versus code emphasis: underlying assumptions and their implications for reading instruction. In Gough, P.B., Ehri, L. C., & Treiman, R. (Eds), *Reading Acquisition*. NJ: Lawrence Erlbaum Associates, pp.343-365.

Liberman, I, & Shankweiler, D. (1985). 'Phonology and the problem of learning to read and write', *Remedial and Special Education*, 6, 8-17.

Liberman, I.Y., & Shankweiler, D. (1991). Phonology and beginning reading: A tutorial. In L. Rieben, & C. A. Perfetti (Eds), *Learning to Read: Basic Research and its Implications*. Hillsdale, New Jersey: Lawrence Erlbaum Associates, pp.3-18.

Liberman, I.Y., Shankweiler, D. Fischer, F.W., & Carter, B. (1974). 'Explicit syllable and phoneme segmentation in the young child', *Journal of Experimental Child Psychology*, 18, 201-202.

Lie, A. (1991). 'Effects of a training program for stimulating skills in word analysis in first-grade children', *Reading Research Quarterly*, 26, 234-250.

LINC materials, (1990). Carter, R. (ed.), *Knowledge about Language and the Curriculum: The LINC reader*. London: Hodder & Stoughton.

Lindamood, C. H., & Lindamood, P. C. (1975). *The ADD Program, Auditory Discrimination in Depth: Books 1 and 2*. Hingham, MA: DLM Teaching Resources.

Lloyd, S. (1993, September). *Phonics Prevents Failure*. Paper presented at the Reading Reform Foundation conference, London, England.

Lloyd, S. (1992). *The Phonics Handbook*, Chigwell, Essex: Jolly Learning Ltd.

Locurto, C. (1990). 'The malleability of IQ as judged from adoption studies', *Intelligence*, 14, 275-292.

Lovett, M. W., Ransby, M. J., Hardwick, N. Johns, M.S. & Donaldson, S. A. (1989). 'Can dyslexia be treated? Treatment-specific and generalized treatment effects in dyslexic children's response to remediation', *Brain and Language*, 37, 90-121.

Lundberg, I, Frost, J. & Petersen, O.P. (1988). 'Effects of an extensive program for stimulating phonological awareness in preschool children', *Reading Research Quarterly*, 23(2), 263-285.

Lyon, G. R. (1985). 'Identification and remediation of learning disability subtypes: Preliminary findings', *Learning Disabilities Focus*, 1, 21-25.

Lyon, G. R. (1992). Current and future research in dyslexia: NICHD perspectives. Paper presented at the meeting of The Orton Dyslexia Society, Cincinnati, Ohio, USA.

Maclean, M., Bryant, P. E., & Bradley, L. (1987). 'Rhymes, nursery rhymes and reading in early childhood', *Merrill-Palmer Quarterly*, 33, 255-282.

Majsternek, D. & Ellenwood, A. (1995). 'Phonological awareness and beginning reading: Evaluation of a school-based screening procedure', *Journal of Learning Disabilities*, 28(7), 449-456.

Manis, F. R., & Morrison, F. J. (1985). Reading disability: a deficit in rule learning? In L.S. Siegel & F.J. Morrison (Eds), *Cognitive Development in Atypical Children*. New York: Springer-Verlag, pp.1-26.

Mann, V. (1986). 'Phonological awareness: the role of reading experience', *Cognition*, 24, 65-92.

Mann, V. (1991a). Phonological abilities: Effective predictors of future reading ability. In L. Rieben, & C. A. Perfetti (Eds), *Learning to Read: Basic Research and its Implications*. NJ: Lawrence Erlbaum Associates, pp.121-134.

Mann, V. (1991b). Phonological awareness and early reading ability: one perspective. In D.J. Sawyer & B.J. Fox (Eds), *Phonological Awareness in reading: An Evolution of Current Perspectives*. NY: Springer-Verlag, pp.191-216.

Mann, V., & Liberman, I.Y. (1984). 'Phonological awareness and short-term memory', *Journal of Learning Disabilities*, 17, 592-599.

Manning, A., & Harste, J. (1994). 'Teacher research: Demonstrations of possibilities', *Reading*, April, 2-4.

Masonheimer, P.E., Drum, P.A., & Ehri, L.C. (1984). 'Does environmental print identification lead children into word reading?', *Journal of Reading Behaviour*, 16, 257-271.

Mather, N. (1992). 'Whole language reading instruction for students with learning disabilities: Caught in the cross fire', *Learning Disabilities Research and Practice*, 7, 87-95.

May, F. (1986). *Reading as Communication: An Interactive Approach.* Columbus, Ohio: Merrill Publishing.

Maxwell, J. (1977). *Reading Progress from a Survey of Attainment and Teaching Practices: Age 8-15 in Scotland.* NFER.

McDowell, E.E. (1982). 'Specific aspects of prompting and fading procedures in teaching beginning reading', *Perceptual and Motor Skills*, 55, 1103-1108.

McGuinness, D. (1981). Auditory and motor aspects of language development in males and females. In A. Ansara, N. Geschwind, A. Galaburda, M. Albert, & N. Gartrell (Eds), *Sex Differences in Dyslexia*. Towson, Maryland: The Orton Dyslexia Society.

McKenna, M. Robinson, R., & Miller, J. (1990). 'Whole language: a research agenda for the nineties', *Educational Researcher*, 19, 3-6.

McKenna, M., Stratton, B., Grindler, M. & Jenkins, S. (1995). 'Differential effects of whole language and traditional instruction on reading attitudes', *Journal of Reading Behaviour*, 27(1), 19-43.

McNee, M. (1990). *Step by Step: A Day-By-Day Programme of Intensive, Systematic Phonics for All Ages.* Norfolk: Mona McNee.

Meek, M. (1982). *Learning to Read.* London: Bodley Head.

Meek, M. (Ed.), (1988). *How Texts Teach What Readers Learn.* Stroud: Thimble Press.

Menard, M., Kosslyn, S., Thompson, W., Alpert, N. & Rauch, S. (1996). 'Encoding words and pictures: A positron emission tomography study', *Neuropsychologia*, 34(3), 185-194.

Moeller, T.G. (1993). 'Self-esteem: how important is it to improving academic performance?' *Virginia Journal of Education*, 87(2), 6-11.

Moeller, T.G. (1994). 'What research says about self-esteem and academic performance', *The Education Digest*, 59(5), 34-37.

Moller, D. (1994). 'Exclusive schools poll: What parents really want', *Reader's Digest*, 145, October, 49-55.

Moorman, G. B., Blanton, W. E., & McLaughlin, T. (1994). 'The rhetoric of whole language', *Reading Research Quarterly*, 29(4), 309-329.

Morais, J. (1991). Phonological awareness: A bridge between language and literacy. In D. Sawyer, & B.J. Fox (Eds), *Phonological Awareness in Reading: The Evolution of Current Perspectives*. New York: Springer-Verlag, p.31-71.

Morais, J., Alegria, J., & Content, A. (1987). 'The relationship between segmental analysis and alphabetic literacy: An interactive view', *European Journal of Cognitive Psychology*, 7, 1-24.

Morais, J. & Kolinsky, R. (1994). 'Perception and awareness in phonological processing: the case of the phoneme', *Cognition*, 50, 287-297.

Morris, J.M. (1966). *Standards and Progress in Reading*. The National Foundation for Educational Research.

Morris, J.M. (1974-1983). *Language in Action*. London and Basingstoke: Macmillan Education.

Morris, J.M. (1983). *Phonics 44*. London and Basingstoke: Macmillan Education.

Morris, J.M. (1990, 1994). *The Morris-Montessori Word List*. London: London Montessori Centre.

Morris, J.M. (1993). Texts for reading assessment. In D. Wray (Ed.), *Literacy: Text and Context*. United Kingdom Reading Association.

Mortimore, J. & Mortimore, P. (1984). *Secondary School Examinations: The Helpful Servants, Not the Dominating Master*. Institute of Education, University of London: Heinemann Education.

Mortimore, P., Sammons, P., Stoll, L., Lewis, D., Ecob, R. (1988a). *School Matters. The Junior Years*. Somerset, England: Open Books.

Mortimore, P., Sammons, P., Stoll, L., Ecob, R., & Lewis, D. (1988b). 'The effects of school membership on pupils' educational outcomes', *Research Papers in Education*, 3(1), 3-26.

NASEN, (1994). *NASEN Newsletter*, 9(1).

NATE (National Association for the Teaching of English) (1986). *The First Twenty-One Years: 1963-1984*. London: Spider Web.

Nelson, T. & Sons. (1991). *General Introduction: Story Chest*. Hong Kong, Australia, Canada: Thomas Nelson & Sons.

Nicholson, R.I., & Fawcett, A.J. (1990). 'Automaticity: a new framework for dyslexia research?', *Cognition*, 35, 159-182.

Nicholson, T. (1989). A comment on Reading Recovery. *New Zealand Journal of Educational Studies*, 24, 95-97.

Nicholson, T. (1991). 'Do children read words better in context or in lists? A classic study revisited', *Journal of Educational Psychology*, 83(4), 444-450.

NUT, National Union of Teachers. (1992). *Testing and Assessing 6 and 7 Year Olds – Final Report: The evaluation of the 1992 Key Stage 1 National Curriculum Assessment*. NUT and School of Education, Leeds.

Obrzut, J.E. (1991). Hemispheric activation and arousal asymmetry in learning-disabled children. In J.E. Obrzut & G.W. Hynd (Eds), *Neuropsychological Foundations of Learning Disabilities: A Handbook of Issues, Methods, and Practice*. London: Academic Press, ch.8.

O'Connor, R.E., Jenkins, J.R., Leicester, N. & Slocum, T.A. (1993). 'Teaching phonological awareness to young children with learning disabilities', *Exceptional Children*, 59(6), 532-546.

O'Connor, R.E. , Jenkins, J.R., Cole, K.N., & Mills, P.E. (1993). Two approaches to reading instruction with children with disabilities: does programme design make a difference? *Exceptional Children*, 59 (4), 312-323.

O'Connor, R.E., & Jenkins, J.R., (1995). 'Improving the generalization of sound/symbol knowledge: Teaching spelling to kindergarten children with disabilities', *The Journal of Special Education*, 29(3). 255-275.

Ofsted (Office for Standards in Education) (1993a). *Boys and English: A Report from the Office of Her Majesty's Chief Inspector of Schools*. London: HMSO.

Ofsted (Office for Standards in Education) (1993b). *English Key Stages 1, 2, 3 and 4: Fourth Year, 1992-93*. London: HMSO.

OFSTED (Office for Standards in Education) (1994). *Primary Matters: A Discussion on Teaching and Learning in Primary Schools.*

OFSTED (Office for Standards in Education) (1995). *Reporting Pupil's Achievement.*

OFSTED (Office for Standards in Education). (1996). *The Teaching of Reading in 45 inner London Primary Schools. A Report by Her Majesty's Inspectorate in Collaboration with the LEAs of Islington, Southwark and Tower Hamlets.*

Ogden, J. A. (1996). 'Phonological dyslexia and phonological dysgraphia following left and right hemispherectomy', *Neuropsychologia*, 34(9), 905-918.

Ohnmacht, D. C. (1969). *The Effects of Letter knowledge on Achievement in Reading in First Grade.* Paper presented at the American Educational Research Association, Los Angeles.

Open School (1995). *Soundworks: Early Literacy Training Programme.* Park Rd., Dartington, Totnes, Devon, TQ9 6EQ.

Osborn, M. & Broadfoot, P. (1991, April). PACE *Primary Assessment, Curriculum and Experience: A Study of Educational Change under the National Curriculum, Bristol Polytechnic, University of Bristol. The Impact of Current Changes in English Primary Schools on Teacher Professionalism.* Paper presented at the American Educational Research Association conference, Chicago, USA.

Parkinson, J. (1994, 7 October). Letters: The proof is in the Recovery. *Times Educational Supplement*, p. 17.

Patten, J. (1994a, 10 March). Turn off the television and tune into reading. *Department for Education News*, p. 2.

Patterson, K.E., & Coltheart, V. (1987). Phonological processes in reading: A tutorial review. In M. Coltheart (Ed.), *Attention and Performance.* Hillsdale, NJ: Lawrence Erlbaum Associates, vol.12, pp.421-447

Pearce, L. (1994, 12 March). Report on partnership in literacy projects. *Acquisition of Literacy for Life: Teachers and Parents Sharing Responsibility.* United Kingdom Reading Association Seminar, Institute of Education, Cambridge.

Peer, L. (1994). *Dyslexia: The Training and Awareness of Teachers.* London: British Dyslexia Association.

Pennington, B. (1991). *Diagnosing Learning Disorders: A Neuropsychological Framework.* New York: Guildford Press.

Perfetti, C.A. (1985). *Reading Ability*. New York: Oxford University Press.

Perfetti, C.A. (1991). Representations and awareness. In L. Rieben, & C. Perfetti (Eds), *Learning to Read: Basic Research and its Implications*. Hillsdale, New Jersey: Lawrence Erlbaum Associates, pp.32-44.

Perfetti, C.A. (1995a). *Recent Advances in Reading Research and their Applications*. Reading 2000: Recent advances in the science of reading, Human Communication Research Centre Seminar, University of Glasgow, 7 April, 1995.

Perfetti, C.A. (1995b). 'Cognitive research can inform reading education', *Journal of Research in Reading*, 18(2), 106-115.

Perfetti, C.A., & Lesgold, A.M. (1979). Coding and comprehension in skilled reading and implications for reading instruction. In L.B. Resnick & P. Weaver (Eds), *Theory and Practice of Early Reading*. Hillsdale, NJ: Erlbaum Associates, vol.1, pp.57-84.

Perfetti, C.A., Goldman, S., & Hogaboam, T. (1979). 'Reading skill and the identification of words in discourse context', *Memory & Cognition*, 7, 273-282.

Perfetti, C. Beck, I, Bell, L. & Hughes, C. (1987). 'Phonemic knowledge and learning to read are reciprocal: a longitudinal study of first grade children', *Merrill-Palmer Quarterly*, 33(3), 283-319.

Pflaum, S.W., Walberg, H.J., Karegianes, M.L., & Rasher, S.P. (1980). 'Reading instruction: A quantitative analysis', *Educational Researcher*, 9, 12-18.

Plowden, B., Chairman of Council. (1967). *Children and their Primary Schools: A Report of the Central Advisory Council for Education*. DES: HMSO.

Pratt, A., & Brady, S. (1988). 'Relation of phonological awareness and reading ability in children and adults', *Journal of Educational Psychology*, 71, 487-503.

Pumfrey, P.D. (1991, December). Apres le deluge. In P.D. Pumfrey (Ed.), *Reading Standards: Issues and Evidence*. Papers presented at a DECP symposium during the London conference for the British psychological society. London: DECP (Division of Education and Child Psychology of the British Psychological Society.

Pumfrey, P.D., Elliott, C.D., & Tyler, S. (1991). Objective testing: Insights or illusions? In P. Pumfrey (Ed.), *Reading Standards: Issues and Evidence*. Papers presented at a DECP Symposium during the London Conference of the British Psychological Society, December, 1991, pp. 39-48.

Pumfrey, P.D. & Reason, R. (1991). *Specific Learning Difficulties: Dyslexia Challenges and Responses*. London: Routledge Press, ch.9

Pyke, N. (1994a, 13 May). Coded messages. *Times Educational Supplement*, p. 2.

Pyke, N. (1994b, 6 May). A special need for deep pockets. *Times Educational Supplement*.

Rack, J.P., Snowling, M.J., & Olson, R.K. (1992). 'The nonword reading deficit in developmental dyslexia: A review', *Reading Research Quarterly*, 27, 28-53.

Rayner, K. (1993). 'Eye movements in reading: recent developments', *Current Directions in Psychological Science*, 2(3).

Rayner, K. (1995). *What the Eye tells the Brain during Reading*. Reading 2000: Recent advances in the science of reading, Human Communication Research Centre Seminar, University of Glasgow, 7 April, 1995.

Rayner, K., & Bertera, J.H. (1979). 'Reading without a fovea. *Science*', 206, 469-469.

Rayner, K., & Pollatsek, A. (1989). *The Psychology of Reading*. Englewood Cliffs, NJ: Prentice-Hall.

Read, C., & Ruyter, L. (1985). 'Reading and spelling skills in adults of low literacy', *Remedial and Special Education*, 6(6), 37-42.

Redfern, A. & Edwards, V,. (1992). *How Schools Teach Reading*. Reading and Language Information Centre, University of Reading.

Reid, I. & Stratta, E. (Eds). (1989). *Sex Differences in Britain*. London: Gower Publishing, pp.103-132.

Reitsma, P. (1988). 'Reading practice for beginners. Effects of guided reading, reading-while-listening, and independent reading with computer-based speech feedback', *Reading Research Quarterly*, 23, 219-235.

Rieben, L. & Perfetti, C.A. (1991). *Learning to Read: Basic Research and Its implications*. Hillsdale, NJ: Erlbaum Associates.

Rodgers, B. (1986). 'Change in the reading attainment of adults: A longitudinal study', *British Journal of Developmental Psychology*, 4, 1-17.

Rohl, M. & Tunmer, W. (1988). 'Phoneme segmentation skill and spelling acquisition', *Applied Psycholinguistics*, 9, 335-350.

Root, B. (1989). *Help Your Child Learn to Read*. Osborne Publishing.

Rosenshine, B. & Stevens, R. (1984). Classroom instruction in reading. In P. D. Pearson, R., Barr, M. L., Kamil, & P. Mosenthal (Eds), *Handbook of Reading Research*. New York: Longman., pp.745-799.

Rosner, J. (1975). *Helping Children Overcome Learning Difficulties*. New York: Walker & Co.

Routh, D.K., & Fox, B. (1984). Mm...is a little bit of May: Phonemes, reading, and spelling. In K. D. Gadow & P. Bialen (Eds), *Advances in Learning and Behavioural Disabilities*. Greenwich, CT: JAI Press, vol.3.

Rozin, P., Poritsky, S., & Sotsky, R. (1971). 'American children with reading problems can easily learn to read English represented by Chinese characters', *Science*, 71, 1264-1267.

Rumsey, J., Andreason, P., Zametkin, A., Aquino, T., King, A., Hamberger, S., Pikus, A. Rapoport, J, & Cohen, R. (1992). 'Failure to activate the left temporoparietal cortex in dyslexia', *Archives of Neurology*, 49, 527-534.

Rusted, J. & Coltheart, V. (1979). 'The effect of pictures on the retention of novel words and prose passages', *Journal of Experimental Child Psychology*, 28, 516-524.

Sammons, P. (1995). *Gender, Ethnic and Socio-Economic Differences in Attainment and Progress: A Longitudidinal Analysis of Student Achievement over Nine Years*. Instiute of Education, University of London.

Sammons, P., Nuttall, D., & Cuttance, P. (1993). 'Differential school effectiveness: results from a reanalysis of the inner London education authority's junior school project data', *British Educational Research Journal*, 19(4), 381-404.

Sammons, P., Nuttall, D., Cuttance, P., & Thomas, S. (1993). *Continuity of School Effects: A Longitudinal Analysis of Primary and Secondary School Effects on GCSE Performance*. Institute of Education, University of London, Department of Curriculum Studies.

Sammons, P, Thomas, S., Mortimore, P., Owen, C. & Pennell, H. (1994). *Assessing School Effectiveness: Developing Measures to Put School Performance in Context*. London: Institute of Education for OFSTED.

Saunders, R.J. & Solman, T.T. (1984). 'The effect of pictures on the acquisition of a small vocabulary of similar sight-words', *British Journal of Educational Psychology*, 54, 265-275.

Sawyer, D. J. (1992). 'Language abilities, reading acquisition, and developmental dyslexia: A discussion of hypothetical and observed relationships', *Journal of Learning Disabilities*, 25(2), 82-95.

Sawyer, D. & Fox, B. (1991). (Eds), *Phonological Awareness in Reading: The Evolution of Current Perspectives*. New York: Springer-Verlag.

SCAA (School Curriculum and Assessment Authority), (November, 1994a). *National Curriculum Final Draft Orders: General Requirements for English: Key Stages 1-4*. London:DFE.

SCAA (School Curriculum and Assessment Authority). (1994b). *Desirable Outcomes for Children's Learning on Entering Compulsory Education*. London:DFE.

SCAA (School Curriculum and Assessment Authority) (May, 1994c). English in the National Curriculum – Proposals. London: DFE.

SCAA. (1994d). *School assessment folder: Key Stage 1. Information and Guidance about Assessment Arrangements in 1994*. London: DFE.

SCAA. (1994e). *Assessment Handbook for English En2 Reading: En 3/4/5 Writing. Key Stage 1*. London: DFE.

Schickedanz, J. A. (1990). 'The jury is still out on the effects of whole language and language experience approaches for beginning reading: A critique of Stahl and Miller's study', *Review of Educational Research*, 60(1), 127-131.

Schwantes, F. M. (1991). 'Children's use of semantic and syntactic information for word recognition and determination of sentence meaningfulness', *Journal of Reading Behaviour*, 23, 335-350.

Scottish Education Department. (1985). *HMI of Schools: Borgue Primary School, Dumfries and Galloway Regional Council. Report of an Inspection in February, 1985*.

Scottish Education Department (1988). *Assessment of Achievement Programme: AAP 1988*. Edinburgh: HMSO, p. 11.

Scottish Education Department. (1989). *English Language 1989 Assessment of Achievement Programme*. Edinburgh: HMSO.

Scottish Education Department (1992). *English Language 1992 Assessment of Achievement Programme*. Edinburgh: HMSO.

Scottish Education Department (Edinburgh) (1995). Personal communication with the Principal Research Officer.

Scottish Education Department (Fife) (1995). Personal communication with the Early Years Advisor.

Scottish Office of Statistical Services. (1994, October). *Statistical Bulletin: Educational Series*. Edinburgh: The Government Statistical Service.

Seaton, N. (1993). *Teacher Training: Public Funding for Progressivism?* No.18. York: The Campaign for Real Education.

Seaton, N. (1994a). 'Developments in education', *The Lantern: Supporting the Policy and Philosophy of the British Housewives League.* vol.1(4), 2-7.

Seymour, P.H.K. (1990). Developmental dyslexia. In M.W. Eysenck (ed.), *Cognitive Psychology: An International Review.* Chichester: Wiley, pp.135-196.

Seymour, P.H.K., & Elder, H.M. (1986). 'Beginning reading without phonology', *Cognitive Neuropsychology.* 3, 1-36.

Seymour, P.H.K., & Evans, H.M. (1994). 'Levels of phonological awareness and learning to read', *Reading and Writing: An Interdisciplinary Journal,* 6(3), 221-250.

Shanahan, T. (1987). 'The early detection of reading difficulties by Marie M. Clay', *Journal of Reading Behaviour,* 19, 117-119.

Share, D.L., & Jorm, A.F. (1987). 'Segmental analysis: Co-requisite to reading, vital for self-teaching, requiring phonological memory', *Cahiers de Psycholgie Cognitive,* 7, 509-513.

Share, D.L., & Silva, P.A. (1987). 'Language deficits and specific reading retardation: Cause or effect?', *British Journal of Disorders of Communication,* 22, 219-226.

Share, D.L., & Stanovich, K.E. (1995a). 'Cognitive processes in early reading development: Accomodating individual differences into a model of acquisition', *Issues in Education,* 1(1), 1-58.

Share, D.L., & Stanovich, K.E. (1995b). 'Accommodating individual differences in critiques: Replies to our commentators', *Issues in Education,* 1(1), 105-121.

Shephard, G. (1995, 17 April). Quoted by O'Leary, J. Militants defy Labour and NUT leaders. *Times,* p. 1.

Shore, R.E., & Marascuilo, L. (1974). 'Programmed approach versus conventional approach using a highly consistent sound-symbol system of reading in three primary grades',. *Journal of Educational Research,* 25. 11-31.

Silver, A.A., & Hagin, R.A. (1990). *Disorders of Learning in Childhood.* New York: Wiley.

Singh, N.N. & Solman, R.T. (1990). 'A stimulus control analysis of the picture-word problem in children who are mentally retarded: the blocking effect', *Journal of Applied Behaviour Analysis,* 23, 525-532.

Smith, F. (1971). *Understanding Reading: A Psycholinguistic Analysis of Reading and Learning to read*. New York: Holt, Rinehart, & Winston.

Smith, F. (1973) *Psycholinguistics and reading*. New York: Holt, Rinehart, & Winston, p. 190.

Smith, F. (1978). *Understanding Reading* (2nd edn). New York: Holt, Rinehart & Winston, pp.7-8.

Smith, F. (1986). *What's the Use of the Alphabet?* Victoria, BC: Abel Press, Reading and Language Information Centre.

Smith, F. (1988). *Understanding Reading* (4th edn). Hillsdale, NJ: Lawrence Erlbaum Association.

Smith, H. (1994a, 11 January). Ban on trendy teaching leads to boost for young readers. *Evening Standard*, p. 14.

Smith, F. (1994b). *Understanding Reading* (5th edn.). NJ: Lawrence Erlbaum Associates.

Snowling, M.J. (1980). 'The development of grapheme-phoneme correspondence in normal and dyslexics readers', *Journal of Experimental Child Psychology*, 29, 294-305.

Snowling, M. J. (1987). *Dyslexia: A Cognitive Developmental Perspective*. Oxford: Basil Blackwell.

Snowling, M. (1995). 'Phonological processing and developmental dyslexia', *Research in Reading*, 18(2), 132-138.

Solman, R.T., Singh, N.N., & Kehoe, E.J. (1992). 'Pictures block the learning of sight words', *Educational Psychology*, 12(2), 143-153.

Sowden, P.T., & Stevenson, J. (1994). 'Beginning reading strategies in children experiencing contrasting teaching methods', *Reading and Writing: An Interdisciplinary Journal*, 6(2), 109-124.

Speed, A. (1994, April). Seen, but not always heard. *Times Educational Supplement*, p. 4.

Stahl, S.A. (1988). 'Is there evidence to support matching reading styles and initial reading methods? A reply to Carbo', *Phi Delta Kappan*, 70, 317-322.

Stahl, S.A. (1990). 'Riding the pendulum: a rejoinder to Schickedanz and McGee and Lomax', *Review of Educational Research*, 60 *(1)*, 141-151.

Stahl, S.A., McKenna, M.C., & Pagnucco, J. (1994). 'The effects of whole language instruction: An update and a reappraisal', *Educational Psychologist*, 29(4), 175-185.

Stahl, S.A., & Miller, P.D. (1989). 'Natural language approaches to beginning reading: A quantitative research synthesis', *Review of Educational Research,*

Stanovich, K.E. (1980). 'Toward an interactive-compensatory model of reading: A confluence of developmental, experimental, and educational psychology', *Remedial and Special Education,* 5, 11-19.

Stanovich, K.E. (1981). 'Relationship between word decoding speed, general name-retrieval ability, and reading progress in first-grade children', *Journal of Educational Psychology,* 73, 809-815.

Stanovich, K. (1984). 'An interactive-compensatory model of reading: A confluence of developmental, experimental, and educational psychology', *Remedial and Special Education,* 5, 11-19.

Stanovich, K. (1986). 'Matthew effects in reading: Some consequences of individual differences in the acquisition of literacy', *Reading Research Quarterly,* 21, 360-407.

Stanovich, K. (1988). 'Explaining the difference between the dyslexic and the garden-variety poor reader. The phonological-core variable-difference model', *Journal of Learning Disabilities,* 21(10), 590-604.

Stanovich, K. (1991). Changing models of reading and reading acquisition. In L. Rieben, & C.A. Perfetti (Eds), *Learning to Read: Basic Research and its Implications.* Hillsdale, New Jersey: Lawrence Erlbaum Associates, pp.19-32.

Stanovich, K.E. (1992). Speculations on the causes and consequences of individual differences in early reading acquisition. In P. B. Gough, L. C. Ehri, & R. Treiman (Eds), *Reading Acquisition.* Hillsdale, NJ: Erlbaum Associates, pp.307-342

Stanovich, K. & Stanovich, P. (1995). 'How research might inform the debate about early reading acquisition', *Journal of Research in Reading,* 18(2), 87-105.

Start, K. B., & Wells, B. K. (1972). *The Trend of Reading Standards.* The National Foundation for Educational Research.

Sternberg, R. (1985). Beyond IQ: a triarchic theory of human performance. In D. Detterman & R. Sternberg (Eds), *How and How Much Can Intelligence Be Increased?.* Norwood, NJ: Ablex, pp.141-146

Stevenson, J. (1992). 'Identifying sex differences in reading disability: Lessons from a twin study', *Reading and Writing: An Interdisciplinary Journal,* 4(4), 1-9.

Stevenson, H.W., Parker, T., & Wilkinson, A. (1976). 'Longitudinal study of individual differences in cognitive development and scholastic achievement', *Journal of Educational Psychology*, 68(4), 377-400.

Stoner, J. C. (1991). 'Teaching at-risk students to read using specialized techniques in the regular classroom', *Reading and Writing: An Interdisciplinary Journal*, 3(1), 19-30.

Stuart, M. (1995). 'Through printed words to meaning: issues of transparency', *Journal of Research in Reading*, 18(2), 126-131.

Stuart, M. & Masterson, J. (1992). 'Patterns of reading and spelling in 10-year-old children related to prereading phonological abilities',. *Journal of Experimental Child Psychology*, 54, 168-187.

Sylva, K., & Hurry, J. (1995). *Early Intervention in Children with Reading Difficulties: An Evaluation of Reading Recovery and a Phonological Training*. London: School Curriculum and Assessment Authority.

Taylor, P., & Miller, S. (1994). *Our Children, Our Future – Primary Education Today*. Primary Schools Research and Development Group.

The Citizen (December 1993). Article regarding children in Gloucestershire with special educational needs. Cited by Seaton, N. *The Campaign for Education Newsletter*.

Thomas, S., Pau, H., & Goldstein, H. (1994). Report on the analysis of the 1992 examination results. London: Association of Metropolitan Authorities.

Times Educational Supplement, (1996, 7 June). Despatches from the home reading background. *TES Primary Update, TES*, p.16.

Tizard, B., Blatchford, P. Burke, J., Farquhar, C. & Plewis, I. (1988). *Young Children at School in the Inner City*. Hove, Sussex: Lawrence Erlbaum Associates.

Torgesen, J.K., Morgan, S.T., Davis, C. (1992). 'Effects of two types of phonological awareness training on word learning in kindergarten children', *Journal of Educational Psychology*, 84(3), 364-370.

Torgesen, J.K., Wagner, R.K., & Rashotte, C.A. (1994). 'Longitudinal studies of phonological processing and reading', *Journal of Learning Disabilities*, 27(5), 276-286.

Treiman, R., Goswami, U, & Bruck, M. (1990). 'Not all nonwords are alike: Implications for reading development and theory', *Memory & Cognition*, 18, 559- 567.

Tregenza, A. (1994). Knowsley Reading Project Report in *Literacy Today*, vol.1, October.

Tunmer, W.E. (1991). Phonological awareness and literacy acquisition. In L. Rieben, & C.A. Perfetti (Eds), *Learning to Read: Basic Research and its Implications*. Hillsdale, New Jersey: Lawrence Erlbaum Associates, pp.105-120

Tunmer, W.E., & Hoover, W.A. (1992). Cognitive and linguistic factors in learning to read. In P. Gough, L. Ehri, & R. Treiman (Eds), *Reading Acquisition*. Hillsdale, NJ: Erlbaum, pp,175-214

Tunmer, W.E., & Hoover, W.A. (1993). 'Phonological recoding skill and beginning reading', *Reading and Writing: An Interdisciplinary Journal*, 5 (2),161-180.

Tunmer, W.E., Herriman, M.L., & Nesdale, A.R. (1988). 'Metalinguistic abilities and beginning reading', *Reading Research Quarterly*, 23, 134-158.

Tunmer, W.E., & Nesdale, A.R. (1985). 'Phonemic segmentation skill and beginning reading', *Journal of Educational Psychology*, 77, 417-427.

Tunmer, W.E., & Rohl, M. (1991). Phonological awareness and reading acquisition, In D.J. Sawyer, & B.J. Fox (Eds), *Phonological Awareness in Reading: The Evolution of Current Perspectives*. New York: Springer-Verlag, pp.1-30.

Turner, M. (1990). *Sponsored Reading Failure*. IPSET.

Turner, M. (1991, 10 January). A disturbing report however you read it. *Daily Telegraph*, p 12.

Turner, M. (1991a). *Reading, Learning and the National Curriculum*. CPS Policy Challenge, April 1991. London: Centre for Policy Studies.

Turner, M. (1991b). 'The reading debate: Finding out', *Support for Learning*, 6(3), 9-102.

Turner, M. (1995). Personal communication concerning number of LEAs from which data were analysed.

Tyk, I. (1993). *The Butterfly Book: A Reading and Writing Course by Irina Tyk*. Potter's Bar: Irina Tyk.

Uhry, J. & Shepherd, M. (1993). 'Segmentation and spelling instruction as part of a first-grade reading programme: Effects on several measures of reading', *Reading Research Quarterly*, 28, 218-233.

UKRA (United Kingdom Reading Association) (1994). Proceedings of the 31st UKRA annual conference, Institute of Education, Cambridge, March 1994.

University of Edinburgh, Centre for Research on Learning and Instruction (1994). *Manual of Instructions: Edinburgh Reading Tests, Stage 1, Ages 7:0 to 9:0*. London: Hodder & Stoughton, pp. 3, 24, 34.

University of London. (1992). *The External Programme – Display Rack 7: Diploma in Education Curriculum Studies and the Primary School.*

van den Bosch, K., van Bon, W., & Schreuder, R. (1995). 'Poor readers' decoding skills: Effects of training with limited exposure duration', *Reading Research Quarterly*, 50(1), 110-125.

Vandever, T.R., & Neville, D.D. (1976). 'Transfer as a result of synthetic and analytic reading instruction', *American Journal of Mental Deficiency*, 80(5), 498-503.

Vellutino, F.R. (1979). *Dyslexia: Theory and Practice*. Cambridge, MA: MIT Press.

Vellutino, F, (1991). 'Introduction to three studies on reading acquisition: convergent findings on theoretical foundations of code-oriented versus whole-language approaches to reading instruction', *Journal of Educational Psychology*, 83(4), 437-443.

Vellutino, F.R., & Scanlon, D.M. (1984). 'Converging perspectives in the study of the reading process: reaction to the papers presented by Morrison, Seigal, and Ryand, and Stanovich', *Remedial and Special Education*, 5, 39-44.

Vellutino, F., & Scanlon, D.M. (1987). 'Phonological coding, phonological awareness, and reading ability: Evidence from a longitudinal and experimental study', *Merrill-Palmer Quarterly*, 33, 321-363.

Vellutino, F.R., & Scanlon, D.M. (1991). The effects of instructional bias on word identification. In L. Rieben, & C.A. Perfetti (Eds), *Learning to Read: Basic Research and its Implications*. Hillsdale, New Jersey: Lawrence Erlbaum Associates, pp.189-204

Vernon, P.E. (1967). *The Scottish Council for Research in Education: The Standardisation of a Graded Word Reading Test*. University of London Press.

Wagner, R. (1988). 'Causal relations between the development of phonological processing abilities and the acquisition of reading skills: A meta-analysis', *Merrill-Palmer Quarterly*, 34, 261-279.

Wagner, R.K., & Torgesen, J.K. (1987). 'The nature of phonological processing and its causal role in the acquisition of reading skills', *Psychological Bulletin*, 101, 192-212.

Walker, C. & Newman, I. (1995). 'What teachers believe', *Educational Research*, 37(2), summer.

Wallach, L. & Wallach, M.A. (1976). *The Teaching All Children to Read Kit*. Chicago: University of Chicago Press.

Warnock, M. (1994, 30 September). Crack the code for the vulnerable 20 per cent. *Times Educational Supplement*, p. 20.

Waterland, L. (1985). *Read With Me: An Apprenticeship Approach to Reading*. Stroud: Thimble Press, p. 9.

Webster, A., Beveridge, M., & Reed, M. (1996). 'Conceptions of literacy in primary and secondary school teachers', *Journal of Research in Reading*, 19(1). 36-45.

White, K.R., Taylor, M.J., & Moss, V.D. (1992). 'Does research support claims about the benefits of involving parents in early intervention programmes?', *Review of Educational Research*, 62(1), 99-125.

Williams, E. (1996, 22 March). Exam advisers brought to book. *Times Educational Supplement*, p. 15.

Williams, J.P. (1979). The ABD's of reading. In L. Resnick, & P. Weaver (Eds), *Theory and Practice of Early Reading*. Hillsdale, New Jersey: Lawrence Erlbaum Associates, vol..3, pp.184-189.

Williams, J.P. (1980). 'Teaching decoding with a special emphasis on phoneme analysis and phoneme blending', *Journal of Educational Psychology*, 72, 1-15.

Williams, J. (1985). Explicit decoding instruction. In J. Osborn, P. Wilson, & R. Anderson. (Eds), *Foundations for a Literate America*. Arlington: Lexington Books.

Williams, S. & McGee, R. (1994). 'Reading attainment and juvenile delinquency', *Journal of Psychology and Psychiatry*, 35(3), 444-459.

Willows, D. M. (1978). 'A picture is not always worth a thousand words: pictures as distractors in reading', *Journal of Educational Psychology*, 70(2), 255-262.

Willows, D. (1996). (Personal communication). Study conducted in Ontario schools. Research to be published. Ontario Institute for Studies in Education, Toronto, Ontario, Canada.

Wimmer, H., Landerl, K., Linortner, R., & Hummer, P. (1991). 'The relationship of phonemic awareness to reading acquisition: More consequence than precondition but still important', *Cognition*, 40, 219-249.

Wimmer, H., & Goswami, U. (1994). 'The influence of orthographic consistency on reading development: word recognition in English and German children', *Cognition*, 51, 91-103.

Wise, B.W., Olson, R.K., & Treiman, R. (1990). 'Subsyllabic units in computerized reading instruction: Onset-rime versus postvowel segmentation', *Journal of Experimental Child Psychology*, 49, 1-19.

Woodhead, C. (1996a, June 3). Interview on *Panorama*, BBC television programme.

Woodhead, C. (1996b, 7 May). Conspiracy of silence on failing schools 'must be broken'. *Times*, p. 1-2.

Wray, D. (1994, 18 March). A sound idea: David Wray welcomes additions to the phonics library. *Times Educational Supplement*, p. 19.

Wray, D., & Medwell, J. (1994). 'Student teachers and teaching reading', *Reading*, November, 43-45.

Wright, A. (1994a). 'Evaluation of reading recovery in Surrey: A reply to Kathleen Hall', *British Educational Research Journal*, 20(1), 129- 135.

Wright, A. (1994a). The trouble with boys. In C. Hymas & J. Cohen (1994, 19 June), *The Sunday Times*, p. 14.

Wu, H., & Solman, R.T. (1993). 'Effective use of picture as extra stimulus prompts', *British Journal of Educational Psychology*, 63, 144-160.

Yates, G.C.R. & Yates, S.M. (1993). 'Teacher effectiveness research: towards describing user-friendly classroom instruction', *Effective School Practices*, summer.

Yopp, H.K. (1988). 'The validity and reliability of phonemic awareness tests', *Reading Research Quarterly*, 23, 159-177.

Education Without the State

JAMES TOOLEY

1. Functional illiteracy, youth delinquency and lack of technological innovation all point to the failures of state schooling. They raise the question of why governments should be involved in education at all.

2. One justification for state intervention in education is that, without it, there would not be educational opportunities for all. However, the great majority of people would not need state intervention for funding or provision of educational opportunities. Intervention would at most be required for a minority in need of financial support.

3. This conclusion is supported by historical evidence from Victorian England and Wales, and from more recent experience around the world, of educational entrepreneurs stepping in to provide desired opportunities where state education is failing.

4. A second justification offered is that equality of opportunity requires state intervention in education. When the record is examined, it is not clear that states anywhere have been able to provide equality. Strong theoretical arguments undermine the suggestion that they ever would.

5. Moreover, arguments against 'markets' in schooling which purport to show how they increase inequality actually point to problems not with markets, but with state regulation and provision themselves.

6. Many influential philosophers and economists agree that justice or fairness requires that everyone has adequate opportunities. But markets – with a funding safety-net – could provide adequate educational opportunities for all, and more effectively than further state intervention.

7. A final justification is that state regulation of, *inter alia*, the curriculum is required.

8. Lessons from the recent history of the national curriculum illustrate the general undesirability of government intervention in the curriculum. The problems of 'competing visions' and the 'knowledge problem' and considerations of the nature of education point to the folly of not leaving decisions to parents and young people themselves.

9. If state intervention in education is not justified, except for a funding safety-net, how can we move towards markets in education? A simple proposal is put forward, linked to recent discussion of the learning society and lifelong learning accounts.

10. Lowering the school leaving age to 14, and simultaneously giving young people two years' state funding for them to use in a Lifelong Individual Fund for Education (LIFE), would help liberate the educational demand side which, coupled with liberation of the supply side, would lead to an enlivening and nurturing of the enterprise of education.

ISBN: 0-255 36380-X

Studies in Education No. 1

The Institute of Economic Affairs
2 Lord North Street
London SW1P 3LB
Telephone and sales: (0171) 799 3745
Facsimile: (0171) 799 2137

£12.00
incl. p&p